HÉLÈNE'S WORLD:

HÉLÈNE DESPORTES OF SEVENTEENTH-CENTURY QUEBEC

SUSAN MCNELLEY

D1452881

Etta Heritage Press

Second printing September 2014

ISBN: 0615738591
ISBN-13: 9780615738598

The cover design is based on the painting *Quebec, The Capital of New-France, a Bishoprick, and Seat of the Sovereign Court*, by Thomas Johnston (Boston, 1759). Courtesy of the John Carter Brown Library at Brown University, Providence, Rhode Island

To Terry, my love

For his unfailing support

—◦◦◦—

Why do some people become stronger in the face of adversity while others quickly lose heart? What separates the bully from the protector? Is it education, spiritual belief, our parents, our friends, the circumstances of our birth, traumatic events, or more likely, some combination of circumstances that spell the difference?

... Madeleine Albright in *Prague Winter*

TABLE OF CONTENTS

PREFACE

Q uebec is an appealing city. It was founded in 1608 by the French explorer Samuel de Champlain and it became the first permanent French settlement in Canada. Now, four hundred years later, the French character of the city is unmistakable. Its language, food, architecture, and culture all reflect its French heritage. This is in spite of the fact that Quebec was conquered by the British in 1763 and France's colonial reign in Canada ended at that time.

As a result of the Official Language Act of 1974, passed by the Parliament of the Quebec Province, French became the official language of the Canadian province of Quebec. In the 2006 census, Quebec City had a population of 491,000. Of that number, 456,000 were French speakers, identifying French as their mother tongue. The city is overwhelmingly Francophone and these Francophones cherish their French roots and their heritage. Their motto, the motto of Quebec, is *Je me souviens* (I remember).

Vieux Quebec, located at the eastern tip of Quebec City, is a living museum: colorful, lively, and steeped in history. Designated a UNESCO World Heritage site in 1985, the district of Old Quebec is the only walled city in North America and offers the visitor a delightful peek into the city's French past. Today's tourists can meander through the charming streets of the Lower Town, along the banks of the St. Lawrence River. The rue du Petit-Champlain is particularly picturesque. A short distance away is the Place Royale and the small stone Church of Notre-Dame-des-Victoires, whose original construction dates back to 1687. In the Upper Town on the cliff above the river, one can wander along the Governor's Promenade or past the bastions and massive stone walls built long ago for the city's protection. The venerable Cathedral de Notre-Dame still stands tall and proud. Monuments and museums pay tribute to heroes and deeds of a previous age. The side streets are lined with eighteenth and nineteenth-century homes, lovingly restored and featuring brightly painted doors and colorful, flower-laden window boxes. Many of the streets and shops carry names of the original French pioneers. In the numerous restaurants and cafes, one can enjoy a meal of duck, pheasant, venison, fish, or other foods also enjoyed by the first settlers. Today, there are celebrations honoring the past with a kaleidoscope of processions, music, feasting, plays, and people dressed in the costumes of a bygone era. Old Quebec now offers comfort and gaiety; it is a place where people come to relax and enjoy themselves.

There is little physical evidence, however, of the seventeenth-century settlement found in the Lower Town at the edge of the river or on the prominence of Cap Diamant above. Fires, sieges, conquests, immigrants from other countries with new ideas, and the ravages of time in an often harsh environment have taken their toll. In the historic district of Old Quebec there are seven hundred old buildings. According to UNESCO, just two percent date back to the seventeenth century. Nine percent date to the eighteenth century and forty-three percent belong to the first half of the nineteenth century. The oldest structures are found in the Lower Town in the area surrounding the Place Royale.

Historians, working with archeologists and architects, have endeavored to uncover, preserve, restore, and protect what remains of this heritage. In recent years, archeologists have conducted excavations of the ground beneath the eighteenth-century buildings which line the Place Royale. They have discovered remnants of stone foundations, floors, ceilings, and fireplaces which date to the seventeenth century. Portions of Champlain's Second Habitation, located beneath the Notre-Dame-des-Victoires Church at the Place Royale, have been exposed. Various seventeenth-century artifacts are now on display: an inkwell purported to have been the property of Champlain, a few cannon balls, pieces of pottery, stone pipes, and porcelain beads. In the Upper Town, the oldest wing of the Seminary of Quebec contains elements dating back to the mid-1600s: windows, walls, ceilings, and a large fireplace in what was once a kitchen. The Ursuline Museum, located nearby, features fine embroideries from that era. However, the great majority of the original buildings, including those of the religious and civic institutions, have disappeared or been greatly modified. The few remaining structural elements and artifacts do not tell the complete story of early Quebec. There is little sign of the wilderness and the precarious nature of life experienced by Canada's first European settlers.

Life was very difficult for the French men and women who settled along the St. Lawrence River in the seventeenth century. It took stamina, courage, and perseverance, along with a measure of good fortune, to stay alive in the early years of the colony. The women who settled in Quebec at that time married young and had large families. Historians tell us that there were altogether only about one thousand married women living in Quebec between 1608 and 1680; fifty years later these women had produced fifty thousand descendants. Today, these same one thousand women and their husbands supply approximately two-thirds of the genetic makeup of six million French Canadians. (Charbonneau et al., *The First French Canadians: Pioneers in the St. Lawrence Valley,* 205.) Around the world, the vast majority of those who claim French Canadian ancestry can trace their family roots to one or more of these pioneer families. These French settlers left an indelible mark on the Quebec City of the twenty-first century.

One of the earliest residents of Quebec was Hélène Desportes, who was born in 1620 in Champlain's Habitation. She was the first child of French parents to be born in Quebec and to survive. Hélène was married at the age of fourteen, had two husbands, fifteen children, and seventy grandchildren. These are the bare facts of her life. What was life really like for this young woman who was born, grew up, and raised a family on the shores of the St. Lawrence in the seventeenth century? What did she experience in her lifetime? This is her story, but it is also the story of the other pioneers of early Quebec. It is the story of those who built a strong French foundation in the New World, a solid French underpinning that has endured to this day.

helene desportes

FOREWORD

We have no idea what Hélène Desportes looked like; no portrait of her exists. There are neither diaries nor memoirs to guide the biographer. The only thing we have that belonged to Hélène is her signature. She was literate to the extent that she could sign her name and she probably received some education in reading and writing as part of her religious preparation for First Holy Communion. However, the extent of her formal education is unknown. Any letters written by Hélène have been lost to history.

This is not to say that we know nothing about her. Her name appears in more than one hundred public records. The *Parchemin* and *Pistard* databases, compiled by the Bibliothèque et Archives nationales du Québec, contain notary records found in the civil archives of Quebec dating back to 1626. Hélène, Guillaume Hébert, and/or Noël Morin (Hélène's two husbands) are named in more than thirty of these records, many of them land transactions. Hélène is first mentioned in the civil archives in the fall of 1639 following the death of her first husband.

The *Programme de recherche en démographie historique (PRDH)* genealogical database has been compiled by the University of Montreal. It is an online database containing all the baptisms, marriages and burials in the parish records of the Roman Catholic Church in the province of Quebec up to 1800. Hélène is first mentioned in the church records in 1634, with her marriage to Guillaume Hébert. After that, she appears in the church records of Quebec seventy-eight times. In these records, there are a number of instances where Hélène is listed as *sage-femme* or midwife. Hélène and Noël are listed in the census records of 1666 and 1667, also recorded in the *PRDH*. The Church of Jesus Christ of the Latter Day Saints has digitized the church records of the province of Quebec and these are available at Family-Search.org, although currently non-indexed.

If we want to know about Hélène, we need to learn something about the early history of Quebec. Her character and her life would have been shaped by events in the settlement and by the people who lived there. Insofar as possible, Hélène's story has been developed through the use of primary materials. Much of what we know about seventeenth-century Quebec comes from the writings of its founder, Samuel de Champlain, the Jesuits who were missionaries in New France, and Marie de l'Incarnation, the Ursuline nun who founded a school for girls in Quebec in 1639. For Champlain's writings, I have used the following compilations: *Voyages of Samuel de Champlain*, edited by Rev. Edmund F. Slafter, and *The Works of Samuel de Champlain*, edited by H. P. Biggar. The Jesuits compiled annual reports on their activities in New France, beginning with an account of their efforts in Acadia in 1610 and continuing for almost two hundred years. These reports came to be known as *The Jesuit Relations*. In 1632, they began to appear in print in France. At the turn of the twentieth century, the material was edited by Reuben Gold Thwaites and compiled into more than seventy volumes. These missionary accounts have proven to be an invaluable resource for historians of New France in the seventeenth century. I have used a number of volumes in my research for this story. The Ursuline nun Marie de l'Incarnation was a prolific writer during the thirty-three years she spent in Quebec. It is believed that she wrote some three thousand letters; of that number, less than three hundred have survived. In her book, *Marie of the Incarnation*, Irene Mahoney included Marie's *Relation of 1654* (detailing her life in Quebec) and selected letters Marie wrote to her superiors in France and to her son, Claude.

These individuals were writing for a particular audience in France and had specific motives. Champlain focused on the natives and the terrain of the New World. The missionaries and Marie de l'Incarnation, writing for their superiors and sponsors in France, were focused on their evangelical mission of conversion and ministering to the aborigines. All of these writers reflected their upbringing and the bias of the times. None of them wrote at length about the early French settlers or life in the French settlements. Hélène is mentioned in Champlain's will. Otherwise, she is not cited in the writings of these individuals. Taken together, however, these early residents of the colony wrote enough to allow me to piece together an outline of life in New France.

There are other histories of New France written in the seventeenth century. The Récollet friar Gabriel Sagard arrived in Canada in 1623 and wrote his *L'Histoire du Canada* in 1636. Father Christian Le Clercq, another Récollet Missionary, wrote *The First Establishment of the Faith in New France* in 1691(translated by John Gilmary Shea in 1881). Although he was not a contemporary of the first missionaries to come to the New World, he availed himself of then-extant documents to compile his history. Hélène's own daughter Marie Morin joined the Hospitallers of St. Joseph in Montreal in 1662 and began writing the *Annales de L'Hôtel-Dieu de Montreal* in 1697. All of these resources have provided additional insight, although much of the earlier writing is hagiographic in nature, that is, idealizing its subject. I have tried to be more balanced in my reporting of the facts.

The original seventeenth-century documents and reports were written in French. Fortunately, most have been translated into English and I have relied on the English translations or I have had help with the French translations.

With respect to the world in which Hélène lived, virtually all of the early writings on Quebec referred to the aborigines of the New World as savages. Indeed, the word "savage" as applied to these natives is found in all of the writings of seventeenth-century Europeans. It was their word for the indigenous peoples of the Americas. Some writers have suggested that the word originally referred to someone growing up close to nature, pure and uncorrupted by the more base side of complex societies. Nevertheless, it came to be a strongly negative and condescending term, often associated with backwardness and cruelty. For this reason, the word is not used again in this book.

The *Dictionary of Canadian Biography Online* offers brief biographical sketches of the explorers, missionaries, and many of the first French immigrants to the New World. This is a research and publishing project of the University of Toronto and the Université Laval, initiated in 1959. I have used this resource, as well as material from other credible writers, to flesh out the story of the world in which Hélène lived. All of these sources are listed in the Bibliography.

I've included a lot of information on what was going on in seventeenth-century France, in Paris in particular. Many of the early settlers had close ties to Paris. Others came from the seaport towns of La Rochelle and Dieppe. The region of Normandy was well-represented. These pioneers were thoroughly French and they brought with them their French attitudes and mores. Hélène's life was certainly molded and shaped by the culture of the mother country.

There are clearly difficulties in reconstructing the life of a woman who lived four hundred years ago. We don't know what Hélène was thinking or feeling. It is difficult to imagine a life in a time and a place so different from our own. In reality, all biographies are incomplete. One can never know all of the hopes, sorrows, and dreams of an individual. These are buried deep within the heart and in the sands of time and that is as it should be. Hélène's life cannot be completely recreated by the limited public documents and histories of France and the New World. However, by painting a picture of the setting and the society in which Hélène lived, my hope is that a more or less faithful portrait of Hélène Desportes emerges.

HÉLÈNE'S
WORLD

Champlain's Habitation, 1608
(Champlain, 'Voyages of Samuel de Champlain, II,' PD)

CHAPTER ONE

DECEMBER OF 1620

Hélène's birth at Quebec; Winter along the St. Lawrence River; Fishermen and fur traders; Earlier explorations; Founding of Quebec by Champlain in 1608; Description of Champlain's Habitation and its inhabitants in 1620

It is believed that Hélène Desportes was born in Quebec in 1620, in the second half of the year, although the exact date of her birth is uncertain.[1] The colony at Quebec had been founded twelve years earlier by Samuel de Champlain and it remained a primitive trading post.[2] Champlain's Habitation, Hélène's first home, consisted of a few decrepit wooden structures surrounded by a wooden palisade. It stood a short distance from the banks of the St. Lawrence River. A small group of missionaries occupied a cabin nearby. On the bluff above was a rudimentary fort and a stone farmhouse belonging to one of the French families.

The small bands of Montagnais natives who camped every summer along the northern shores of the St. Lawrence had finished their eel fishing in the autumn and left for their wintering grounds. The sixty French men and women spending the winter of 1620-21 in Quebec were thousands of miles from their homeland and alone except for the occasional small band of aborigines that might stop by the settlement seeking food. Otherwise, there was no contact with the outside world. There would be no ships from France, or from any other country for that matter, for another five or six months. It was a harsh environment, and the survival of the French colonists would depend on knowledge gained from the trials and tribulations of those who had come before them, on their limited resources, and on their own determination. Hélène's survival was by no means certain; indeed, the odds were stacked against an infant.

The French, along with Basques, Spanish, English, and Portuguese, had been making the trip across the Atlantic to the North American coast for more than one hundred years before Champlain established the settlement of Quebec.[3] Beginning early in the sixteenth century, French fishermen set sail from the ports of Dieppe, Honfleur, Le Havre, La Rochelle, and Saint-Malo in the late spring of each year. They fished for cod, mainly on the Grand Banks of Newfoundland, but also off the mainland of North America. Basque whalers came to ply their trade near the coast of Labrador and in the Gulf of St. Lawrence. By 1580, it is estimated that there were 10,000 fishermen in some five hundred vessels making the voyage across the Atlantic to the Grand Banks each year.[4] This was in spite of the risks of ocean travel in the sixteenth and seventeenth centuries. The sailors encountered violent storms, dense fog, and mountains of ice that towered above their sailing vessels, and they often feared for their imminent demise.[5] In the late summer, the fishermen headed for home, avoiding the more severe tempests which would strike the North Atlantic in the autumn.

The Frenchmen who visited North America in the sixteenth century included explorers and adventurers, as well as fishermen and traders. Like other European visitors, many dreamt of finding riches. Some had ventured far inland along the rivers of the new continent. They had explored the St. Lawrence River valley, seeking a waterway that would lead them across the continent to the lucrative markets of Asia. The men who searched the northern reaches of this new continent and its coastal waters never found a northwest passage; nor did they find gold.[6] However, they did find wealth in furs and fish. Cod fishing in Newfoundland was one of Europe's most important transatlantic commercial ventures. Long before the establishment of Quebec, and lasting until the end of the French regime in Canada, France would import more cod than fur.[7]

Initially, it was the fishermen who brought animal skins back from New France. Beaver furs were particularly popular in France at that time and the pelts found a ready market in Europe. Increasing demand for beaver fur had enticed the French up the St. Lawrence River and, by the end of the sixteenth century, the fur trade along the St. Lawrence River had become established.[8] In addition to the French, there were ships from rival European nations making regular trips up the St. Lawrence River, seeking a share of the trade and commerce in the lands bordering this waterway.[9]

Champlain was not the first Frenchman to attempt a settlement in the vicinity of Quebec. Jacques Cartier was the first of the French explorers to spend a winter in Canada and he was the first to claim the territory for France. In September of 1535, Cartier encamped on the north shore of the St. Charles River, near the junction of the Lairet and St. Charles Rivers. This was approximately one league (three miles) from the site later chosen for Quebec. Nearby was the Huron-Iroquois settlement of Stadacona. Cartier stayed until the following spring, leaving the area in May of 1536. In 1541, he would attempt to establish a fort and settlement at Cap Rouge on the St. Lawrence River, a short distance to the west of Cap Diamant and the future Quebec. Two years later, the French explorers abandoned their settlement and returned to France, sorely discouraged by the failure to find either gold or a route to Asia. The ravages of scurvy and other diseases had sapped their strength. Relationships with the natives had seriously deteriorated.[10] It was to be more than sixty years before the French would again attempt a settlement on the St. Lawrence River.

As to be expected, the politics in France would play a vital role in the establishment and maintenance of a colony in the New World.

In the last half of the sixteenth century, planning for French colonization was disrupted by the Wars of Religion which raged in France
between 1562 and 1598. During these years, there were shortages of
food and a great deal of suffering in many parts of France. Armies
on both sides of the conflict set upon cities and villages, comman-
deered crops and livestock, and forced residents from their homes.
French life was in complete disarray; destruction was everywhere.
With the end of these wars in 1598, Henry IV, the monarch who had
ascended the throne in 1589, began to think of rebuilding France
and profiting from the resources in North America, if not about colonization.[11] There followed a series of commercial trade monopolies
given to various merchants and noblemen in the hopes of developing a successful business enterprise in the New World.[12]

The man to undertake another French settlement in the St. Lawrence River Valley was Samuel de Champlain. Although the financing
would come from the merchant companies, he would serve as lieutenant of the King in New France and would have personal command over the colony.[13] Champlain was a seasoned explorer. Prior to
the establishment of a settlement at Quebec, he had spent a number
of years in the New World. His first trip to New France was in 1603.
At this time, both the French and the English were exploring the
Atlantic Coast of North America, intent upon finding locations suitable for the establishment of settlements. Following a six-month trip
to the North American continent in 1603, Champlain wrote a "small
discourse" for the benefit of the King. He wrote about the natives,
their way of life, lodging, diet, clothing, religion, celebrations, and
warfare. He also made drawings of the rivers, harbors, native settlements, and plants he discovered. After a winter in France, Champlain
sailed again to the New World in May of 1604. He did not return
to his native country until 1607, more than three years later. During
that time he explored the New World from Nova Scotia south to the
coast of Massachusetts. As before, Champlain provided the King
with detailed narratives, maps, and drawings of the region.[14]

On April 13, 1608, Champlain departed from Honfleur, France
with the intention of establishing a permanent settlement in New

France. On June 3, he dropped anchor at the seasonal trading post of Tadoussac, established by French merchants at the mouth of the St. Lawrence River in 1600.[15] From there he traveled west. For the site of his settlement, Champlain chose a flat area at a narrow point along the St. Lawrence River where it is joined by the St. Charles River. This narrow strip of land lay at the base of a promontory which the French named Cap Diamant. The bluff rising steeply above the river would provide good defensive possibilities, as it offered a commanding view of the river and the surrounding countryside. Below the promontory and at water's edge, the land was covered with walnut trees. The Algonquins had named this area along the river "Kebec" which meant the "Narrows." Champlain borrowed this word for the naming of his new settlement which he determined to build here, believing that this would be an ideal location for protecting French interests in the fur trade against merchants from other countries. It was upstream from Tadoussac and about five hundred miles from the mouth of the river.[16] The St. Lawrence River valley was, for all purposes, virgin territory when the French immigrants established settlements in the seventeenth century. Although there were various bands of Native Americans camping, hunting, and fishing in the area, there were no permanent Amerindian settlements. Apparently, the Iroquois village of Stadacona had long since disappeared.[17]

When he had decided upon the site for the first colony, Champlain immediately set all of his men to work. Some labored at felling trees. Others were put to work digging a moat around the settlement. The first priority was to construct a storehouse to protect the provisions the men had brought with them, and Champlain wrote that this was accomplished in short order. Before the winter of 1608-09 had set in, Champlain and his men had completed a crudely constructed wooden fort and living quarters. Champlain offered a description of the settlement in his writings. The Habitation consisted of lodging for the governor, a storehouse, a dove-cote, a kitchen, a munitions warehouse, lodging for the workmen, a blacksmith's shop, and a cellar. A second-story gallery encircled the structure. The Habitation was surrounded by a wooden stockade; outside the walls of the stockade was a promenade, ten feet wide, extending to the borders of a moat. Eventually the moat would become fifteen feet wide and six feet deep. A drawbridge to the Habitation could be raised, if necessary. Cannon were mounted on platforms inside the stockade. There was open space between the Habitation and the river bank, as well as a garden for Champlain.[18]

In spite of all of Champlain's efforts, Quebec's founding was anything but auspicious. Twenty-eight men spent that first winter at the settlement. Of those, all but eight had died before spring arrived the following year, including ten from scurvy and five from diarrhea.[19] In the years between 1608 and 1620, Champlain divided his time between France and the New World. When he was in France, Champlain was working to promote the interests of the new colony.

In 1620, it was an odd assortment of people gathered together in Champlain's Habitation at Quebec. One would not ordinarily expect them to be sharing close quarters in a primitive settlement in this vast wilderness. They came from widely varied backgrounds and had different motives for being there.

Of course, Samuel de Champlain, as founder and administrator of Quebec, was the community's most prominent member. In the summer of 1620, Champlain had returned to Quebec with his young Parisian wife, Hélène Boullé, and their servants.[20] The small party left Paris that spring, setting sail from the French seaport of Honfleur on May 8 on the ship Saint-Etienne. After a rough passage, they arrived at Quebec in mid-July, two months later.[21] Champlain had married Hélène ten years earlier, when he was thirty-six and she was a child of twelve.[22] The pre-nuptial contract with her family was signed on December 27, 1610. Three days later, on December 30, they were joined in matrimony in a hastily arranged ceremony at Saint-Germain l'Auxerrois, the parish church of the late Henry IV. The bride came with a dowry of six thousand *livres*. Of this sum, Champlain received 4,500 *livres* the day before the wedding. The wedding guests included the physician, apothecaries, and counselors of the deceased King, as well as some of the leading merchants of Paris. The couple's wedding documents were signed by the King's notaries and record keepers.[23]

In seventeenth-century Europe, marriage was very much a business transaction. Champlain's marriage to Hélène was likely an effort on his part to forge a strong alliance with the French nobility and the administrators of state, as he would need a solid base of support for his ambitions in the New World. Hélène was the daughter of Nicolas Boullé who, as secretary of the King's Chamber, was responsible for carrying out the decisions of the King. Champlain had made his acquaintance during his military service in Brittany.[24]

In recognition of her young age, the pre-nuptial contract specified that Hélène was to remain at home with her family for two years. In the spring following the marriage, Champlain sailed alone for New France and Hélène remained with her family, as agreed.[25] How much time they spent together is unknown. Champlain was often away. Seven years later, in 1617, the couple would be sharing a home in Paris on the rue Saint-Germain de l'Auxerrois. It was close to the Louvre and to Hélène's family. Champlain, determined to provide for the comfort of his wife, had contracted with a young woman named Isabel Terrier to serve as a lady's maid to Hélène. She was the daughter of Richard Terrier, a reputable merchant. Apparently the arrangement suited both of the women. Isabel sailed with her mistress when the Champlains left France for the New World in 1620. Ten years after their marriage, Champlain and his wife had no children.[26]

Hélène, wife of Champlain, was the person who seemed most out of place in the tiny settlement of Quebec. Her dress, her style, and her mannerisms set her apart from the other women. Undoubtedly, Champlain had gone to some effort to see that his wife was as comfortable as possible. She would have had the best accommodations in Champlain's Habitation. But they paled in comparison to the luxury to which she was accustomed in France. Champlain and his wife had little in common. There was the discrepancy in age. Furthermore, they came from different rungs of society. Hélène came from a prominent Parisian family. She had been born and bred in the upper-class society of Paris and was accustomed to the finer things in life. Tradition has it that she was young, beautiful, and high-spirited. Champlain came from the coastal French town of Brouage; his parents had no particular standing in society.[27] While he had friends in high places, Champlain was a well-seasoned seaman of modest means. He was completely at home with the rank and file of soldiers, sailors, and the natives of the newly discovered world across the Atlantic Ocean. Fortunately, Hélène's brother Eustache had been a companion of Champlain in Acadia and in the settlements along the St. Lawrence River in New France. Eustache was also spending the winter of 1620-21 in Quebec and his presence must have been of no small comfort to his sister.[28]

There were other Parisians wintering in the little settlement of Quebec in 1620. Louis Hébert, an apothecary from Paris, was a veteran of early exploration and settlement in New France. He had come to Quebec at the encouragement of Champlain, with whom he had traveled on earlier voyages to the New World. Louis had been born in a home near the Louvre, the son of the apothecary Nicolas Hébert and Jacqueline Pajot, the sister of a notary. Louis Hébert must have been a man of some means. He is mentioned in the Paris archives in 1601 as having sold his interest in two houses, one located on the rue Saint-Honoré (just outside of Paris at the time) and the other in the Marais district, that he had inherited from his mother.[29] In 1590, his niece had married Jean de Biencourt de Poutrincourt, a member of the French nobility. It was presumably through Poutrincourt that Louis Hébert had met Champlain. In the summer of 1606, Hébert set out across the Atlantic with Champlain and Poutrincourt to explore the east coast of North America, seeking an appropriate site for a settlement. From 1610 to 1613, Hébert was in Port Royal with other Frenchmen, attempting to establish a permanent French settlement there. Port Royal was destroyed by the English in 1613 and Hébert was required to return to France.[30]

In the winter of 1616-17, Champlain was again in Paris trying to garner support for the settlement at Quebec. Champlain had noted with delight that many of the trees and the vines found along the St. Lawrence River were the same as to be found in Europe. Champlain described this land as "fine fertile country," and he envisioned Quebec as a permanent French settlement in the New World, rather than merely a seasonal trading post.[31] He was able to convince Hébert that this latest attempt at colonization had a good chance of success. In 1617, after selling his home and garden in Paris, Hébert traveled to Honfleur and sailed for Quebec.[32] He brought with him his wife, Marie Rollet, and their children, Anne, Guillemette and Guillaume.[33] The Hébert family would earn the title of "First Family of Quebec." It was their arrival and their determination to establish a home and a farm in this new country that laid the foundation for a truly permanent French settlement.

The tiny establishment at Quebec could not have been more different from the Paris familiar to Champlain, his wife, and the other Parisians who found themselves at Quebec that winter. Paris in the early seventeenth century was one of the largest cities in Europe. It was also one of the older cities, dating back to a Celtic settlement established there in 250 B.C. It was a city marked by great contrasts. On one hand, it was the home of the French king and aristocrats, an exciting and fashionable center for European art and culture. The landscape featured the Notre-Dame Cathedral, the Sorbonne, the Louvre Palace, and the Pont Neuf. However, the Wars of Religion had taken their toll on Paris. The city had experienced years of siege fighting. The city's population was reduced by as much as a third, to about 200,000 residents at the beginning of the seventeenth century. Buildings throughout the city were in poor repair. Streets were filled with filth and rubble.[34] There were shortages of goods in the markets. Neighborhood fountains no longer functioned and clean water was in short supply. When Henry IV settled into Paris in 1594, he immediately set out to rectify these problems and was able to make a number of improvements within a few years. The quality of life in the French capital improved significantly. Still, it remained dirty, smelly, and noisy; it was home to merchants and tradesmen of all sorts, as well as to pickpockets and prostitutes.[35]

Françoise Langlois and Pierre Desportes, the parents of the infant Hélène, along with Françoise's sister Marguerite Langlois and her husband Abraham Martin, made up a third family unit. They had arrived in 1619 in a party of thirteen Frenchmen.[36] Hélène's mother, as well as her aunt and uncle, came from the port city of Dieppe on the northern coast of France. Almost nothing is known about Pierre Desportes, Hélène's father, but it is likely that he was from the same general area. Seventeenth-century Dieppe bustled with maritime activity. It was the home of merchants and mapmakers, as well as shipbuilders, sailors, explorers and pirates.[37]

There were just six women among the sixty individuals in the settlement.[38] No doubt these ladies shared in each other's joys, sorrows, and labors. Marie Rollet, wife of Louis Hébert, was the oldest and most experienced, a woman highly respected by Champlain and the Récollet missionaries. Her presence would have been invaluable to the younger women of the group: the Langlois sisters, Champlain's wife, her servant, and Marie's daughter, Guillemette. In all likelihood, Marie Rollet attended Hélène's birth, serving as midwife. It must have been a bittersweet experience for Madame Rollet: joy in welcoming this infant into the world and sadness that she had lost her own eldest daughter Anne and Anne's newborn infant in Quebec only the year before.[39] The infant Hélène was named after Champlain's wife, who was chosen to be her godmother.[40] In 1620, the only other child in the colony was Guillaume Hébert, who had been born in Paris some time prior to the departure of the Hébert family for Quebec in 1617. Champlain had great hopes for the women of the settlement and for the children born there; he understood that they were key to the building of the colony. In the years to come, Hélène Desportes would play no small part in that effort.

A small band of French missionaries was also spending the winter of 1620-21 in Quebec. The Récollet Fathers LeBailly and Jamay, along with Brother Bonaventure, had arrived the previous summer accompanying Champlain and his wife.[41] The first missionaries in the young colony had arrived five years earlier, on April 24, 1615. They were four friars from the Récollet order [42] who had secured the blessing and the financial support for the missionary effort from the Cardinal and Bishops in Paris. Champlain had been given money by the French-Catholic authorities to meet the needs of the friars who would come to New France: clothing, vestments, chapel ornaments and other necessities for their mission.[43]

Also in Quebec that year was Baptiste Guers, the Commissioner representing Charles de Montmorency, viceroy to New France. There was a small posting of the King's soldiers. The others who made up the population of the settlement were clerks, workmen, builders, stone masons, carpenters, a butcher, a needle-maker, and farm laborers. Not all of the Frenchmen who had sailed to the New World wintered in Quebec. Some found the rigors of life in this untamed wilderness too difficult to endure; they returned at the end of the summer with the ships that sailed back to France. Over the years, Champlain sent others who sailed with him to spend the winter with the natives so that they might learn their language, their customs, and more about this land which the French were just beginning to explore.[44]

The quiet and stillness that surrounded the Habitation in December of 1620 were in sharp contrast with the flurry of activity which followed Champlain's arrival the previous summer. When Champlain returned from France, he had found his little settlement in shambles. People were living in squalid conditions. The few cottages within the Habitation were in great disrepair. Roofs leaked and the flimsy walls did little to protect against the cold and wind. The storehouse was on the verge of collapse. Nothing remained of his attempts to till the soil and raise crops. Champlain immediately set out to rehabilitate the cottages and rebuild Quebec. This time, the storehouse and a few other buildings were constructed of stone. It was also in 1620 that Champlain began construction of Fort Saint-Louis on the cliff above the river to better defend the city against its foes.[45]

The early settlers of Quebec were dependent on France for all of their provisions. Back in France in 1619, Champlain was able to persuade the Sieur de Monts and his partners in the fur trading company to support the ongoing needs of the fledgling colony. They drew up a statement whereby they agreed to send sufficient provisions to sustain a total of eighty persons at Quebec. One mattress, one straw bed, two blankets, and three pairs of new sheets were allotted for every two people. For clothing, each settler was to receive two coats, six shirts, four pairs of shoes and a cloak. For the defense of the colony, the following were to be purchased: forty muskets, twenty-four pikes, one thousand pounds of fine powder, one thousand pounds of cannon powder, one thousand pounds of balls for the cannon, six thousand pounds of lead and a good supply of cannon-match. To aid in the construction of the buildings, four thousand pounds of iron, two barrels of steel, ten thousand roof tiles, and ten thousand bricks were to be sent. An order for ten tons of lime was also placed, although later a source of lime was discovered near Quebec. The company also recognized that it would have to provide for the sick, so it requested a dozen stuffed mattresses to be stored in the warehouse for the sick and wounded, as needed.[46]

Champlain's dream of establishing a permanent French colony in the New World was ambitious. Each year brought challenges to threaten the existence of the tiny community. However, the man was not one to give up. So it came to be in 1620, twelve years after the founding of Quebec, that Champlain was determined to persevere in this isolated part of the world.

The first frosts heralding the coming of winter generally came toward the end of October. The leaves of the deciduous trees, which had turned brilliant reds, oranges, and yellows in early autumn, began to drop. Now, in December, the piercing cold and the hush of winter had settled over the land. The branches of the trees hung heavy with snow. When the wind was calm, the surrounding quiet was broken only by an occasional thud made by snow falling from the branches of one of the nearby trees or by water dripping from an icicle hanging from the roof of the Habitation. Winter generally brought gray, overcast skies, although, occasionally, there were days that were clear and sunny, so much so that the sun would be dazzling against the snow. Beyond the clearing, vast stretches of forest lined the river banks, peaceful and pristine in their virginal beauty. Looking northeast, low mountains in hues of blue and purple were clearly visible from the settlement. Across the river and to the south, the softer and more distant hills of the Appalachians might be seen.

Champlain was intent on seeing that French traditions were followed even in the most remote of outposts. This year, he had his wife with him and, of course, was anxious to see to her pleasure to the extent that it was possible in these circumstances. The Christmas celebration would have begun with the ceremony and pageantry of Midnight Mass in the humble chapel of the Récollet missionaries. Afterward would follow a feast of the finest food and the best French wine to be found in the storehouse. The commander and his guests would dine in style. Part of the provisions for the colony shipped over in 1619 included a dining service consisting of thirty-six each of platters, bowls, and plates, six salt-cellars, six jugs holding two pints each, six pint-pots, six half-pints, and six quarter-pints, all of tin. There were also two dozen table cloths and twenty four dozen napkins. For the kitchen, a dozen copper cauldrons, six pair of andirons, six frying pans, and six gridirons were brought.[47]

When the French at Quebec finally settled down to sleep in the early morning hours, some might have dreamed of fortunes to be made in furs, while others, of the souls they would save for God. A few might have dreamed of crops they would plant in the spring. To be certain, there were those who dreamed of returning home to France as soon as they were free to do so. The infant Hélène, if she dreamt at all, dreamt the dreams of newborns who trust in those that surround them.

CHAPTER TWO

LATE SUMMER OF 1621

Later generations of French-Canadians would only read or hear of the fragility of life in the infant colony; Hélène Desportes would live those years. Winters in Quebec were long and harsh. The cold winds, the snow, the sleet, and the ice would often come with the first of November, maybe earlier, and last through May. It was not unheard of to find snow on the ground in the month of June. Eventually, the days would grow warmer. The ice on the river thawed and the snow melted. Trees began to leaf out. A myriad of birds filled the air with song. Wildflowers, in various shades of pinks and purples, blues and yellows, dotted the river banks and filled the meadows. Woodland creatures, large and small, reappeared in the nearby forest. Spring arrived in the St. Lawrence River valley, with summer close on its heels. Along with it came new life and renewed hope.

Hélène was now a year old and had survived her first winter. In 1621, she and Guillaume Hébert were still the only children in the settlement. The marriage of Guillaume Couillard with Guillemette Hébert was celebrated on August 26, 1621.[1] Marguerite Langlois and Abraham Martin, Hélène's aunt and uncle, were expecting a child in the fall.[2] The colonists could look forward to having additional children in the community.

The French settlers, confined in close quarters for the long winter, were happy to be outdoors again. However, there was much work to be done in the summer months. When Champlain was around, he made sure that everyone was busy. Fort Saint-Louis was not yet finished. There were the annual repairs to the compound. Land had to be cleared and planted. The settlers had no equipment for tilling the soil. The first person to use a plow would be Guillaume Couillard, Louis Hébert's son-in-law, in 1628.[3] Men and women alike were employed in the business of sustaining the colony. Whatever could be obtained by hunting, fishing, gathering, or cultivating the land had to be in quantities sufficient to address immediate needs; it also had to last through the long winters. A later missionary to Quebec would describe the workload thus:

> It must be confessed that the work is great in these beginnings; the men are the horses and oxen; they carry or drag wood, trees, or stones; they till the soil, they harrow it. The insects in summer, the snows in winter, and a thousand other inconveniences, are very troublesome. The youth who in France worked in the shade find here a great difference. I am astonished that the hardships they have to undergo, in doing things they have never done before, do not cause them to make a greater outcry than they do.[4]

A short distance from Champlain's Habitation, the Récollet fathers were hard at work at their enclave along the banks of the St. Charles River. They were putting the finishing touches on their convent and chapel which they had begun the previous year, in 1620, and had named Notre-Dame-des-Anges.[5] The convent was a wooden structure measuring thirty-four feet long and twenty-two feet wide. The building had two floors, with a tower built above the front door. The chapel and the kitchen were on the first floor. The second floor included one large room and four small rooms. Two of the smaller rooms were set apart to accommodate the needs of the sick. The building was in the middle of an enclosure and looked more like a dungeon. Privacy and warmth were provided by curtains made out of fur. There were three turrets and a moat constructed to defend against possible attack by the natives. Gardens were established in the four corners of the enclosure. The Récollet friar Gabriel Sagard, who first came to Canada in 1623, might have exaggerated when he remarked that their home was very comfortable and resembled more the country home of a French nobleman than a monastery.[6]

The small settlement of French immigrants along the St. Lawrence River was still in peril. Supplies in the storeroom ran low over the winter. The waterway which coursed past the outpost was the lifeline for the settlers. With the coming of spring came anticipation of the arrival of a ship from France. Eyes automatically turned toward the water in the hope of spying a shallop or pinnace making its way toward the small bay at Quebec. Due to delays in leaving port and the unpredictability of weather in the North Atlantic and along the St. Lawrence, it was impossible to know when a sailing vessel would appear. In 1611, Champlain's journey to New France had taken seventy-four days. He had left the French seaport of Honfleur on the 5th of March, but had encountered foul weather and rough seas. His ship did not arrive at Tadoussac on the St. Lawrence River until May 13. When the weather was fair, the journey was much quicker. In 1615, the same journey from Honfleur to Tadoussac took only a month. Champlain and four Récollet friars left on April 24 of that year and arrived on May 25. They had encountered neither snow nor ice and remarked that it had been a pleasant voyage.[7]

Champlain was eager to establish a colony that could sustain itself in the New World. In the summer, fish were plentiful in the rivers; the meadows and forests in the St. Lawrence River valley were teeming with wildlife. However, these were not enough to support a growing colony. From the beginning, Champlain had set his sights on establishing farming in New France. He wanted settlers who were willing to become farmers. He had high hopes for agriculture in the area around Quebec. Champlain, ever interested in the world about him, had discovered a number of familiar plants in the area. In the woods along the St. Lawrence, he had found cherries, plums, raspberries, strawberries, gooseberries, red currants, and other small fruits. Although wild and uncultivated, these fruit-bearing trees and vines were recognizable to the French. In 1608, the year in which Champlain founded Quebec, he had instructed his men to prepare the land around the settlement for garden plots. He believed the soil was fertile, that all manner of grains and seeds could be brought to maturity. Before the end of October of that first year, fields had been sown with wheat and rye. Champlain later noted in his reports that, after he left the colony the following year, the settlers neglected the fields. All of the crops had died, much to his distress.[8]

In the first years of the colony, only two men saw the possibilities of Quebec beyond that of a trading post: Champlain and his friend Louis Hébert, the apothecary from Paris. For many years he and Champlain were the only Frenchmen who had any interest in cultivating the land, and they faced significant opposition from the fur traders in the colony.[9] Champlain believed that agriculture was key to the colony's success. He was determined to establish farming in the colony so that the settlers would not be dependent on the mother country for their foodstuffs. Toward that end, he had convinced the trading company to send scythes, sickles, spades, pickaxes, and two mill-stones. Also provided were grains for sowing, in as great a quantity as could be managed, as well as other seeds for the kitchen gardens. Bulls, heifers, sheep, and other livestock were also to be transported to New France.[10]

If winters brought severe cold, summers might also be unpleasant. It was often hot and humid. Sudden thunderstorms appeared in the summer, with fierce winds that whipped the waves of the St. Lawrence River and were strong enough to make the ships at anchor roll violently in the heavy waves or break anchor. In these tempests, ships were driven into the mud or slammed into the rocks. In the summer, the woods were filled with a multitude of mosquitoes, flies and various other stinging insects which greatly tormented the French colonists.[11]

Several thousand years before the arrival of Europeans, aborigines had learned to survive in the harsh environment along the St. Lawrence River. In Cartier's time, Algonquin and Iroquois peoples hunted and farmed in the area that is now Quebec.[12] As mentioned in the first chapter, the name of Quebec came from an Algonquin word meaning point where the river narrows. The Huron-Iroquois natives called the area Kanata (Canada), which meant settlement or village in their language. Their capital, Stadacona, was situated on the bluff named Cap Diamant by the French and now the site of Champlain's Fort Saint-Louis. Initially, when the French used the name Canada, they were referring to this small sliver of land along the St. Lawrence River. In 1535, the explorer Cartier gave the name of St. Lawrence to a small bay on the gulf west of Newfoundland. By 1613, the name was extended to include the Gulf and the mighty river which flowed into it. Although it became known as the St. Lawrence River, it was also called the River of Canada. Champlain sometimes referred to the natives who camped in the area of Quebec as Canadians. Over time, the name Canada come to be applied to the whole territory north of the St. Lawrence River.[13]

The Montagnais, also known as Montagnards, were one of the Algonquin tribes that inhabited eastern Canada and were native to the Tadoussac region. The word they used to refer to themselves was Ilnout, meaning men-hunters of moose. Their main trading post was at Tadoussac, but they were semi-nomadic, roaming over a vast territory stretching north, south, east and as far west as Quebec. They did not cultivate the soil; instead, they lived off of what was found naturally in the woods and in the rivers and streams. When winter came and the rivers and lakes froze over, the Montagnais headed inland into the woods north and south of the St. Lawrence River, where there was the possibility of finding large game. In summer, they camped around Quebec and Tadoussac. There were other Algonquin tribes that settled along the Ottawa River, to the west of the Montagnais.[14]

In 1621, as in previous years, the Montagnais tribes had returned to their summer campsites along the St. Lawrence River. A number of families camped in the shadow of Champlain's settlement. Summer days for the French settlers were long and filled with hard work. This was not the case for the indigenous people. Life was much less demanding in the summer. Fish, fowl, and small game were readily available in the river and nearby forest. The indigenous peoples along the St. Lawrence didn't worry about storing food to last the winter. To the consternation of their French neighbors, the natives spent much of their time sleeping and socializing with their friends. There were games, story-telling, feasting and opportunities for young people to meet and court.[15] Summer was a time of replenishment and fortification for the rigors of winter.

These Amerindians were frequent visitors to the French cabins. The Jesuit Father Le Jeune would later describe the natives as patient and indulgent with children.[16] One can imagine that they admired and fussed over the French infant at the Habitation. When Hélène was not at her mother's breast, she would have been swaddled and placed in a wooden cradle fashioned by her father or perhaps the Habitation's carpenter. The cradle was the safest place for a baby in the crowded living quarters. When she began to walk, she would have been dressed, French style, in a frock that reached the ankles and was worn by boys and girls alike for the first couple of years.[17] In contrast, Amerindian babies were strapped to a board when they weren't in their mother's arms. As they grew, the young indigenous children scampered from place to place, naked, smelling of smoke, and smeared with bear grease. Champlain encouraged interaction between the French and these natives. He would have liked to see them become one people, albeit behaving more like the French and living under the Christian god.[18]

The lodges of the Montagnais were conical in shape. Cedar poles, arranged in a circle and tied together at the top, provided the framework. In the summer, these poles were covered with bark. Animal skins covered the structure in winter to provide extra warmth. The top was left open to allow smoke from the fire pit to escape. Each hut was between twelve and eighteen feet in diameter and might be inhabited by a dozen or more people. The cabins provided sleeping quarters and shelter from the elements; most activities took place out-doors. The native lodges were not permanent. As winter approached, the cabins were dismantled, to be transported and reconstructed in the winter hunting grounds.[19]

There were other indigenous people who came to the French settlement, mainly for trading purposes. Champlain was acquainted with most of these tribes through his many years of exploration in the New World. Two powerful tribes were the Hurons and the Iroquois. These natives were culturally and linguistically similar to each other and, at the same time, different from the Montagnais in culture and language.[20]

The Hurons had settled in the southern region of Georgian Bay in a comparatively small area measuring some twenty miles by forty miles. The land was relatively flat, with many meadows and lakes and a scattering of villages. The Hurons, as they were called by the French, referred to themselves as Wendat. They were the richest and most powerful of the natives in the Great Lakes area. These Amerindians controlled the fur trade to the West and transported furs to the trading posts on the St. Lawrence River; the language of the Hurons had become the language of commerce.[21] Their lodges, called long-houses, were described by Champlain in one of his reports:

> Their cabins are in the shape of tunnels or arbors, and are cov-ered with the bark of trees. They are from twenty-five to thirty fathoms [150 to 180 feet] long, more or less, and six [36 feet] wide, having a passage-way through the middle from ten to twelve feet wide, which extends from one end to the other. On the two sides there is a kind of bench, four feet high, where they sleep in summer, in order to avoid the annoyance of the fleas, of which there are great numbers. In winter they sleep on the ground on mats near the fire, so as to be warmer than they would be on the platform. They lay up a stock of dry wood with which they fill their cabins, to burn in winter. . . . They have pieces of wood suspended, on which they put their clothes, pro-visions, and other things, for fear of the mice, of which there are great numbers. In one of these cabins there may be twelve fires and twenty-four families.[22]

According to Champlain, there were seventeen villages in the country of the Hurons and numerous people. Around each village was constructed a triple wooden palisade to provide protection against Huron enemies.[23] Here, too, were a variety of animals, birds, and fish, the wildlife being much the same as found in France. In contrast to the Montagnais who did not raise any crops, the Hurons grew beans, maize, and squash on the land around their village. However, at the end of ten to twelve years, the soil was exhausted and the natives were obliged to move their village to a new site.[24]

Another group of indigenous peoples who would figure prominently in the lives of the early French settlers were the Iroquois. The Iroquois, sworn enemies of the Hurons, were divided into five nations, namely Mohawk, Oneida, Cayuga, Seneca, and Onandaga. These tribes lived south of the St. Lawrence River in what is now southern Ontario and the western part of New York State, and as far to the west as Lake Erie. The word "Iroquois" is Algonquin in origin and means "serpents." The name these people gave themselves was Hodinonhsioni, meaning "people of the great lodge." They lived together in large, oblong huts, each one sheltering a number of families. Like the Huron, they cultivated the land and lived in semi-permanent villages, moving when the top soil was exhausted.[25]

There were no roads in the wilderness, only a few paths. There were no horses or beasts of burden; there were no carriages or carts.[26] Rivers were the main routes of transportation and canoes the vehicle. The native modes of travel and transporting goods were readily adopted by the French who came to the New World and soon concluded that the canoe was the vessel of choice for these rivers and lakes. They were lighter, swifter, and easier to maneuver than the French sailing vessels. The canoes were constructed of birch bark, with ribs of white cedar forming the framework. These craft varied somewhat in size but generally measured 8-9 paces (20-22 feet) long and 1- 1 ½ paces (2 ½ to 4 feet) wide in the center, growing narrower at each end. The smallest could carry four or five persons, along with baggage. Two persons would row the canoe, one in the front and one in the back. If there was a woman on board, she would sit at the stern and steer the canoe. Great skill was required in handling the canoes as they tipped easily. They were light enough that the natives could carry them on their shoulders between rivers as they traveled between summer encampments and winter hunting grounds.[27]

When loads to be transported across land were too heavy for the shoulders of the natives, they were transported by a sledge or toboggan. This kind of sleigh was made of two boards, hewn by the native from the trunk of a tree with a stone axe and with perhaps the aid of fire. Each board was five to six feet long and about six inches wide, with the tip curved upward. The boards were bound together with wooden crosspieces. Strips of wood were attached to the sides and served as brackets to which bundles of furs and other baggage were fastened. The sledge was purposely narrow so that it could be drawn easily around trees and undergrowth through the pathless wilderness. These sledges were pulled by Amerindians over the rough terrain by means of a rope or leather strap which was positioned around the native's chest and fixed to the end of the toboggan.[28]

In winter, in addition to the narrow toboggans, large snowshoes and warm robes of beaver, bear, elk, and other animal fur allowed the natives to live and travel in the cold and snowy forestland north of the St. Lawrence. The natives made a snowshoe that was two or three times the size of snowshoes that were used in France. The French learned from the natives that the only way to get around in the deep winter snow was by wearing these snowshoes.[29]

Each year, the small community of French colonists looked forward to two events with great anticipation. One was the arrival of a ship from France bringing needed provisions; the other was the lucrative annual fur trade with the natives. Along the St. Lawrence River, the Montagnais controlled this traffic, trading in their own furs and controlling commerce with natives farther afield. Notwithstanding, the Montagnais peoples were forced to share the business with the powerful Hurons who controlled the fur trade farther to the west. Although there was trading at Quebec, the big trade fair was held each year at a spot which came to be known as Trois-Rivières, thirty leagues (ninety miles) upriver from Quebec. The indigenous people often traveled in great numbers and for great distances in order to attend the trade fests. They would join other Amerindians eager to exchange their bundles of furs for prized French wares. In the early years of the colony, before the great Huron nation was destroyed by disease and warfare, this trade yielded an abundance of animal furs to be sent to France to satisfy European demand.[30]

Hurons coming from Georgian Bay left their settlements in May. Traveling by canoe, their journey would take some six weeks: it would often be the first part of July before they reached the trading post at Trois-Rivières. When the Huron came, there might be hundreds of bark canoes on the St. Lawrence River. It was thrilling for the early French settlers to see these craft skimming lightly through the water. The trip between the Huron country and the French settle-ments was an arduous journey of some three hundred leagues (nine hundred miles) by water. The trip took the voyagers past more than sixty waterfalls and many long and dangerous rapids. There were a number of places along the route where the Amerindians had to leave the river and carry the canoes and baggage on their shoulders around the area of the river which was not navigable. Some areas of rapids stretched along the river for a distance of two to three leagues (six to nine miles). In addition, the Huron traders often faced attack from hostile tribes.[31] No doubt the journey required considerable courage, strength, and skill on the part of the natives. Yet they did come for many years and were a welcome sight for the French. One of the Jesuit missionaries would write of the arrival of the Huron at Quebec:

> Already a few canoes had arrived on different days, sometimes seven or eight, sometimes ten or twelve at a time; but at last . . . there arrived about one hundred and forty all at once, carrying easily five hundred Hurons . . . with their merchandise.[32]

For the Native Americans, as well as the European explorers and traders who came later, the mighty St. Lawrence River was the main artery for travel into the heartland of North America. It originated at the northeast corner of Lake Ontario and flowed over seven hundred miles to empty into the north Atlantic. Dense forest and verdant meadowland spread north and south along the river's edge. The river brought life; it could just as quickly bring death. This powerful river changed with the weather and with the seasons. When the days were warm and calm, the water flowing past the settlement was tranquil and welcoming. However, when storms blew in, the waters became perilous for anyone who found himself on the river. Strong winds whipped the surface into treacherous, white-capped waves. In deep winter, the St. Lawrence was stilled by a thick covering of ice and mounds of snow. The water froze first at the edge of the river banks; gradually the ice would extend all of the way across the river. When the river was frozen solid, the *habitants* could walk across the ice to the opposite bank. It was hazardous to cross the St. Lawrence in winter before it was frozen solid. There was danger that one could fall through thin ice; underneath, the current was swift and the water a numbing cold. As springtime approached, the water warmed and the ice melted, with chunks, large and small, drifting along the river; it was again a dangerous time to try to navigate the waterway.[33]

Champlain understood that it was the commercial possibilities offered by New France, in particular the fur trade, that drew many of the first Frenchmen to journey across the Atlantic Ocean. It was also what enticed the investors and sponsors of the transatlantic voyages. The discovery in New France of a new source of beaver furs was welcome news to the French. The demands of fashion in France were a major impetus for the establishment of a French commercial enterprise in the New World. By the end of the sixteenth century, wide-brimmed felt hats had become popular with both the French aristocracy and the Parisian bourgeoisie. It wasn't long before demand for the beaver felt hats had reached all levels of male society. By 1630, these hats had become a part of the standard French military uniform. Beaver skins were the ideal fur for producing felt. The process of felt making, known to hat-makers since the Middle Ages, converted the fur into a material that was warm, soft, pliable and weather-resistant. However, by this point, the beaver population in Europe had been depleted. Importation from Russia was declining. Furs from the New World were needed to support the fashion industry of seventeenth-century Europe.[34]

Native families along the St. Lawrence River required the killing of some thirty beavers each year to meet their needs for food and clothing. *Castor sec*, or dry beaver, was a fresh pelt, with just the flesh removed. *Castor gras*, or greasy fur, was a skin that had been worn by the natives for two or three years and was ready to be discarded. At this point, the beaver skin had become oily and had lost its long hair, thus exposing the short hairs that Europeans required in the felting process. These "used" pelts were thus more valuable to the French, and the natives were more than happy to find a market for their cast-offs. It has been estimated that several hundred thousand used pelts might have been available each year in the St. Lawrence-Great Lakes Region.[35]

In the beginning, seasonal trading posts met the needs of the trading companies. Tadoussac was the first trading post to be established on the mainland of New France and was located about 130 miles east of Quebec on the north shore of the St. Lawrence River. It had been established in 1600 as a trading post by François Gravé du Pont, a French merchant who had received a fur trade monopoly from Henry IV. It was also a seasonal settlement for cod fishermen and whalers. In the seventeenth century, ships from Europe would sail up the St. Lawrence as far as Tadoussac, which had a harbor large enough for twenty vessels. After this point, the river became more difficult for large ships to navigate: it was too narrow for them to tack back and forth to go upstream. Smaller vessels were generally employed to carry people and supplies up the river to Quebec.

For the natives, trade was a form of social exchange, accompanied by ceremony which included games, feasting, speech-making, and smoking of pipes. Goods of generally equal value were exchanged in the form of gifts. Before the arrival of the Europeans, the meat and furs collected by hunter/gatherers were traded for the food grown by the tribes who cultivated the land. Hurons traded tobacco and corn for the pelts of the semi-nomadic tribes of the northeast. Trading with Europeans simply expanded the options.[36]

By the time Quebec was established in 1608, the indigenous peoples were very familiar with European traders and used to exchanging furs and fish for metal tools and utensils. In the storeroom of the little settlement at Quebec could be found all sorts of things to exchange with the natives. There were blankets, cloaks, shirts and hats. Swords, ice picks, knives, iron axes, and kettles were popular with the natives. Other items for trade included foodstuffs such as raisins, peas, and sea biscuits. It would not be long before the Amerindians favored guns, gun powder, and brandy above other articles. The French, along with other Europeans, exchanged these goods for animal skins. While beaver pelts made the finest hats and other articles, the French also traded in otter, fox, marten, mink, raccoon, bear, deer, moose, wolf, and seal skins. The number of furs collected each year varied, generally ranging from 9,000 to 12,000 a year, although one year the French were able to obtain 22,000 pelts.[37]

For all but a handful of people, there were four incentives for travel from France to the New World in the sixteenth and early seventeenth centuries: fish, furs, the search for an inland water passage to India and Asia, and the conversion of the natives to Christianity. For the most part, the French wanted to get along with the natives and vice versa. The small number of French could easily have been wiped out by the Amerindians. That didn't happen: the French wanted to trade with the indigenous people and the indigenous people wanted to trade with the French. Neither group was interested in annihilation. While Champlain and a few others of like mind wanted to see more integration of the two cultures, that would not happen either.

There would be a succession of commercial monopolies that dominated affairs in New France in the first half of the seventeenth century. These trading companies were interested in profit and not in establishing a permanent colony in the New World. The promises to support the development of a permanent settlement were often forgotten and the needs of the fledgling colony at Quebec were ignored. The monopolies sustained the settlement at Quebec only insofar as it also benefited the fur trade. These companies did little to help establish agriculture or any kind of self-sustaining economy. The companies felt that once a colony was established, it would compete for the profits of the fur trade. Champlain's efforts at building a settlement were greatly hindered by the trading companies. The efforts of the missionaries were also thwarted; the men hired by the trading companies did not always share the religious and moral values of the religious men of the colony.[38]

The settlement at Quebec needed attention. Champlain worried that the King of France was distracted with other issues in the mother country. He, along with the Récollets and others interested in settling the land, had grown increasingly concerned about what they termed the "imminent ruin of the country." On August 18 of 1621, the inhabitants of Quebec assembled and chose the Récollet Father Georges Le Baillif to present a summary of concerns from the colonists and a petition to Louis XIII, requesting assistance in addressing the problems that threatened the survival of the young colony. This document was signed by Samuel de Champlain and by Baptiste Guers, the Vice Roy's Commissioner. The Récollet friars Denis Jamay and Joseph Le Caron added their signatures, as did a half dozen other Frenchmen at Quebec. Louis Hébert, Eustache Boullé, and Hélène's father, Pierre Desportes, were among those who signed this petition.[39] Over the years, there would be many letters and many pleas on the part of the colonists to the king and other powerful figures for support.

CHAPTER THREE

FALL OF 1625

———

More births among the French at Quebec; Departure of Champlain and his wife for France; Récollet activity and the arrival of the Jesuits; Amerindian dress, face-painting, lifestyle, and spirituality

Years had passed and Hélène was now five years old. Her world was well defined. Its boundaries extended from Fort Saint-Louis on the cliffs above the Habitation to the St. Lawrence River at the foot of the tiny settlement. Also included were the chapel of the Récollets on the nearby St. Charles River, the stone farmhouse of the Hébert family next to the fort in the Upper Town, and the scattered pole lodges of the Montagnais and other natives who camped nearby from the spring through the fall of each year.

It had been four years since a petition had been drafted by the colonists imploring the king for support for the little colony. There was little to show for their efforts. The population of Quebec in the fall of 1625 was only fifty-six.[1] That was four souls fewer than the number present during the winter of Hélène's birth. The number was small enough that the child knew every one of the French settlers, or at least their faces. No more families had arrived to join their ranks.

That is not to say that there were no changes in the little community. There were two new infants in the settlement. Hélène's Uncle Abraham and Aunt Marguerite were the parents of a little girl whom they named Marguerite and baptized on January 4 of 1624.[2] A year later, in January of 1625, Guillaume Couillard and Guillemette Hébert had also given birth to a baby daughter. She was baptized by Father Joseph LeCaron on January 30 and given the name of Louise.[3]

Hélène was dressed as a miniature French woman. No doubt her mother had fashioned her clothing with whatever material was at hand. Her dress would have had a long-sleeved, fitted bodice and a full skirt that skimmed the ground when she walked. She may have had additional petticoats, and nothing else, beneath her skirt. There would be a bonnet to cover her hair and shield her face from the sun. In the winter, a lined cape would offer some protection against the cold.[4] The garments were mended, patched, and refashioned as Hélène grew. In many ways, Hélène's dress reflected the thinking of the era. She was dressed as a little adult because children were expected to assume adult tasks as soon as they were physically capable of performing them. Older children assumed childcare duties in order to free the mothers for other tasks. Hélène would certainly have helped to care for Marguerite and Louise, the infants in the Couillard and Martin families. Before long, these girls would join the native children as Hélène's playmates.

It had also been one year since Hélène and the other settlers had seen their governor. On August 15, 1624, after four years in Quebec, Champlain, his wife, and their servants left the settlement, along with Champlain's brother-in-law Eustache.[5] Champlain's wife, Hélène Boullé, was never to return to the New World.[6] There is no record of any letters or other contact between the wife of the governor and Hélène Desportes, her godchild and namesake. It is easy to imagine that Hélène would grow up with only the most vague of memories, if any, of her godmother. Folk legends suggest that the pretty, young wife of the governor had made quite an impression on the natives.[7] Certainly, Hélène Desportes would hear many stories about this woman in the years to come.

The settlement was bustling with activity in the warm-weather days of 1625. Probably the biggest surprise of the summer was the arrival of four Jesuit missionaries. The religion of the Roman Catholic Church had been a cornerstone in the development of the colony from the first. By 1624, five Récollet missions were established in New France: Quebec, Trois-Rivières, Tadoussac, a mission in the Huron country, and another among the Nipissing natives. The Récollets realized that the evangelization of the natives was more than they could handle alone with their limited resources. The rules of their order, more severe than those of other Franciscan orders, forbade them to own personal property. The Récollet missionaries in New France had to rely on the support of the trading companies. They had become discouraged at the amount of work, particularly among the semi-nomadic tribes along the St. Lawrence River, the few conversions, and the lack of support from the merchants, many of whom were Protestant. They wanted the assistance of the Jesuits, in the form of laborers and financial resources, in expanding missionary efforts in New France. Father Joseph le Caron, a Récollet missionary who first arrived in Quebec in 1615, had spent the better part of ten years in the New World. He had returned to France to convince the King and the religious superiors of the Society of Jesus to send Jesuits to assist in the evangelization of the country.[8]

The Jesuits traveled in 1625 with only the oral approval of the King. When they arrived at Quebec, they were rebuffed by the settlers. No one wanted to receive them without specific orders from the King regarding their establishment in the colony. It was the Récollets who were able to convince the settlers that both they and the Jesuits could share in the missionary activity in the New World. And so the Récollets boarded the ship and invited the Jesuits to stay with them in their convent on the St. Charles River. The Jesuits were offered half of the Récollets' accommodations and half of their gardens. The Jesuits would remain with the Récollets until the spring of 1626, when their own lodging was sufficiently complete to shelter them.[9]

Father Charles Lalemant, the priest who led the first group of Jesuits to set foot in the little settlement of Quebec, was a learned and accomplished man with an illustrious career before immigrating to the New World as a missionary. Lalemant was born on November 17, 1587, the son of a criminal court lieutenant in Paris. In 1607, at the age of nineteen, he entered the Jesuit novitiate in Rouen. Between 1609 and 1612, he studied philosophy at the Jesuit College of La Flèche, and he returned there in 1615 to study theology.[10] In 1620, he was teaching logic and physics at the Collège of Bourges. In 1622, he moved on to serve as principal of the boarding-school at the Collège de Clermont. In 1625, he was appointed the first superior of the Jesuits of Quebec and given the task of setting up a Jesuit mission in New France.[11]

The Jesuits lost no time in acquainting themselves with the natives who had returned to their summer camping grounds on the banks of the St. Lawrence River near the settlement of Quebec. The missionaries were not the only ones closely observing the indigenous people. Like any five-year-old, Hélène would have been fascinated by everything happening in the native encampment, particularly after a long winter when there was no interaction with anyone other than the few French settlers. Her first playmates were the Amerindian children. Governor Champlain had been delighted to welcome the children into the compound. Children learn language quite easily. Certainly Hélène would have learned at least a few words in the language spoken by her young friends.

The indigenous peoples who camped at Quebec in 1625, as well as those who came to trade, were robust and notably healthy. As was the case every year, only the strong survived the winter. The ready availability of food over the summer months and into the fall contributed to their health. The native men were tall and agile. The women, too, could be quite tall and nicely proportioned. This was in contrast to Europeans of that era who were smaller in stature, with countenances that were often pock-marked. Champlain was to observe that a number of the young Amerindian girls had pretty faces, nice figures, and pleasant dispositions.[12]

Native clothing was generally utilitarian and limited to the resources on hand. Clothing served as protection against the elements, not a fashion statement. In the winter, the natives wore robes fashioned of the skins of beaver, bear, fox, deer, otter, elk, and other woodland animals. Men and women dressed in similar fashion. They arranged these furs around their bodies, with the skins wrapped under one arm and draped over the opposite shoulder. Sometimes the women fastened the skins with cord at the shoulders. The fur garments generally extended to the knee and were cinched at the waist with a rope made of dried animal intestine. In the winter, natives also wore leggings and shoes made of moose skin treated in such a manner to make it soft and pliable.[13]

When the days were warm, the men were all but naked, wearing only a strip of animal skin belted at the waist and falling below the navel to the thighs. A beaver skin might be slung across their shoulders as a sort of mantle. Many of the men smoked: a pipe and a pouch filled with tobacco were common accessories. The women were modestly dressed, although their breasts were not always covered. The natives smeared their bodies and those of their children with animal grease, mainly bear fat, in order to protect themselves from the elements: the sun, wind, and insects.[14]

Some of the natives went to greater effort than others to embellish their dress. Champlain noted that the Algonquins and Montagnais who camped in the vicinity of the French settlement paid particular attention to their attire. Some fastened bands of porcupine quills, dyed scarlet red, to their dress. These adornments were prized possessions and could be detached to be used over other robes when they wanted a change. Furs were trimmed and cured in such a way that a garment might be composed of bands of various styles and colors of red, brown and white. Some of the natives were also more skillful at fitting the fur skins to the body.[15]

Amerindians were often eager to trade their animal skins for blankets and French clothing. Early in the seventeenth century, natives had begun to wear French shirts, jackets, stockings and shoes. They also favored the European woolen blankets for use as capes in the winter. Although traditionally native men and women wore nothing on their heads, the men soon adopted the French felt hats as part of their dress.[16]

Humans have decorated their bodies from the beginning of time. The indigenous peoples of the St. Lawrence River valley enjoyed having their faces painted. Plant pigments were mixed with oil obtained from sunflower seeds, bear grease, and the fat renderings of other animals. Women painted their own faces, along with those of the men and children, in shades of red, brown, black, and blue. The particular design was left to the creativity of the individual woman. Dyed porcupine quills were also used to adorn the face. Men wore their coal-black hair in a variety of styles: long, short, or on one side only. Sometimes the men dyed their hair. Women generally wore their hair long and straight. For celebrations, the natives would dress their hair with bear or moose grease, then apply feathers, eel-skin bands, and other decorative elements. As opposed to European men, Amerindian males did not sport beards or other facial hair.[17]

When preparing for war, natives painted their faces in bold colors to resemble masks. Some had their countenances painted entirely in black. Other faces were more colorful: noses might be painted blue, while eyes, eyebrows and cheeks were colored black, and what remained of the face painted red. Some had a single, thick black stripe painted across the face in a wide band which stretched from ear to ear.[18] Equipped with spears, shields, bows, and a quiver filled with arrows, the natives looked fierce indeed.

Some years later, Father LeJeune would remark that the natives also painted their faces prior to making friendly visits, "just as a man in Europe arranges his toilet with care when he is going to pay a visit to some respectable family."[19] He had observed a young native preparing to visit the settlement at Quebec: "I saw his mother grease him and paint him red; she did the same to her husband. They find this so agreeable that the little children do not think they are beautiful unless their faces are smeared over with something."[20]

In addition to face-painting, Amerindian women took pleasure in adorning themselves with large quantities of porcelain beads.[21] The girls delighted in dressing up for the dances which accompanied many native celebrations and were much enjoyed by all in the encampments. Champlain described the young women he observed on one such occasion. They were:

> loaded with quantities of porcelain, in the shape of necklaces and chains, which they arrange in the front of their robes and attach to their waists. They also wear bracelets and earrings. They have their hair carefully combed, dyed, and oiled. Thus they go to the dance, with a knot of their hair behind bound up with eel-skin, which they use as a cord. Sometimes they put on plates a foot square, covered with porcelain, which hang on the back. Thus gaily dressed and habited, they delight to appear in the dance, to which their fathers and mothers send them, forgetting nothing that they can devise to embellish and set off their daughters. I can testify that I have seen at dances a girl who had more than twelve pounds of porcelain on her person, not including the other bagatelles with which they are loaded and bedecked.[22]

Dogs were everywhere in the Amerindian encampments. Descended from wolves, they were the only animals domesticated by the natives of North America.[23] These creatures were treated like members of the family and slept in the pole huts along with the other family members. The shelters were often wall-to-wall bodies, wherein man and beast each kept the other warm. The warmth was certainly welcome in the winter. In the summer, fleas were a constant torment. The dogs competed with the aborigines for whatever food was available. In spite of their liabilities, these animals did serve a function in the family unit. Dogs protected the women and children while the men were away hunting. They acted as companions for the younger and older folks.[24]

While the young children played and the dogs wandered about or lounged in the shade, the native women worked. Labor in the tribes was divided along gender lines. The French were amazed at the amount of work shouldered by the females of the tribe. They were the ones who carried the heaviest responsibilities within the camp and family unit. To them fell the burden of setting up camp, making a home, preparing the meals, and caring for the children. Women prepared the animal hides and made the clothes, using needles made of bone. They collected nuts and berries in the woods. Women broke camp, dismantling the lodges and bundling the materials to be used in the construction of the next shelter. When the group moved from place to place, it was the women who carried the heaviest loads so that men would be free to hunt along the way.[25] Of the Huron women, Champlain wrote:

> They till the land, plant the corn, lay up a store of wood for the winter, beat the hemp and spin it, making from the thread fishing nets and other useful things. The women harvest the corn, house it, prepare it for eating, and attend to household matters. Moreover they are expected to attend their husbands from place to place in the fields, filling the office of pack-mule in carrying the baggage, and to do a thousand other things.[26]

For the native men who lived along the St. Lawrence River, hunting was a year-round activity. Particularly in winter, the survival of their families depended upon their skills in finding and killing their woodland prey. The native diet of wild animals felled in the woods was augmented by fishing in the rivers and streams from late spring through the late fall. The men were also responsible for the construction of canoes, snowshoes, toboggans, stone axes, spears, bows and arrows. Champlain wrote that "having done these things, they then go to other tribes with which they are acquainted to traffic and make exchanges. On their return, they give themselves up to festivities and dances, which they give to each other, and when these are over they go to sleep, which they like to do best of all things."[27] Champlain was undoubtedly referring to life in the summer encampments. The search for game in sufficient quantity over the long winter was demanding and taxed the men to the limits of their endurance. Trading and festivities, along with making war and taking revenge on enemies, were activities pursued in the warmer months when life was much easier.

The missionary Paul LeJeune provided more details concerning the specific and distinct roles of men and women in the indigenous community. He was to observe that

> The order which [the natives] maintain in their occupations aids them in preserving peace in their households. The women know what they are to do, and the men also; and one never meddles with the work of the other. The men make the frames of their canoes, and the women sew the bark with willow . . . or similar small wood. The men shape the wood of the [snowshoes], and the women do the sewing on them. Men go hunting, and kill the animals; and the women go after them, skin them, and clean the hides. It is they that go in search of the wood that is burned. In fact, they would make fun of a man who, except in some great necessity, would do anything that should be done by a woman.[28]

The native value system differed significantly from French values. Chieftains exercised control through respect and consensus. The opinions of everyone in the tribe were to be respected. Natives disliked coercion. Even though the individual's role in society was defined by gender, natives valued individual freedom. Indigenous women had relative autonomy over their bodies, their sex lives, and the organization of their activities of daily life. Other values included sacrificing for the family unit, stoicism in the face of adversity, hospitality, and generosity toward the less fortunate. The "haves" were expected to share with the "have-nots." Individual ownership was unknown; everything was community property. Families were responsible for the misdeeds of their family members. Major transgressions were addressed through reparations provided by the family. The amount of the reparation depended on the nature of the crime and the sex and status of the victim.[29]

The missionary LeJeune would also record,

> Having spent a long time on that day in one of the large cabins of the [natives], where there were a number of men, women, and children of all kinds, I noticed their wonderful patience. If so many families were together in our France, there would be nothing but disputes, quarrels, and revilings. The mothers do not get impatient with their children, they do not know what it

is to swear. . . . There is no jealousy among them; they aid and relieve each other very generously, because they expect a return of the favor. If this expectation fail, they respect the person no longer, whoever he may be.[30]

While the majority of colonists were concerned with their own survival, the Jesuits and Récollets were concerned primarily with saving the souls of the natives. This was the reason that compelled them to leave the comforts of their monasteries in France to come to this foreign land. Those who arrived in the New World were filled with the missionary fervor which had developed as a response to the Protestant Reformation. These men wanted others to know and believe in God as they had come to know Him. They could not accept anything outside of their own belief system as valid. Seventeenth-century Roman Catholicism was a complex system of doctrines and traditions that permeated every aspect of daily life for the believer. God the Father, as well as Jesus, Mary, and the saints of the church were honored with Masses, processions, song, prayer, and other special devotions spread throughout the year. Outward manifestations of the Catholic faith also included elaborate churches and cathedrals, religious paintings, sculptures, rosaries, and other artifacts.

Native spirituality was seen by the French who came to the New World through the prism of the European experience and interpreted from a Christian perspective. The natives had no houses of worship and no formal religious ceremony; each prayed to God in his heart as he so wished.[31] The lack of a formalized religion among the natives was seen by the French as a serious failing. Champlain was among those who sought to bring Christianity to the indigenous people. He was fiercely loyal to his God, his King, and his Country. He worked tirelessly to plant a permanent colony in the New World that would bring glory and riches to France, but would also spread the word of God to the natives so that they, too, might one day enjoy a heavenly kingdom as envisioned by the French.[32] Champlain wrote in his journal, "I believe that they would soon become good Christians, if people would come and inhabit their country, which they are for the most part desirous of."[33] The French, with their focus on religion as they practiced it, did not accept the spirituality of the natives and their strong belief in a world beyond the physical world.

Champlain did observe that the Amerindians believed in the immortality of the soul. There were often elaborate funeral ceremonies to honor the members of their tribe who had died. A pit was dug and the deceased was buried with all of his belongings, which might include candlesticks, axes, bows, arrows, robes, kettles, and knives. Upon death, a person's soul left the body and traveled to the netherworld to join the souls of family and friends already there. It was believed that, although the items mentioned remained in the grave, the "souls" of the items would be useful to the deceased in the next world. The gravesite was marked with large pieces of wood, including one which was placed upright and painted red. If the deceased was a person of some distinction, the tribe celebrated with a banquet three times a year, followed with singing and dancing around the grave.[34]

The Amerindians along the St. Lawrence River believed that all of the woodland creatures were endowed with spirits and the natives took pains to honor these spirits. When a bear was killed, his bones were buried and not given to the dogs. This was to avoid offending the spirit family of the bears. The sun, the moon, the rivers, and other such objects to be found in the natural world were also animate and might respond to supplications from humans.[35] For instance, gifts were offered to the spirit of the river to ensure a safe voyage. In this manner, many aspects of the native lifestyle had spiritual undertones.[36]

Amerindians took great stock in their dreams, believing these visions foretold the future. As such, it was wise to act upon them. As one of the Jesuit missionaries would later put it: "They consider the dream as master of their lives. It is the God of the country; it is this which dictates to them their feasts, their hunting, their fishing, their war, their trade with the French, their remedies, their dances, their games, their songs."[37] The natives lived in fear of their adversaries. They often dreamed of their enemies and believed that the dreams were true. Those that camped near the settlement at Quebec were frequently alarmed at night. At times, Champlain allowed the native women and children to sleep inside the fort. Amerindian men were not extended the same courtesy: they were required to stay outside. However, Champlain would send five or six Frenchmen into the woods to reassure the natives that there were no enemies lurking nearby.[38]

For the aborigines, interaction between the physical and spiritual worlds was facilitated by soothsayers or medicine men. These individuals held positions of power and advised tribal members on a variety of issues. They ministered to the sick and dying. The natives were not of a mind to disregard or disobey the instructions of these men.[39] It is not surprising that the relationship between the native shaman and the missionaries was generally based on mutual suspicion.

The Jesuit Charles Lalemant wrote of the difficulties in evangelizing the Amerindians. In a letter to his brother Jérôme in 1626, he observed that the conversion of the natives would take time:

> The first six or seven years will appear sterile to some; and, if I should say ten or twelve, I would possibly not be far from the truth. But is that any reason why all should be abandoned? Are not beginnings necessary everywhere? . . . I shall hold myself only too happy to employ my life and my strength, and spare nothing in my power, not even my blood, for such a purpose.[40]

Years later, in 1648, Father Ragueneau, the Jesuit superior to the Huron mission, would remark, "One must be very careful before condemning a thousand things among their customs, which greatly offend minds brought up and nourished in another world."[41]

The daily life of the French pioneers was governed by the weather, by the seasons, by limited resources, by interaction with the Amerindians, by what transpired on the river, and by the traditions and dictates of Roman Catholic faith. Hélène, at the young age of five, was rapidly learning what she needed to do to fit into life in the settlement at Quebec. Champlain would soon return to the colony, and he would continue to be a significant figure in young Hélène Desportes' life.

CHAPTER FOUR

SUMMER AND FALL OF 1626

———∞∞∞———

Food for survival: the farm at Cap Tourmente, Louis Hébert's farm, Jesuit and Récollet gardens; French diet in the seventeenth century; Amerindian diet and banquets; Scarcity of food and the threat of starvation

On July 5 of 1626, Champlain returned to Quebec, having sailed from Dieppe, France with five ships. The first order of business was to expand the farming enterprise at Cap Tourmente. He had previously determined that this area on the north side of the St. Lawrence River, some 10 leagues (thirty miles) east of Quebec, would be a good site for a farm. Here there was a large meadow: open grassland that would not require labor-intensive clearing of trees. It would be a good place to raise the cattle that Champlain had imported from France. In July of 1626, Champlain employed every available man in Quebec in the construction of the farm. In his report, Champlain noted that the farmstead consisted of two cottages, eighteen feet wide by fifteen feet long, and a stable, sixty by twenty feet. A strong wooden palisade surrounded the settlement. The cottages were built in the style of the cottages of Normandy: half-timbered constructions of wood and clay. The structures were low and dark; fireplaces were made of clay and windows were covered with oiled paper. Two months after beginning construction, the farm was ready for its first inhabitants. Nicolas Pivert, his wife Marguerite Lesage, and their young niece became the first farmers of Cap Tourmente. Later excavations revealed that their diet included a healthy mix of fresh beef, pork, fish, geese, duck, corn, and beans. There would certainly have been provisions from the mother country: the wine, flour and other dry items prized by the French and not yet produced in New France.[1]

In the early years of the colony, food was never far from the minds of the French settlers. For at least the first half of the seventeenth century, the colonists in Quebec lived precariously from year to year, dependent upon the annual supplies from France to meet their basic needs. For Hélène, as well as for everyone else, it could be feast or famine: the availability of food was never certain. Each year, those who had spent the winter in Quebec eagerly awaited the arrival of the ships from France.

The vast majority of French immigrants to Quebec were not interested in farming. In his earliest explorations of the region, Champlain had noted that the soil along the St. Lawrence River was rich and fertile. However, clearing even a small parcel of virgin land for planting was extremely hard work. In spite of Champlain's enthusiasm for the establishment of an agricultural enterprise in Canada, he was unsuccessful in convincing many others of the worthiness of the effort. Indeed, in the first twenty years following the establishment of Quebec in 1608, only a handful of men were engaged in farming: Louis Hébert and his family, the Récollets, the Jesuits, and lastly, Nicolas Pivert at Cap Tourmente.[2]

In the nine years since his arrival in New France, Louis Hébert, with stubborn determination and hard work, had been able to clear some land and raise crops. The Upper Town had plenty of spring water. It was a good site for agricultural endeavors, as well as defense of the colony. It was here, a short distance from Fort Saint-Louis, that Hébert built his home and established his farm.[3] He would become known as the first French-Canadian farmer. Over the years, his skill as an apothecary and his small store of grain and vegetables would be life-saving for sick and hungry settlers. Louis Hébert was certainly the largest private landowner in Quebec at that time. He had been granted the Fief du Sault-Au-Matelot in 1622 and Seigneuries of Lespinay and Saint Joseph in 1626.[4]

Louis XIII had given the Récollets a property of two hundred *arpents* (approximately 170 acres) in the vicinity of their convent and seminary at Quebec. By 1626, the Récollets had cleared eight *arpents* (seven acres) of this land and were growing vegetables and grains.[5] It was a good beginning, as it amounted to half the total property under cultivation by the French settlers. The Récollets were intent on making themselves independent of the mother country for survival. It wasn't long before they had added animals to their enterprise: cows, goats, pigs, donkeys, and geese.[6]

The Jesuits, anxious to have a place of their own, were also busy getting settled in the New World. On March 10, 1626, the Jesuits received a concession of land from the Duke de Ventadour on the St. Charles River a short distance from Quebec and on the site where tradition says Jacques Cartier established his fort in 1535. When the Jesuits arrived in 1625, the Récollets had generously offered them a frame for their house, measuring forty feet by twenty-eight feet, which the Récollets had originally planned to use in the extension of their seminary. The construction of the Jesuit's cabin was described by Father Charles Lalemant in a letter to his brother Jérôme in 1626. The work was begun in late winter, apparently soon after receiving the land. Carpenters from the settlement helped the missionaries build their home, which was eight or nine hundred paces (steps) from the Récollet compound. Some 250 wooden planks were needed to add rafters, roof, and walls to the frame given the Jesuits by the Récollets. Even with inclement weather (there was still more than a foot of snow on the ground), they were finished by Holy Week. All of this was done in the spirit of collaboration to ensure the success of the missionary effort in the New World. Soon, the Jesuits would have their own fields under cultivation.[7]

There were gardens at Champlain's Habitation as well. In addition to the produce from these plots, the French colonists enjoyed all manner of fish, fowl and game as it came into season. This was especially true in the summer and fall. The other settlers who were not actively cultivating the land also spent time obtaining and preparing food. When not engaged in the fur trade or in construction projects about the Habitation, Hélène's father, along with the other men, would have spent a lot of time hunting and fishing. Her mother would have been among those caring for the small garden of the Habitation. She would also search for edible plants in the nearby woods. Hélène learned by watching and doing. She would certainly have been able to help in the garden with weeding and harvesting. She would also have accompanied her mother on forays into the forest where she would learn which bark, berries, and roots were edible and which were not. However, all of these efforts to obtain food were not enough to erase the constant threat of famine in the colony.

Bread was a staple of the French diet. In the New World as well as in France, inventories compiled after a death by those responsible for administering an estate would make note of the contents of the flour bin, the granary, and sown fields. Grains used to make bread included barley, oats, millet, rye, and wheat. After maize was brought to France from the Americas at the beginning of the seventeenth century, it was also used in bread-making. In France, bread had long been a symbol of spiritual as well as physical nourishment. The breaking of the bread by the head of the household was a solemn tradition, a gesture signaling the start of the meal. A peasant family might well have spent half of its income on flour and bread. An adult could consume as much as three pounds of bread a day. It was a source of cheap calories. The flour used in the making of bread depended on what could be sown in the region and it was often an uneven mix of grains. The process of turning a field of grain into bread was labor-intensive. At harvesting, the grain was thrashed by hand with flails, a hard job requiring strong workers. Once placed into storage, grain was vulnerable to parasites, rodents, moisture, and sometimes fermentation if temperatures were high in the granary. Eventually, grain was taken in sacks to a mill which turned it into flour. Bread-making included kneading and baking in a communal oven or in the oven of the seigneur. Sometimes *habitants* had individual ovens built onto one end of the house. Enough bread was baked at one time to last for a week or two. Large round loaves, weighing ten or more pounds, were produced. Thick crusts prevented the bread from going stale quickly. However, it didn't really matter if it did become stale, as this bread was often softened with a soup or porridge.[8]

Soup was also a mainstay of the diet in the households of seventeenth-century Frenchmen on both sides of the Atlantic. Soup or porridge might be consumed three times a day: in the morning (*déjeuner*), in the middle of the day (*dîner*), and in the evening (*souper*). A large pot would be hung on the hook over the fire in the hearth. This pot was filled with water, hauled from the river, lake, a nearby spring, or perhaps a rain barrel. The task of fetching the water might well have been the job of a younger child. Into this pot would be cast a variety of vegetables from the kitchen garden: peas, cabbage, carrots, turnips, leeks, and radishes. Edible roots and mushrooms from the nearby woods, and possibly a bit of meat or fish, would be thrown into the pot. Grains were also used in porridges. The soup might have been flavored by a variety of *fines herbes*, the exact mix depending on the local climate and terrain. The French were familiar with chives, tarragon, sage, thyme, basil, shallots, and garlic. This broth would simmer over the fire all day. The soup was thicker, richer in variety, and tastier in the fall after the harvest. At the end of the winter it was considerably thinner. At mealtime, everyone would gather around the hearth with their wooden or earthenware bowl. Soup would be ladled over a piece of bread placed in the bottom of the bowl.[9]

Peas were one of the first crops to be planted by the French in the New World. The French loved their peas and considered them a basic necessity. To prepare them, the women had to soak the peas in a kettle of water overnight. A bit of salt pork and vegetables from the family's garden or root cellar were added during the cooking.

For a beverage, the men much preferred to drink French wine and brandy, although some beer would eventually be brewed in the colony. Women typically drank water.[10]

In writing to his superiors in 1634, Father Le Jeune would note that the workmen on the Jesuit property each required the following in food rations:

> two loaves of bread, of about six or seven pounds a week, ... two pounds of lard [pork fat], two ounces of butter, a little measure of oil and of vinegar; a little dried codfish, that is about a pound; a bowlful of peas, which is about a [pint], and all this for one week. As to their drinks, they are given a [pint] of cider per day, or a quart of beer, and occasionally a drink of wine, as on great Feast Days. In the winter they are given a drop of brandy in the morning, if one has any. What they can get from the country, in hunting or fishing is not included in this [list].[11]

If summer and fall were seasons of bounty in New France, late winter and early spring were often times of scarcity. For the most part, the winter diet of the settlers consisted of rough bread, lard, peas, beans, preserved pumpkin, root vegetables, and salted eel or sturgeon. There wasn't much variety in winter and, as previously noted, the soup became much more dilute in the early spring, when the supplies from the storeroom and root cellar were almost exhausted. In this matter, the diet of the French colonists was not much different from the daily fare consumed by the common Frenchman in the home country. However, when supplies dwindled in France, it was easier to obtain food from other regions in Europe. In Quebec, the colony still depended on the foodstuffs brought by ship each summer.

Certainly, a number of the first settlers in Quebec were from the more privileged classes of people in France. This would have included Champlain and his wife, his wife's brother, the Commissioner of the Vice Roy, and the missionaries. Most, if not all, of these individuals had spent some time in Paris. Like their Parisian counterparts, they had an appreciation for good wine and an appetite for an array of well-prepared food.[12] Perhaps they enjoyed their wine a little too much. Champlain kept a close eye on the supply at the Habitation. The entrance to the wine cellar was through Champlain's living quarters.[13] Even as bread and soup formed the core diet, there were a number of holidays in the course of the year which would have been celebrated with a banquet of the best of available food. Champlain was a generous man; natives were invited to these feasts, as were the other Frenchmen in the small community.

The French had long had a love affair with food and spices imported from other parts of the world.[14] One historian was to observe:

> The vigor of [French] culinary tradition in the sixteenth century is apparent when one considers the assimilation of foods originating in the Americas. Dozens of edible plants and animals were introduced to Europe in the decades following Columbus's voyages. Some of these were readily accepted as food – turkeys, beans, chili peppers, for example - while others, such as potatoes and tomatoes, were not. . . . Large fowl, both domestic and wild, were highly prized in the medieval kitchen. Capons, geese, swans, cranes, herons, and even peacocks were the pièce de résistance of many feasts and were thought to be especially appropriate for the tables of the nobility. The turkey had significant advantages over all of these – it was larger than the capon, meatier than the goose, and moister than other game birds. Accordingly, its rise to the pinnacle of European gastronomy was swift. In 1534, Marguerite, queen of Navarre, arranged for a farm near Alençon to raise turkeys for her table. Fifteen years later, sixty-six turkeys constituted the roast course at a banquet given for Catherine de'Medici.[15]

The settlers of Quebec were quite willing to experiment in preparing various foods, depending upon what was at hand. On one occasion, natives presented the Jesuits in Quebec with a gift of a piece of bear meat. It so happened that Champlain was dining with them that evening. When he had tasted the meat, he laughingly noted, "If they knew in France that we were eating bears, they would turn their faces away from our breath, and yet you see how good and delicate the meat is."[16]

Meat and grains were the main ingredients of the French diet of the seventeenth century, but there was also a renewed interest in vegetables. Beginning in the fourth century, practicing Catholics were required by the Roman Catholic Church to abstain from meat and other animal products during Lent and at other times of the year as a part of their religious devotion. Because vegetables were the basis of the diet on such days, these foods became associated with penance and deprivation, and were valued less than meat and grains.[17] The Renaissance in Europe brought a new appreciation for a diet that included a variety of vegetables. In the late sixteenth century, the Frenchman Olivier de Serres put together a list of more than thirty vegetables and herbs that were desirable for cultivation. These were "artichoke, asparagus, beetroot, cabbage, cardoon, carrot, cauliflower, chard, turnip-rooted chervil, chicory, cucumber, endive, fava beans, garlic, horseradish, leek, lettuce, melon, onion, parsley, parsnip, peas, pumpkin, radish, rampion, salsify, scallion, shallot, spinach, squash, and turnip."[18]

The French also found new ways of preparing the produce from their gardens. In the mid 1600s, two books appeared in France which revolutionized French culinary practice. François Pierre La Varenne, considered the founder of modern French cooking, published his cookbook, *Le Cuisinier françois,* in 1651. La Varenne's book provided recipes for some 150 dishes in which vegetables served as the primary ingredient. Nicolas Bonnefons published his *Les Délices de la campagne* in Paris in 1654. His book had sixty-seven pages devoted to the preparation of more than one hundred vegetable and fruit dishes. Breads and pastries were featured on forty-nine pages. There were twenty-one pages for egg dishes and nineteen for dairy products, as well as forty-five for fowl, fifty-seven for meat, and fifty for fish. Recipes for wine and other beverages filled forty-six pages. The diverse dishes featured in the cookbooks required access to the freshest of produce from farms and kitchen gardens as well as from the sea. While the best of these foods would have been available only to the more affluent French households, these books set the standards for French cookery and taste.[19]

Clearly, a variety of vegetables were in vogue in the French cuisine of that era and the early colonists wanted them in their diet as well. In his journal of 1618, a year after Hébert had arrived with his family, Champlain noted the contents of the former's cultivated land. In addition to "fine grain", the gardens of Hébert included cabbages, radishes, lettuce, sorrel, parsley, squashes, cucumbers, melons, peas, and beans, "as fine and forward as in France."[20] It was unfortunate that so few of the French immigrants were interested in putting in the effort required for preparing and maintaining these kitchen gardens. In addition, Mother Nature didn't always cooperate, so that a bountiful harvest was not guaranteed.

In contrast, the diet of the Algonquin natives, including the Montagnais, was fairly simple. In the summer the natives who camped near Quebec nourished themselves on a diet of fish, migratory birds, and small game. This largely meat and fish diet was supplemented by berries and nuts found in the forest. These natives did not sow corn or otherwise occupy themselves with sowing and reaping crops. From the middle of September to the middle of October, the main employment of the Montagnais was in catching eel. That in excess of immediate needs was dried to provide sustenance for the colder months when availability of other foods was limited. When they had dried enough eel, the natives left their summer encampment to hunt for beaver. Around January, when the weather had turned very cold and when the supplies of eel and beaver were exhausted, natives along the St. Lawrence divided into small bands and headed inland in search of moose, caribou, deer, and bear.[21] Natives did not simply roam the woods in winter. They had specific routes and territories which they knew from experience would be the best source of big game and would not infringe on the territory of the other bands. Survival depended upon cold weather and a heavy snowfall which would slow down prey and make the kill easier.[22]

The process the Montagnais natives used for preserving the eel was described in Father Le Jeune's journal:

> This work is done entirely by the women, who empty the fish
> and wash them very carefully, opening them, not up the belly

but up the back; then they hang them in the smoke, first having suspended them upon poles outside their huts to drain. They gash them in a number of places, in order that the smoke may dry them more easily. The quantity of eels which they catch in the season is incredible. I saw nothing else inside and outside of their cabins. They and the French eat them continually during this season [fall].[23]

The practice of tilling the soil and growing crops did not take hold among the Amerindians who populated the St. Lawrence River valley. Although they did obtain maize through trade with tribes who cultivated the soil, the Montagnais preferred to remain semi-nomadic hunters and gatherers. Consequently, they faced the real threat of starvation each winter. Their numbers were smaller than those of the tribes to the west and farther south.

Huron and Iroquois natives, as described in an earlier chapter, sowed corn as well as squash and beans.[24] The cultivation of this food helped them survive the winters. Native corn was productive, sometimes yielding one hundred grains for one sown.[25] *Sagamité*, a staple of the native diet, was a stew made from ground corn to which additional ingredients were added, depending upon availability. These could be vegetables, wild rice, animal fat, beans, fish, or wild game. In this dish, the corn was ground to a fine meal using a wooden mortar; the bran may or may not have been removed. If the bran was removed, it was done so with the aid of a fan made of tree bark.[26]

Many years later, in his *Jesuit Relations*, Le Jeune included a description of a visit to a Huron village made in 1639 by Father François du Peron, another of the missionaries. It offers insight into both the hospitality and the diet of the Huron peoples:

> They immediately spread a mat upon the ground for me to rest upon, and afterward brought four ears of corn which they roasted and presented to me, as well as two squashes cooked under the ashes, and a dish of *sagamité;* I assure Your Reverence that this food was delicious to me. The little children and others ran wonderingly into the cabin, to see me. My ignorance of the

language rendered me mute; and their custom, which is to say
not a word except chay, to one who arrives, made them silent
also; they merely surveyed me from head to foot, and all wished
to try on my shoes and my hat, each one putting the hat on his
head and the shoes on his feet.[27]

The missionary went on to further describe *sagamité*, which was
consumed each morning and evening. At times this dish was seasoned with pieces of cinders. The natives might also toss in

> a handful of little waterflies, which are like the gnats of Provence;
> they esteem these highly, and make feasts of them. The more
> prudent keep some fish after the fishing season, to break into
> the *sagamité* during the year; about half of a large carp is put in
> for fourteen persons, and the more tainted the fish is, the bet-
> ter. As for drinks, they do not know what they are—the *sagamité*
> serving as meat and drink; when not on their journeys, they will
> go six months without drinking.[28]

The natives prepared corn in other ways as well. Sometimes they
would take an ear and bury it under water in the mud, leaving it there
for a couple of months until it had rotted. It was then roasted or
boiled with meat or fish. "The women and children take it and suck
it like sugar-cane, nothing seeming to them to taste better, as they
show by their manner."[29]

The Jesuits who established missions among the Amerindians
ate much the same food and in the same manner as the natives.
They dined around the fire, seated on a log, with the ground serving as a table, and plates of bark holding the food. Provisions were
left to divine providence: "One person will bring us three ears of
corn, another six, someone else a squash; one will give us some fish,
another some bread baked under the ashes."[30] The missionaries kept
a store of glass beads, rings, small pocket knives, and awls to use as
currency in exchange for food. There were none of the luxuries and
delicacies to which the missionaries were accustomed in France.

The natives enjoyed partying and feasting as much as any other
people. Banquets were organized to honor the dead or to celebrate

victory over enemies. Many of the banquets were "eat-all" feasts: everything had to be eaten or one lost his reputation for bravery. If the feast was given in honor of someone who had died, a portion of the food was set aside, which was later thrown into the fire. In these feasts, care was taken that nothing was left, even for the dogs.[31] When there was something to eat, the natives gorged all day and into the night, without thought to saving anything for a later date. They lived in the moment, not concerning themselves with what tomorrow might bring.[32]

Winters were unpredictable. The indigenous peoples could not always count on finding enough wildlife to sustain them over the course of the long and brutal winters. In his journal recounting his first winter in Quebec, Champlain noted that in February, a band of Amerindians had appeared on the other side of the river desperately seeking the assistance of the French. Frantic for food, women with children on their backs, as well as men, set their canoe in the river which was still only partially frozen. Midway across, the vessel was splintered by a drifting piece of ice. Fortunately, the little group was able to jump on a large mass of ice which drifted to the shore where Champlain and his men waited. The French leader was amazed that the natives had the strength to cross the river. They were so emaciated and weak with hunger that they could barely stand. Champlain had his men take them to the Habitation where they were offered beans and bread. Champlain added that later, while the natives were setting up their lodging, they ate the rotting remains of a dog and a sow that had been cast aside by the French and exposed to the elements. On another occasion, the natives cut down a tree to reach the body of a dog that had been hung as bait to attract weasels and birds of prey. Champlain and his men warned them that the meat was unfit for consumption. Such was their hunger that the stench of the meat and the warnings of the Frenchmen were ignored. The fare was devoured as if it were a feast. There were times when the natives suffered so much from a lack of food that they would eat anything they could find, including the animal skins which they wore as clothing.[33] There were reports that, in the face of famine, natives sold their children as slaves in order to obtain corn.[34] Although the French did try to be generous, they rationed the distribution of provisions to the aborigines out of necessity. Otherwise, the food would not have lasted a month.

While Champlain saw the possibilities for agriculture along the banks of the Saint Lawrence River, he did not clearly appreciate the challenges. In the years ahead, the aborigines would not be the only ones in the St. Lawrence River Valley to suffer from hunger and be haunted by the specter of famine. Champlain, and later the missionaries and nuns, would often write about the scarcity of food in the colony. Undoubtedly Hélène experienced hunger and near starvation as a child. One can be certain that there were years when she, along with the rest of the colonists, grew quite thin and listless from a shortage of food over the winter months. She would learn how much effort it took to feed a family, and that, when she grew up, much of her day would be spent in preparing meals. She would also come to appreciate the French love of good food and great variety; it would contrast sharply with the simplicity of the Amerindian diet. Although starvation was perhaps the greatest danger the colonists faced, it was by no means the only threat to survival in the New World.

CHAPTER FIVE

FALL OF 1627

───❦───

Murder in Quebec; Strained relations with the Montagnais; Warfare among the Amerindians; Native and French methods of torture and punishment; Formation of the Company of One Hundred Associates; Deaths among Frenchmen in the early years of the colony

In the fall of 1627, two Frenchmen were murdered just outside of Quebec. An argument over a loaf of bread led to the crime. The French were not the only ones who liked their bread; the natives had also grown quite fond of it. The trouble started at the Hébert farm when one of Madame Hébert's employees refused a Montagnais native this staple of the French diet. To the native way of thinking, this was a clear breach of hospitality. Feeling wronged and desiring revenge, this Amerindian killed the first two Frenchmen he came across: Henri, a servant of Madame Hébert, and the commissioner Dumoulin. The men were killed with a hatchet and their mangled bodies thrown into the river. Champlain, returning from the settlement at Cap Tourmente, came upon what remained of the bloody scene. By this time the murderer had fled into the woods.[1]

It would not take long before word of the killings spread through the small settlement, along with the attendant fears and anxieties.

The men at Fort Saint-Louis on Cap Diamant would have been placed on high alert. In the Lower Town, the women and children, including Hélène, would certainly have been instructed to stay inside the Habitation. The relationship between the settlers and the Montagnais natives was tenuous at best. When the colonists were feeling less than charitable, they described the aboriginals as untrustworthy. They lied, stole, broke promises, and liked to take revenge.[2] There was no security in life among the natives; there were so many Amerindians and only a handful of French settlers!

Champlain was to note that in the native world, wrongs were addressed by retaliation against the wrongdoer's family or tribe. The natives took vengeance on the first person or people they met from that tribe or village. If a native was offended by a Frenchman, he took revenge on the next Frenchman he met. It might be the women or the children instead of the person who had committed the offense. To appease an aggrieved family, it would be necessary for the captains of those guilty of the crime to make presents to the relatives of the deceased. This was the native system of justice.[3]

The Montagnais were anxious not to break the ties they had with the French. Following their tradition and knowing that Champlain encouraged the natives to bring their children to the settlement to be reared in the Christian faith, the Montagnais offered three of their daughters in an effort to placate Champlain in this matter.[4] Champlain, well aware of the necessity of maintaining peace between the two groups, readily accepted their gift. He welcomed the girls into his home and treated them like daughters, seeing to it that they were instructed in the Christian faith, in needlework, and in other women's "exercises." Champlain became their godparent when Father Joseph Le Caron baptized them, christening them Foi, Espérance, and Charité, that is, Faith, Hope and Charity.[5]

There were still few children in the French settlement. Hélène was now seven years old and considered by the Church to have reached the "age of reason." At this point, she was old enough to receive some rudimentary education and her First Communion as well. It is likely that she learned alongside Champlain's adopted daughters. At some point during her childhood, Hélène learned to sign her name. Might she have learned this from the missionaries who could also have taught her to read and write? The little education French girls received generally came in convent schools. However, there were no religious sisters in Quebec at this time. The Jesuits and Récollets taught the native children, both boys and girls, their catechism and a few religious hymns. It is quite plausible that these learned men living at Quebec might have decided to give Hélène some basic instruction, particularly when all were often confined indoors over the long winter months. Hélène might also have been taught to read and write by Guillemette Hébert. Guillemette was literate, at least to the extent that she could sign her name.[6] She had probably received a basic education in Paris, before the family immigrated to New France.

Among the natives throughout the Americas, there were frequent conflicts with neighboring tribes. In New France, warfare generally occurred only in summer. During the winter, all energy was devoted to survival: finding enough to eat and not freezing to death. The cause of conflict was generally a desire to avenge a perceived wrong or to increase one's status, not to conquer the opposition. A few warriors, faces rendered fierce with war paint, would surprise their opponent along a forest path. There would be the rush of arrows and angry cries filling the air. Sworn enemies were killed, or captured and tortured. The attack was soon over. Women and children were often spared, although it was not unusual for them to be abducted and forced to join their assailants. These summer attacks were brief and mild when compared with European warfare of the time.[7]

Since time immemorial, men have engaged in the most horrific of cruelties when it comes to treatment of a vanquished enemy. The Native Americans were no different. Still, the French were horrified by their methods of torture. The writings of Champlain and the seventeenth-century missionaries offer a number of descriptions of the cruelties the natives inflicted on their prisoners. In 1610, Champlain and a group of Frenchmen accompanied a war party of Montagnais natives in an assault on the Iroquois, their traditional enemy. Champlain wrote of the torture perpetrated by the captors:

> They took the prisoners to the border of the water, and fastened them perfectly upright to a stake. Then each came with a torch of birch bark, and burned them, now in this place, now in that. The poor wretches, feeling the fire, raised so loud a cry that it was something frightful to hear; and frightful indeed are the cruelties which these barbarians practice toward each other. After making them suffer greatly in this manner and burning them with the above-mentioned bark, taking some water, they threw it on their bodies to increase their suffering. Then they applied the fire anew, so that the skin fell from their bodies, they continuing to utter loud cries and exclamations, and dancing until the poor wretches fell dead on the spot.[8]

Champlain went on to add:

> As soon as a body fell to the ground dead, they struck it violent blows with sticks, when they cut off the arms, legs and other parts; and he was not regarded by them as manly, who did not cut off a piece of the flesh, and give it to the dogs. Such are the courtesies prisoners receive. But still they endure all the tortures inflicted upon them with such constancy that the spectator is astonished.[9]

Missionary descriptions of the torture inflicted by the Amerindians were similar to those noted by Champlain. Captured enemies, regardless of their injuries, were made to sing and dance, amid much shouting and screaming from the victors. Prisoners were admired for bravery if they were stoic in their endurance of pain, although their lives were not necessarily spared. After death, the chest was cut open and the heart and other parts of the body were devoured by the persecutors. In many cases, the victim was eventually scalped. Women as well as the men participated in these brutalities.[10]

A number of French pioneers would fall victim to the cruelty practiced by the aboriginal peoples. Later in the century, a Jesuit missionary would write in his annual report that a French woman living in Montreal had been captured by a band of Iroquois in retaliation for the death of eight of their warriors who had been killed in battle that summer. After they had torn off the woman's breasts and cut off her nose and ears, the natives subjected her to a cruel burning.[11]

It was not that torture was unheard of among the Europeans. New France in the seventeenth century had its own methods of punishment and persecution. For offenses committed in early Quebec, flogging and branding were often used and considered a deterrent, as well as a public diversion. Property might be seized and the offender exiled from the settlement. More serious crimes called for a stronger sentence. The most common form of capital punishment in the colony was hanging from the gallows. Other measures of castigation included burning at the stake, beheading, and breaking on the wheel. This last punishment consisted of lashing the condemned to a wheel and braking his limbs with an iron bar.[12] The French, as well as the Spanish and other Europeans, used burning at the stake in the execution of heretics and witches. For Christians of the Middle Ages, this was a particularly horrific punishment. Destroying the body and scattering the ashes meant that there would be no Christian burial and no hope of resurrection. It meant eternal damnation.[13]

If there were tensions between the colonists and the aborigines, there were also serious conflicts among the colonists themselves. This surfaced in the first winter Champlain spent along the St. Lawrence. On the trip undertaken in 1608 to found a settlement at Quebec, Champlain uncovered a plot by his locksmith, Jean Duval, and three other of his men to assassinate him. Champlain condemned Duval to death for having conspired against him. The man was beheaded and his head placed on a spike, a grim reminder of the consequences of mutinous behavior.[14]

Fortunately, there were few serious misdeeds among the French in the early years of the colony. There were, however, tensions of a different sort. It is no surprise that, from the beginning, there was dissension in New France along religious lines. Roman Catholics were pitted against Protestant Huguenots. In France, Huguenots were generally better off financially and were hated as much for their economic successes as for their differing religious views.[15] Both religions were represented in the men who came to the New World in the early seventeenth century.

Dieppe, La Rochelle, and other coastal seaports had been Huguenot strongholds since the sixteenth century. In addition to the seamen, a majority of the shareholders in the commercial companies based at these ports were Protestant and a part of an international Protestant network. French seafarers enjoyed a life of freedom and independence. Some historians suggest that this is one reason that they were attracted to the Protestant Reformation.[16] Since Cartier's explorations in the mid-sixteenth century, private trading companies had been given responsibility for settling New France in exchange for a monopoly on the fur trade. In November of 1620, a new company had been formed and came to be known as the Compagnie de Caën. At the head of this company were Guillaume de Caën and his cousin Émery. The De Caëns came from Dieppe and were a bourgeois family of merchants and shipbuilders. Although Émery was Roman Catholic, Guillaume and a majority of crew members on their ships were Huguenots.[17]

The Compagnie de Caën was interested in trading for furs and reaping the profits. To the De Caëns, Quebec was nothing more than a base for the trading operation. They were not interested in supporting the establishment of a colony or the evangelization of the natives. The agreement signed by the King stipulated that in return for a monopoly on trade, the company De Caën would pay the stipends for Samuel de Champlain and the duc de Montmorency, Viceroy of New France. It specified that Champlain would be given ten men each summer to assist with building and protecting the settlement at Quebec. The company also agreed to support six Récollets and to settle six families, each family consisting of at least three persons.[18]

The terms of the agreement were routinely ignored, much to the frustration of Champlain and those few others who were interested in establishing a viable colony. The endeavors of Champlain and a few other settlers, principally Louis Hébert, were regularly thwarted by the merchants and traders. Champlain was to note that the trading companies themselves had not so much as cleared an arpent and a half of land (about one acre) in all the years during which they were to bring colonists and help to establish a permanent settlement at Quebec. At the same time, the merchants made claims on Hébert's annual harvests, requiring him to sell only to the company and at specified prices.[19]

Whether it was based more on religious affiliation or on conflicting objectives, Protestants and Catholics in New France were often in disagreement.[20] In 1621, the more prominent members of Quebec signed a petition asking, among other things, that the Huguenots be excluded from trade and settlement in New France. This petition had been taken by the Récollet Le Baillif to Louis XIII; however the King decided to respect the rights of the Huguenots granted to the Protestants under the Edict of Nantes. Nothing was done at that time to impede Protestant involvement in New France.[21] Over the years, the missionaries traveled back and forth between France and the colony to deliver messages to dignitaries, to promote the interests of the mission, to seek funding, and to collect needed supplies for the inhabitants. In 1626, Charles Lalemant noted in a letter to his brother Jérôme that this was his sixty-eighth letter, and not his last, destined for benefactors and for those who had written to him. Eventually, their pleas for support would have the desired outcome.[22]

In January of 1627, Cardinal Richelieu founded the Company of One Hundred Associates. The charter, ratified by the French Council of State in May of 1628, gave the company complete control of trade as well as settlement of the colony. Under the charter of the Company of One Hundred Associates, only Catholics would be allowed to emigrate. Huguenots were excluded from settling in the colony. It was the end of the Compagnie de Caën and the end of Protestant involvement in trade and colonization of New France.[23] The exclusion of the Huguenots in 1627 would be a turning point in the history of New France. Quebec would become Catholic and the French Protestants would find a welcome in the Dutch and English colonies to the south.[24]

The Company of One Hundred Associates was to be controlled and managed by Cardinal Richelieu, who held the position of number one on the list of associates. The other members of the company included noblemen, wealthy merchants and officials in high positions. Champlain was number fifty-two. He was still in New France when the Company of One Hundred Associates was formed in France. Champlain's wife, Hélène Boullé, supported her husband's membership in the company and, on his behalf, paid the capital investment of three thousand *livres* required of each investor.[25]

Apparently one thing that Champlain and his wife did have in common was the path they took in religious matters. Both were born to Protestant families, but eventually converted to Catholicism. It is likely that Champlain was drawn to the Catholic Church at some point in his travels and that he influenced his wife's decision to practice the faith of her husband. Both embraced their new religion with enthusiasm, although Champlain's friends included people of both persuasions. He showed no partiality in his treatment of Protestant and Catholic; however he recognized that the hostility that accompanied relations between people of the two faiths could cause serious disruption of attempts to establish a viable French colony in the New World.[26]

The charter of the Company of One Hundred Associates would require the company to send two to three hundred artisans representing a variety of trades in 1628 and to bring four thousand settlers to New France within the space of thirteen years, that is, before 1643. The company was obligated to support each colonist for a period of three years. At the end of that period, each man would be given enough land to sustain himself and his family through agricultural enterprise. Even before the charter had been ratified, the company had outfitted a convoy of eighteen transports filled with emigrants and supplies for the New World.[27]

There was no privacy and therefore few secrets in Champlain's Habitation. The great majority of the settlers at Quebec still lived within this little compound at water's edge. It is likely that Hélène

Desportes and her parents shared one small room with her uncle Abraham and his family. Hélène would witness many adult conversations and activities. Champlain, the Hébert family, and the missionaries were devoutly religious. However, many of the men who stayed at the settlement were adventurers, soldiers, and workmen under contract; they were a rough breed. The religion and social background of Hélène's parents are unknown. They came from an area in France known to be heavily Protestant. Like Champlain, his wife, and even some of the missionaries, this might have been their religious background as well. However, tradesmen and peasants generally assumed the religion of those in power. For this reason, they were probably practicing Catholics in Quebec, regardless of their religious affiliation in France. Certainly, Hélène was exposed to a range of language and behavior. Who knows what fears and prejudices she internalized from the adults surrounding her during her growing-up years?

In 1627, events taking place in France had yet to impact the colony. The settlers had more immediate concerns. In addition to hostilities with the natives, accidents and sickness had taken their toll on the French settlers. The specter of death had haunted the colony since its founding. The survival of only eight of the twenty-eight men who wintered in Quebec in 1608-09 was recounted in the first chapter. In 1616, Michel Colin and Marguerite Vienne had come to Quebec. In fact, Marguerite was the first European woman to come to New France. Both died that same year, the cause of death unknown. In 1618, the small group of settlers celebrated the marriage of Anne, daughter of Louis Hébert and Marie Rollet, to Étienne Jonquest. Just a year later, Anne died in childbirth. In October of 1621, Abraham Martin and Marguerite Langlois gave birth to a little boy, christened Eustache, who died before the year had ended. A man had been killed by a falling tree in 1621; two years later another man was crushed by a log. On January 25, 1627, Quebec's first farmer, Louis Hébert, died as a result of a fall on the ice and his widow was left to manage the farm with the help of her son-in-law.[28]

On the other hand, there were new lives to celebrate. On August 10, 1626, a second daughter, baptized Marguerite, was born to Guillaume Couillard and Guillemette Hébert. Governor Champlain was present and served as godparent. In 1627, Abraham Martin and Marguerite Langlois added another daughter to their family.[29] There were now five little girls in the settlement, with Hélène Desportes being the oldest.

After the departure of the sailing vessels in September of 1627, fifty-five Frenchmen remained in Quebec.[30] There were only about one hundred colonists in all of New France.[31] Across the Atlantic, England had declared war on France. This would soon have a major impact on the little settlement that was struggling to survive on the banks of the St. Lawrence River. Hélène's life would change dramatically.

CHAPTER SIX

NOVEMBER OF 1629

———⊰⊱———

Hélène arrives in Dieppe; Hunger in Quebec; Capture of Quebec by the English; Settlers return to France; Travel across the Atlantic: tales of storms, shipwreck, drowning, pirates, plague; Hébert family remains in Quebec

Nine-year-old Hélène was now three thousand miles from Quebec, the only home she had ever known. Her world had been turned upside down. She had just arrived with her parents in the small city of Dieppe, France. A series of misfortunes had brought her to the homeland of Pierre Desportes and Françoise Langlois.

For much of the preceding two years, the colony in New France had been in desperate straits. The last ships from the mother country had arrived in 1627. No supplies reached the French settlement in the summer of 1628. The winter of 1628-29 was long and brutal; there had been little food in the colony over many wintry months. Hélène and the other inhabitants were once again facing starvation.[1]

In the spring of 1629, as soon as the weather permitted and the ground had thawed sufficiently, the widow Hébert and her son-in-law planted six to seven *arpents* of land (about 5 acres) in peas and other grains. The four Récollet missionaries had four to five *arpents* of their land sown with various grains, vegetables, roots, and herbs. The four Jesuits and their servants, twelve men in all, had planted only enough to meet their own needs. By June, these crops had still not ripened. While waiting for the harvest, the colonists at Quebec went out every day to scavenge for edible roots, sometimes traveling a distance of six or seven leagues (eighteen to twenty-one miles) to find them in sufficient quantities. Others tried to catch fish, but it was difficult because they lacked fish lines, nets, and hooks. There was discord among the settlers. People in the Lower Town and on the farms had been reluctant to share with the men in the fort. Champlain would complain that he and his men were the last to receive any food.[2]

The previous fall, Champlain had sent twenty Frenchmen to be sheltered and fed by the Hurons in their country. In July of 1629, the men who had wintered with the Hurons returned. Much to Champlain's disappointment, they brought no food and became that many more mouths to feed. Champlain was desperate. The colonists had exhausted what remained in their storerooms. Even with strict rationing, the supply of peas had run out by June. Champlain had decided not to use the small amount of gunpowder remaining at the fort for hunting: he needed it for the defense of the colony. The settlement at Quebec had had to make do with a few sacks of corn purchased from some natives, edible roots and acorns from the woods, and fish from the river. Though minimal, these provisions kept the colonists alive.[3]

Since 1627, there had been no new emigrants from France to augment the scant numbers in the colony. Twenty years after its establishment, the settlement of Quebec included only five women and seven children. In addition to Hélène, the children included her cousins Marguerite and Hélène, the two daughters of Abraham Martin and Marguerite Langlois. Guillaume Couillard and Guillemette Hébert were now parents of Louise, Marguerite and the infant Louis, who had been baptized on May 18, 1629. Lastly, there was Guillaume Hébert, the son of Louis Hébert and Marie Rollet. Guillaume, the only one of these children not to be born in Quebec, was approaching adulthood.[4] By the late spring of that year there had been only three marriages and seven baptisms recorded in the church registers of Quebec.[5]

The underlying cause of the present difficulties in New France was the war that had broken out between the French and the English in 1627. The following year, the English began to harass the French and the Basque fishermen along the St. Lawrence River. In April of 1628, under the sponsorship of the Company of One Hundred Associates, the fleet of ships commanded by Claude Roquemont had sailed from Dieppe for Quebec, bringing much needed supplies and settlers. The squadron was intercepted by English ships sailing under the command of David, Thomas and Louis Kirke. The Kirke brothers captured the French fleet, sending those ships not sunk back to France. The following month, Father Lalemant and others were on their way to New France when the ship carrying them was also intercepted by the English flotilla. The Jesuits were rescued by Basque fishermen and eventually made their way back to France. They were to learn later that the English had blocked the arrival of all French ships to the colony. The French settlement was under siege.[6]

In early summer of 1628, the English appeared in the harbor at Tadoussac. In July, they attacked the French farm at Cap Tourmente. Frenchmen were killed, their fields plundered, their livestock slaughtered, and their home burned. The Kirke brothers sent a letter to Champlain demanding the surrender of Quebec on July 10 of that year. The settlement was in need of gun powder, muskets, and match, as well as food. In spite of very limited resources, Champlain was able to resist their efforts to capture the colony, somehow convincing the English that the struggling colony was stronger than it was in fact. If they were not successful in capturing Quebec in 1628, the Kirke brothers did succeed in keeping others away. No friend appeared in the summer of 1628, nor in the following fall, winter, or spring.[7]

A year later, in the summer of 1629, the settlers learned that the English Kirke brothers were again sailing the North Atlantic and blocking French ships to the New World. That June, a shallop arrived in Quebec from Gaspé.[8] On the boat was the Frenchman Desdames who reported that there were sightings of eight English vessels in the area around Acadia. Some of them were fishing while others scoured the coast for prey and booty. Desdames brought the settlers at Quebec one and a half barrels of salt, plus some extra for the friars. "More prized than gold" was Champlain's remark when he was presented with the salt.[9]

That spring, Champlain felt compelled to release an Amerindian who was suspected of murdering a Frenchman. They had nothing to feed him. Even though execution seemed a just punishment, Champlain did not want to kill him and incur the wrath of the natives:

> We had to let him go or live in continued alarm and apprehension with these [natives], who would not have been disposed to render us any help in our necessity. Indeed, seeing us feeble, and weak in number and left without help they might have made an attack upon us, or on those who went to look for roots in the woods.[10]

On July 9, 1629, a fleet of British vessels commanded by Louis Kirke appeared in the river across from Quebec. The English had come with five large sailing vessels, each of three to five hundred tons, well equipped with cannon and other firearms. There were 120 men on each ship.[11] In sharp contrast, Champlain had sixteen men and less than fifty pounds of gunpowder to defend the fort: powder for two or three cannon volleys and munitions for eight to nine hundred shots from the muskets. Hélène, along with the rest of the French settlers, was ordered inside the fort. Samuel de Champlain, with no food and little to defend Quebec, had no recourse but to surrender. On July 19, 1629, Captain Louis Kirke captured the settlement and raised the British flag.[12]

Making defeat even worse for Champlain was the fact that four Frenchmen decided to stay and serve the English: Étienne Brûlé, interpreter to the Hurons; Nicolas Marsolet, an interpreter to the Montagnais; Pierre Raye, a wagon-maker; and Le Baillif, an employee of the De Caën company who was known to have stolen a number of items from the company storehouse as well as from the missionaries.[13] Champlain and others found it hard to understand the motives of these Frenchmen; however, not everyone in the colony was interested in settlement. Some were opportunists and saw better prospects with the English.

On a more promising note, the Kirke brothers, who sailed under the English flag, had some sympathy for the French. While their father, Gervais Kirke, was an Englishman from Derbyshire, their mother was Elizabeth Goudon, the daughter of a French merchant of Dieppe. David, Thomas, and Louis Kirke had actually been born and raised in Dieppe in a community of Scotsmen who lived on the rue Ecosse. This family had business enterprises on both sides of the English channel.[14] Undoubtedly because of their family ties to France, the Kirke brothers, in particular Louis, treated the French settlers with great courtesy. The Governor of Quebec asked for the best terms possible and was able to negotiate the safe return of the colonists back to their native France.[15]

The Hébert family, who had been in the New World since 1617, was given the choice of staying or leaving. They were treated well by the English and encouraged to stay for at least one year; if not happy at that point, they could return to France. The Hébert family had invested a dozen years of toil in creating a new life in the New World. The fruits of their efforts would be lost if they returned to France, and they would face the possibility of begging for their bread. However, staying in Quebec meant residing among the Protestant English, deprived of their French compatriots and the solace of their religion. In the end, the Hébert family decided to stay, at least for the time being.[16]

On July 24, 1629, Champlain, along with the small band of French colonists who had decided to accept the offer of the English to return to the mother country, sailed away from Quebec.[17] Hélène sailed with her parents, her aunt Marguerite and uncle Abraham, and her cousins Marguerite and Hélène.[18] It must have been a very frightening and confusing time for Hélène. She was leaving the only home she had ever known. She was leaving behind her childhood playmates: Louise and Marguerite Couillard, as well as Guillaume Hébert. Would she ever see them again?

Two other playmates of Hélène would eventually be left behind. Espérance and Charité, the Amerindian girls whom Champlain had adopted in 1627, were also on the ship for the first leg of the journey, that is, the trip downriver to Tadoussac.[19] In his report of what happened in 1629, Champlain wrote that he had come to view these girls as his own daughters. For two years he had taught the girls their religion, French manners, and needlework, "plain and fancy." He wanted to take them back to France and he maintained that they wanted to go with him. However, one man had raised questions about whether they should be going. Marsolet, one of the French traitors, strove to keep the two native girls from leaving on the ships bound for France, stating that their native families did not want them to leave the country. Champlain bitterly accused Marsolet of debauchery and lascivious intentions concerning Espérance, who was twelve years old at the time. Champlain described in colorful detail the condemnation of Marsolet by Charité as her fate was being decided by the English Captain Kirke. Facing Marsolet one evening while the men were dining on board the ship, the girl spoke her mind, angrily denouncing the man and adding, "If I had your heart in my grasp, I would eat it more readily and with better courage than the meats that are on this table."[20] In the end, and much against the wishes of Champlain and the girls, the captain sent Charité and Espérance back to Quebec. Champlain entrusted them to the care of Guillaume Couillard, begging him to treat them kindly and preserve them from harm. Champlain noted that the girls would be useful in that household in many ways. Couillard, in turn, responded that as long as they wished to stay with him, he would treat them as his own daughters.[21]

Before crossing the Atlantic, the ship with the French on board stayed a while at Tadoussac. Supplies were replenished; the ship needed to be tarred and otherwise readied for its ocean voyage. Champlain and the other Frenchmen were allowed to hunt and fish with their captors. To everyone's great relief and delight, there was no longer a scarcity of food. Game was abundant. The French as well as the English dined on snipes, plovers, and sandpipers, as well as salmon and trout taken from the river. One can imagine the exhilaration felt by the colonists. Certainly Hélène and the other French must have savored every bite, after so many months of deprivation. Fortified with nutritious food, they would be better able to withstand the perils of the upcoming voyage. On September 14, all was ready and the fleet of ships weighed anchor and set sail for England.[22]

Those who crossed the Atlantic in the seventeenth century faced many dangers. It was, at the very least, most uncomfortable. There are many accounts of the terrible conditions faced by those who ventured upon the seas. Food was limited and often spoiled. Passengers were crammed into tight, poorly ventilated spaces. There was no privacy. Basic hygiene was lacking. Travelers sometimes shared the hold with animal cargo. They endured rough seas, storms, and illnesses such as dysentery, scurvy, yellow fever, and plague, as well as common seasickness. Not infrequently, there were shipwrecks when all on board were lost.[23] The more vulnerable individuals did not make it. It has been estimated that nearly ten percent of seagoing passengers perished at sea. If there was an outbreak of disease on the ship, that figure could be much higher.[24]

These travelers were also at risk of a frightening and, quite possibly, deadly encounter with pirates. Throughout the seventeenth century, seagoing vessels were plagued by buccaneers. Even the English Channel was not a safe haven. In September of 1624, one of the ships of the merchant De Caën was intercepted by Turks off the coast of Brittany and its French sailors forced into bondage. The Récollet missionary Sagard wrote in 1636 that, on his trip to the New World, his sailing vessel was menaced by a Dutch pirate before leaving the harbor of La Rochelle.[25] In 1635, one of the Jesuit missionaries to New France wrote that "when seeing that we were pursued by the Turks in leaving [the English Channel], I expected nothing else than to fall into their hands, to be loaded with chains, and to live in slavery."[26]

The fishermen who plied their trade off the banks of Newfoundland were constantly harassed by pirates. Between 1612 and 1620, more than one thousand fishermen and mechanics were carried away by buccaneers. On August 12, 1625, the Mayor of Plymouth, England informed his council that there had been twenty-seven ships and two hundred men captured by Moorish pirates in a ten-day period.[27]

Those who fell into the hands of the pirates could expect great suffering and untimely death. If they were not tortured and executed immediately, they were sent to the galleys where few survived. The treatment of the galley slaves was extremely cruel; sometimes wooden plugs were thrust into the mouths of the condemned to stifle the screams from the whippings they regularly received.[28]

The French were not innocent bystanders in this matter: they also engaged in piracy. In 1584, the Frenchman Jean le Frère noted that nearly all seafaring men in France, particularly those who came from the ports of Normandy, were Protestant. In peacetime, these French Huguenots used their boats for fishing or to transport goods. However, in the sixteenth century, during the war between France and Spain and in the religious wars between Protestants and Catholics in France, the Norman ship owners and sailors became privateers. These pirates from Dieppe, Honfleur, and La Rochelle transformed their fishing boats into warships by adding lightweight artillery. By this time, the sailing ships had become nimble and fast. They were rigged to allow sailing with the wind or against it. They were ready to trade, but also ready to raid and plunder. They sailed the seas, hunting for vessels belonging to Spanish and French Catholics, in order to bring back supplies which would aid the Protestant cause in France.[29]

Unbeknownst to the colonists from Quebec making their way across the Atlantic in 1629, Father Charles Lalemant, their beloved Jesuit superior, was facing perils of his own upon the sea. Failing to return to Quebec in 1628, Lalemant was again attempting an Atlantic crossing in June of 1629. This time, the group was shipwrecked in the Strait of Canso, which divides the Nova Scotia Peninsula from

Cape Breton Island. Father Lalemant survived, but Father Noirot and Brother Malot were drowned. Father Lalemant wrote of his experiences at sea upon his return to France at the end of October.[30] In later years, Hélène would hear about his travails; more than likely they would be repeated by family and friends gathered around the hearth. She would have been grateful that her own crossing of the Atlantic was not as harrowing.

Lalemant described the disaster at sea as beginning with a strong gale that blew in from the south-east, on the evening of the 26th day after they had departed from France. The sea was running high and the wind was great when, in short order, the vessel hit a rock and was smashed to pieces. Lalemant, who had been on deck at the time, found himself wedged between four pieces of wood. He had been struck hard in the chest and in the back. Suddenly another large wave engulfed him and freed him from the floating timbers. Fortunately, he was able to grab onto another plank of wood before what remained of their ship sank to the bottom of the ocean. The waves towered above him and crashed around him but, hanging onto the wood, he remained afloat in the darkness. After drifting for some time, he perceived that he was near what was most certainly an island. He looked around him and noted that other men were also floating toward land. Eventually the small group of survivors made it to the shore. Father Lalemant, missing his hat and shoes and with his robe in tatters, was so badly injured that the others had to help him onto the land and into the shelter of the woods. The first thing that Father Lalemant and the others did was to thank God for having spared them and to pray for those who had perished. There were twenty-four men on the vessel and only ten lived.[31]

Lalemant observed that God had been good to those who had survived the shipwreck:

> We found many things upon the shore which had been thrown up by the sea; I found there two slippers, a cap, a hat, a cassock, and several other necessary articles. Best of all, God sent us as food five barrels of wine, about ten pieces of lard [bacon];

oil, bread, and cheese; also an arquebus, powder, and everything necessary to make a fire.[32]

Such was their good fortune that the survivors were rescued by a Basque ship that had been fishing in the area. The master of this boat offered to take the Frenchmen home at the end of the fishing season. So Lalemant stayed with the fishermen until the end of September. There would be one more adventure at sea before Lalemant eventually reached France:

> So we left the coast on the 6th of October; and after having suffered the most furious tempests that we had yet experienced, we entered the fortieth day after our departure, the port near St. Sebastien [San Sebastian, Spain], where we were wrecked a second time, the Ship being broken into a thousand pieces and all the codfish being lost. All I could do was to escape in a shallop into which I threw myself, in my slippers and nightcap, and in this outfit I went to find our Fathers at St. Sebastien, whence I departed eight days later and arrived at Bourdevac, near Bordeaux [France], the 20th of this month.[33]

Father Lalemant would be surprised to learn that Champlain and the other French colonists captured in Quebec by the Kirke brothers the previous July, were also in France. Of this trip across the Atlantic, Champlain would later write that

> We were kept back by very bad weather accompanied with fogs till we reached the Grand Bank. . . . On the sixteenth of the month of October we came into soundings, and on the eighteenth we came in sight of the Scilly Islands. . . . On the twentieth, we ran into Plymouth [England]. . . . On the twenty-seventh, we passed Dover, where Kirke landed all our men, including the Jesuit and Récollet Fathers, to whom he gave passage, as well as to all others who wished to go to France."[34]

So it was that the young Hélène, in the company of her parents, the missionaries, and various tradesmen, that is, a majority of the other settlers from Quebec, landed in France at the end of three months of trials and tribulations on board ship.[35] No doubt soon after her arrival, sometime late in the fall of 1629, Hélène Desportes found herself in the lively French port of Dieppe. This was the birth-place of Hélène's mother, Françoise Langlois, and her aunt, Margue-rite Langlois. Marguerite's husband Abraham Martin, the Scotsman, was also from Dieppe.[36]

Dieppe was a walled city situated between two limestone cliffs on the Normandy coast of France. It was only a short distance across the English Channel to Britain. When Hélène arrived in Dieppe in 1629, it was already a very old city. Its history dated to the eleventh century, when a fishing village was known to have existed on the site. Vikings discovered Dieppe during their raids southward along the coast of Europe. During the Middle Ages, it became a town of some substance. Dieppe was a battleground in the Hundred Years War between France and England, waged from 1337 to 1453; both sides were intent on claiming its port. In the fifteenth century, sailors from Venice stopped in Dieppe on voyages between the Mediterranean and Flanders. Some settled there and added Italian words to the local dialect.[37]

In the sixteenth and seventeenth centuries, seamen from Dieppe were among the first to set sail for other continents.[38] The most advanced school of cartography in France in the sixteenth century was located in Dieppe. Privateers from the port city, authorized by the King of France, sailed against Portuguese interests and succeeded in breaking their monopoly on trade with West Africa and the East Indies. From Africa, sailors brought back ivory tusks that would be carved by Dieppe craftsmen, renowned for their skill, into a variety of articles. The wine, brandy, sugar, and salt trade of western France was an international concern. Ships regularly came into port from England, Spain, and the Netherlands. Merchants not only engaged in trade with these countries, but they also sent their sons abroad to learn the business of commerce. There were, at the same time, trad-ers from other countries based in Dieppe.[39]

Beginning a century before Hélène's birth, French vessels sailed from Dieppe to the Grand Banks of Newfoundland for cod fishing. Thomas Aubert of Dieppe had visited the newly discovered fisheries off these banks in 1508 and was the first Frenchman to bring a native back to France. In the seventeenth century, thousands of French citizens would emigrate from France to the New World from the port of Dieppe. The city was a major port of embarkation for New France.[40]

In Dieppe, there was much to take in for a young girl who had never been beyond the boundaries of the small settlement of Quebec. Wandering along its narrow and winding streets brought all manner of new sights, sounds, and experiences. Hélène had never seen so many people, so many buildings, so many ships in the port. She had never seen a horse or a carriage.[41] In the eleventh century, a wall had been built around the city with seven gates, five of which opened to the sea. Overlooking the city was a massive stone *château*, or castle complex, with its ramparts and turrets, built primarily in the fourteenth and fifteenth centuries. The time-worn stone pinnacles and buttresses of the Church of Saint-Jacques could be seen rising above the homes and businesses. Dieppe was one of the towns visited by pilgrims making their way to the Cathedral of Santiago de Compostela in northwestern Spain (El Camino de Santiago).[42] The Church of Saint-Jacques was built in the twelfth century on this ancient pilgrimage route. The original structure was destroyed by fire, but the church was rebuilt in the fifteenth century in Norman Gothic style. In 1562, the church was pillaged by the Huguenots, but again rebuilt. Now, in the seventeenth century, the oldest part of the church was the thirteenth-century nave. A beautiful stained glass rose window graced the west front of the church. Many beautifully decorated side chapels lined the nave and these were built with donations from the wealthy shipbuilders of the sixteenth century. Not far away was the Church of Saint-Remy, dating back to the thirteenth century. The city also had a school run by Jesuits and a hospital for the poor run by an order of Augustine nuns. How different Dieppe was from the tiny hamlet on the shores of the St. Lawrence River![43]

This is not to paint a rosy picture of Dieppe. In the late fall of 1629, the air would have a distinct chill to it. Darkness descended early, before the day's work was done. Dieppe's citizens would not have welcomed a group of bone-weary travelers, sick at heart and quite possibly sick in body from the grueling trans-Atlantic voyage. They came without money or means of employment. In crossing the ocean, there must certainly have been many times when Hélène was filled with terror and certainty that she would perish on the high seas. Now, although thankful to be on land and alive, Hélène must have wondered what the future held for her.

CHAPTER SEVEN

OCTOBER OF 1634

Hélène's marriage to Guillaume Hébert; Her stay in Dieppe; Return of the French to Quebec: first De Caën and the Jesuits, then Champlain; Quebec in shambles; Le Jeune's description of his winter with the Montagnais natives

Five years after Hélène was taken from the shores of the St. Lawrence River and transported across the Atlantic Ocean, she was again in the land of her birth, again in the small settlement of Quebec, and again making a big change in her young life.[1] Hélène had left Quebec in 1629 as a child. Her parents had both died during their exile in France. When she returned to the New World, she was an orphan in the company of her aunt and uncle. At the age of fourteen, she was considered a girl of marriageable age. So it was that on October 1, 1634, Hélène Desportes was wed to Guillaume Hébert, son of Louis Hébert and Marie Rollet.[2] Henri Pinguet and Robert Giffard de Moncel, two men who had arrived in Quebec a few months earlier, served as witnesses to the marriage. The couple married in the little chapel of Notre-Dame-de-la-Recouvrance, located near Fort Saint-Louis on the bluff above the settlement. Champlain had ordered the construction of the chapel in 1633, in thanksgiving for the return of Quebec to the French. The Jesuit Father Charles

Lalemant performed the ceremony. Lalemant, undeterred from his harrowing experiences at sea in 1629, had returned to Quebec in 1634.

Had Hélène been promised to Guillaume by her parents? Was this a decision made by her aunt and uncle? Did Hélène have any choice in the matter? These are questions for which there are no answers. However in that era, the marriages of young girls were often arranged by their parents or guardians.

It might well have been a day of very mixed emotions for the fourteen-year-old. The previous five years, beginning with the conquest of Quebec by the English in 1629, had been tumultuous years for Hélène. Champlain and the other French exiles from New France had reached the English port of Plymouth on October 20, 1629. A week later, those who were returning to France disembarked at Dover for the trip across the Channel. It was in England that the French received the news that peace between England and France had actually been declared two months before Quebec had been captured by the English in July of 1629. Before returning to his homeland, Champlain was able to extract the promise that Quebec would be returned to the French.[3] However, it would be years before Champlain and the settlers would again set foot in Quebec.

There is no record of the reception that the Langlois sisters and their families received upon their return to France. It is very likely that they were given, at best, a frosty welcome in Dieppe. In his *Voyages*, Champlain had remarked that the returning settlers would be reduced to having to beg for their bread: he foresaw the difficulty the families would have in returning to their homeland.[4] The immigrants to the New World would be dependent upon their families and charitable institutions. Hélène's parents had been gone for ten years. They were returning to France without any assured means of supporting themselves. There is no indication that either the Langlois sisters or Abraham Martin came from well-to-do families. Life was difficult enough for the working-class families of Dieppe; one can imagine that extra mouths to feed were not welcomed by those already struggling to survive. Unlike in the little settlement of Quebec, families could not look forward to ships bringing annual supplies of food and wine to supplement what they themselves could produce or otherwise obtain. Although Hélène's family circumstances are unknown, the reality of their lives was harsh enough that both Hélène's mother and father perished in the years following their return to France. Hélène's mother died on April 20, 1632 and her burial was noted in the records of the Church of Saint-Jacques.[5] According to one record, her father had already died in Lisieux; perhaps he had gone there looking for work to support his family.[6] With her parents gone, Hélène turned to her aunt and uncle. She had shared close quarters with them in Champlain's Habitation during the years in Quebec. No doubt she was attached to them and at this point very dependent upon them.

Quebec remained under British rule until March 29, 1632. On that date, the Treaty of Saint-Germain-en-Laye returned Canada to the French.[7] The merchant Émery De Caën and three Jesuits were the first to return to the colony on the St. Lawrence River, leaving Honfleur on April 18, 1632. De Caën had been appointed provisional governor of the settlement. Father Paul Le Jeune, a Jesuit from Champagne, France, had been selected by Cardinal Richelieu to be Superior General of the Mission in New France. Le Jeune had recently come from Dieppe, where he was in charge of the Jesuit residence. He was making his first trip to the New World in 1632. Along with him were Father de Noüe and Brother Gilbert.[8]

Those traveling to the New World in the spring of 1632 enjoyed fine weather at first, but it quickly turned out to be a stormy crossing. The ship encountered one tempest after another and was continuously buffeted by winds and angry seas. It sailed past enormous icebergs and the passengers and crew were prepared for death at any moment. Even though it was May, the weather was cold and wintry; at times, the sailing vessel was completely enveloped in a chilling fog. Accommodations on board were most uncomfortable. The men were unable to stand up in their small cabins. For sustenance, they had only salted food and no fresh water. It was with great relief that they eventually reached the Outer Banks of Newfoundland. Here they came across numerous vessels fishing for cod, including another ship from Honfleur. They were able to do some fishing themselves and the enormous quantity of fresh cod they caught was a welcome treat. When they entered the Gulf, they found whaling ships, as well as great numbers of white porpoises and seals. On June 1, the group sighted the mainland. On the land, they found good-sized partridges and hares. In the woods, wild fruit was beginning to ripen.[9]

Émery de Caën and the Jesuits arrived in Quebec on July 5, two months and eighteen days after leaving Honfleur. Quebec in July of 1632 was still very cold. There was snow in the woods and the deciduous trees were just beginning to leaf out. De Caën brought a letter requiring Quebec to be turned over to the French. A week later, on July 13 and with little ceremony, the British were relieved of their command. That same day, they sailed away on two boats anchored off shore. No one observing their departure would miss them.[10]

The French found that the settlement had been, for the most part, destroyed by the English. Champlain's Habitation below the fort was in ashes. Nothing but a few stone walls remained. Father LeJeune found the Jesuit house also in a sad state of disrepair. Doors, windows and sashes were gone. Two wooden tables remained inside; everything else in the way of furniture had been carried away. In addition, most of the detached buildings which Father Charles Lalemant had erected had been burned. The cabin and compound of the Récollet fathers was in just as sad shape. The lands that had been cleared by the Fathers and planted with wheat, barley, and corn, were now covered with peas grown wild and weeds.[11]

The Jesuits and other Frenchmen were greeted with great joy by the Hébert family.[12] Their home on Cap Diamant had remained untouched by the English. Their cattle were in good condition and their fields were producing grain. The children were healthy and the family was growing. In 1631, while the colony was still under English rule, a daughter Elizabeth had been born to Madame Hébert's daughter Guillemette and son-in-law Guillaume Couillard. This child was initially baptized by a Protestant minister, who was among the English living in the settlement, and was baptized again in the Roman Catholic faith by the Jesuits upon their return in 1632.[13] While they had been treated kindly by the British, the family had lost hope that the French would return to the settlement, and they were seeking a way to return to France.[14]

There had always been a diverse group of people at the Hébert/ Couillard farm. Champlain had left Espérance and Charité, his two adopted Native-American daughters, in Couillard's care in 1629. Over the years, there would be other indigenous children, as well as laborers under contract who would stay at the family compound in the Upper Town: work on the Couillard farm required lots of hands. Another person to find a place with the family was Olivier, a black child who came to the settlement on the ships of the Kirke brothers in 1629. According to Father LeJeune, he had been born in Madagascar. In 1629, upon the defeat of the French in Quebec, Olivier was sold to a French clerk who had collaborated with the English. When the French returned to Quebec in 1632, the child was given to Guillaume Couillard, now the head of a large household.[15] Father Le Jeune taught the lad his catechism and baptized him in May of 1633. The boy took the name of Olivier Le Jeune to honor his teacher.[16]

Much to the consternation of the Récollets, only the Jesuits were allowed to return to the colony in 1632. The powerful Cardinal Richelieu had denied the Récollets permission to go back to their missions.[17] To the Jesuits alone he gave the task of converting the natives to Christianity. Before leaving New France, the Récollets had buried their vestments and church vessels. In a spirit of generosity, they had instructed the Jesuits on where to find them and these were retrieved by the Jesuits upon their arrival in Quebec. The Jesuits also claimed the Récollet convent, chapel, and lands for their use, and transferred the title Notre-Dame-des-Anges to their convent and church.[18] One of their first projects was to establish a school for natives at Notre-Dame-des-Anges. The Jesuits believed that it would be through the children that conversion of the adults to Christianity could be achieved. Toward that end, the priority would be to establish schools for the native children. In 1633, Father Le Jeune reported how delighted he was to have two small native boys entrusted to his care by their parents. Soon there were twenty Amerindian children in the Jesuit school.[19] In addition, the Jesuits were charged with the spiritual care of the French inhabitants. Father Le Jeune would comment in his *Jesuit Relations* on the religious devotion and good behavior of the French in the small colony.

A year later, on May 22, 1633, Samuel de Champlain arrived to resume his position as governor.[20] Natives, as well as the few French settlers already at Quebec, were thrilled to see him and gave him a hero's welcome. French soldiers fired their cannon and muskets in salute; the Amerindians danced, chanted, and beat their drums.[21] One can imagine the sadness and anger Champlain must have felt at seeing his settlement in ruins; a lesser man would have given up the fight to establish a colony on these river banks.

Now in 1634, it had been two years since the first French had returned to the little settlement at Quebec. Champlain was happy to be living again in his adopted land. He was anxious to do whatever he could to assist other pioneer immigrants. Champlain had become especially close to Robert Giffard, one of the most active of the French in recruiting settlers for Quebec.[22] Giffard, a native of Perche, had originally come to New France as a naval surgeon in 1627, but had returned to France shortly thereafter. However, he had stayed long enough to make up his mind that he wanted to settle in the colony. In 1628, he was returning with a shipment of desperately-needed supplies when he was met by the English ships under the command of Kirke. His cargo was confiscated and he was turned back. On January 15, 1634, Robert Giffard was granted one of the first seigneuries in New France: land that extended a league (three miles) along the shores of the St. Lawrence river and a league and a half inland, at the point where the Notre-Dame-de Beauport river flowed into the St. Lawrence. Now, in the summer, Giffard had returned to New France with his very pregnant wife and two young children, in a convoy of three ships also bringing a number of other families from the rolling hills and farm country of the Perche region in northwestern France. These families carried the names of Guyon, Cloutier, Boucher, Le Gardeur, Juchereau, and Pinguet. Between 1634 and 1638, Giffard would bring fifty families to New France; they established homes in Beauport, on the côte de Beaupré, and on the Îsle d'Orléans. Most of the men had signed contracts with Robert Giffard, committing themselves to a period of work in the New World. Some would return home, but many would stay to become leaders in the community, leaving a rich legacy for the generations of French-Canadians to follow.[23]

Some of the French pioneers were moving farther up the St. Lawrence River to set up their homesteads. On July 4, 1634, Champlain established a fortified French settlement at Trois-Rivières, in order to have an outpost for the defense of Quebec and to protect the French fur trade with Algonquin and Huron tribes. The natives had long used this site as a rendezvous point for their fur-trading operation. There had been a French presence in the area since 1615: the Récollets had established a mission there in June of that year and had maintained it until 1629. In February of 1634, the Jesuits were granted six *arpents* (five acres) of land at Trois-Rivières. The first French settler in Trois-Rivières was Jacques Hertel, who had obtained a grant of land there in 1633.[24]

The French colonists might have been more depressed by the sad state of their settlement upon their return if it had not been for Father Le Jeune. He would certainly have reminded them of how fortunate their circumstances were, compared to life for the indigenous who had lived in the valley of the St. Lawrence for many generations. It had been six months since Father Le Jeune walked into Quebec in the spring of 1634, greatly surprising the small group of colonists who had given him up for dead. In the autumn of 1633, Le Jeune had readily accepted the invitation of one of the groups of Montagnais natives to travel with them to their winter hunting grounds. He welcomed the opportunity to learn the language and customs of the natives as a necessary step in bringing about the conversion of the aborigines. Now his tales of survival in the wild would have been repeated in front of the hearth in the cottages of the French settlers. He later wrote a lengthy and detailed account of his adventures in his journal to his superiors in France.[25]

Father Le Jeune and the band of Montagnais natives left Quebec on October 18, 1633. Initially, the group numbered nineteen men, women, and children, but eventually this number would grow to forty-five natives in Le Jeune's traveling party. Exposure to the elements was constant and death by starvation was always a threat. For the natives to survive the winter in the woods, there had to be sufficient snow and plenty of large game. Heavy snowfall was necessary to slow these creatures enough to allow the natives to kill them. Food and adequate shelter were in a very real way the only concerns. The Montagnais moved when the supply of game ran out within a reasonable hunting distance of their campsite, that is, within two to four leagues (six to twelve miles).

There were no inns, no cabins in the woods to provide a refuge for the travelers. At each campsite, the first order of business was to build a shelter. Sometimes it was snowing or raining, making the job much less pleasant. However, each person knew what was expected; the natives were efficient and could erect a pole hut in about three hours. At times they worked to the steady beating of drums, which made the process more agreeable. First, an outline for the pole huts was drawn in the snow. The men then dug out a square or circular hole in this snow, leaving walls two to four feet high on three sides to form the sides of their cabin. While the adult males were thus employed, the women cut poles from nearby trees. Twenty to thirty poles were required; these poles were stuck in the snow and angled to form a roof. Over the poles were fastened sheets of bark which the women had collected and which they had sewn together for this purpose. The roof was too low to allow anyone to stand straight, so everyone had to either sit or lie down. A crude door was made in one side of the shelter by attaching an animal skin to two poles stuck in the snow. The ground inside was strewn with fir branches to afford some protection from the cold, hard earth. This floor served as bed, table, and chair.

The fire in the center of the hut provided a means for cooking game, heating water, and warming the shelter. A hole was left in the center of the roof to allow campfire smoke to escape. Heat emanating from the fire was not enough to melt the snow walls, but it often became uncomfortably hot. Smoke from the fire could be unbearable. It burned the eyes, the nose, and the throat; it permeated their clothes. At times it was so thick that all inside had to keep their faces pressed against the ground in order to breathe. The severe cold outside, the wind, and the danger of getting lost often kept the group confined within their snow lodges. Between ten and fifteen individuals lived in each primitive cabin, which was barely large enough to accommodate its occupants.

Moving from one campsite to another was laborious. All in the group had large snowshoes; it would have been impossible to move through the woods without them. They had to squeeze through closely spaced trees, dodge low-lying branches, climb over fallen trunks, and navigate around large boulders. It was easy to slip going downhill and the ground was cold and hard. In moving from camp to camp, the women carried the heaviest loads. In deep snow, they made narrow sledges to carry some of the supplies. Travel through the woods in winter was dangerous and exhausting.

One of the few things Father Le Jeune carried was a blanket. During the daytime, it served as a coat. At night, he wrapped himself up in it; thus, it served as both mattress and coverlet. The warmth of other bodies in close proximity generated heat and provided some comfort from the cold. The dogs, large, numerous, and considered very much a part of the family, also slept in the huts, providing another source of heat, less scorching than the fire in the center.

The group of Montagnais with whom Le Jeune was traveling began their winter sojourn on the wooded islands in the St. Lawrence River, moving from one island to the next to find sufficient food. Here, the group had to contend with the rain and blustery weather of sudden storms. During one such torment, a particularly strong wind blew their canoe and sloop from their moorings. The group might well have been stranded on the island; fortunately, both vessels were found intact a short distance away.

Eventually, as the small game dwindled, the group headed for the territory south of the St. Lawrence. As the natives ranged over the heavily-forested land, the all-consuming drive was to find something to eat. Father Le Jeune would recall that it was not at all unusual to go a couple of days without food. The group had started out with a store of provisions. Le Jeune had provided a barrel of sea biscuits, a sack of flour, a barrel of wine, a few ears of corn, prunes, and parsnips from the store of supplies at the Jesuit house in Quebec. As was their tradition, the aborigines feasted until the supplies were exhausted. No thought was given to saving some provisions for days when game could not be found. When the supply of smoked eel and the rations supplied by the missionary were gone, the hunt for wild-life to sustain them through the long winter began in earnest. They found beaver along the small streams of the land. Porcupine, which Le Jeune noted were as large as suckling pigs, were another vital part of the diet. For the first couple of months of their travels, the snow was not deep enough to catch elk and moose.

A porcupine or a beaver was not much to sustain this group of travelers, but enough to stave off death by starvation. It was by no means certain that they would find game every day. The usual course of events was to breakfast on porcupine one morning and fast until the evening of the second day, when the group might again dine on porcupine. The native diet during the winter consisted of meat washed down with water. Without bread or corn to accompany their meal, the natives needed a lot of meat to survive. Le Jeune found it difficult to drink the water. It often had a brackish taste that resulted from its being made from snow heated in a copper kettle encrusted with dirt. The water was much better when the natives set up their campsite near a stream.

The day before Christmas, Le Jeune and his Amerindian "family" broke camp, cheered on by the beating of the native drums which pierced the quiet of their winter wonderland. They left without eating and trudged through the snow to their next campsite. After setting up their snow shelters for the evening, they feasted on porcupine for dinner. Christmas was a day of fasting: there was simply no food to be had. The wine had long since been consumed.

As the winter wore on, they might go three or four days without food. On these days, Le Jeune considered that he had dined well when he could consume an eel skin previously used as a strap. At other times, he gnawed on old moose skins. He was also reduced to foraging in the woods for bits of tender bark. From time to time, they encountered other emaciated natives also searching for food who admitted to having gone as many as five days without a meal.

At last, the deep snows came and the men in the party could hunt elk, moose, and caribou. When a large animal was killed, it was an eat-all feast, with drums and singing again accompanying the celebration. Le Jeune remarked with a certain insincerity that the best singer was the one who yelled the loudest. Food was generously shared with any other natives who might be in the vicinity. However, it was alarming to find others camped nearby; there was only so much game to go around. An elk killed every two days was enough for their little band to eat well enough without suffering. From February through April, if there was no fresh meat, there was at least smoked meat.

Father Le Jeune often mentioned the filth of the meat and other food consumed by the natives. They ate on bark plates, seated on the bare ground of their snow cabins. In competition for the food were the dogs who were also starving and would snatch the food off the plate, if one was not constantly vigilant. Le Jeune got very sick with a gastro-intestinal ailment at the beginning of January. The severe cramps and diarrhea lasted about ten days, leaving him weak and dehydrated. He wasn't at all sure he would make it back to the French settlement alive. He suspected that his illness was due to smoked moose, improperly prepared. A few mouthfuls of the tough and dirty smoked meat were all that Father Le Jeune could stomach. While this was enough to keep him from starving, he suffered with the consequences.

Over the winter months, the Montagnais made their way across low-lying flatlands, into deep valleys, and over mountains in their search for game. They crossed ice-covered streams and lakes, and trudged through forests of pine, cedar and fir. Snow was always on the ground. The bitter cold was their constant companion. Le Jeune wandered with these Montagnais through the vast forest south of Quebec from November 12, 1633 to April 9, 1634, when at last they returned to the banks of the St. Lawrence River and recovered their canoe and sloop. Their last challenge: crossing the Great River without being hit by an ice floe and being thrown into the glacial, swift-moving water. The group succeeded; Le Jeune had made it home to Quebec.

During that winter and early spring, Father Le Jeune observed that the Montagnais changed campsites twenty-three times. For six months, Le Jeune had slept inside their crude shelters, sharing limited space and food with his host and family members. He had endured hunger, sickness, cold, snow, rain, smoky cabins, and scrappy dogs. He had only the clothes on his back. There had been little opportunity for personal hygiene. He had made time for the recitation of the prayers of his office, but as with the others in the group, most of his energies had been directed toward finding enough food to survive and protecting himself against the elements.

Hélène heard these stories and many more from the other missionaries and Frenchmen who wintered among the natives. She would have been glad for the comforts, basic as they were, afforded the French colonists at Quebec. And she would be very glad to see the French ships that dropped anchor each year in the late spring and summer, bringing much needed supplies and a few luxuries. Perhaps she would have had a deepening respect for those who had to depend solely upon their own resources for survival in the wilderness of the New World.

CHAPTER EIGHT

DECEMBER OF 1635

———⚬∞∞⚬———

Champlain's death; A review of his life and his character; Beneficiaries of his estate; His role in Hélène's life; Other father figures and role models for Hélène; Quebec in 1635

Christmas Day of 1635 found the colonists in Quebec in deep mourning. They had lost Samuel de Champlain, their beloved leader and truly their best friend. Early in October, after the summer crops were harvested, Champlain had been stricken with paralysis in what was apparently a stroke. In spite of every effort by his friends to nurse him back to health, Champlain lost the battle and died two and a half months later, on this Christmas day.[1]

Volleys of gunfire from the fort, interspersed with the tolling of the chapel bells, would have punctuated the day. This year's celebrations had a somber tone, as the community turned to planning a funeral and procession worthy of their leader. Certainly Hélène and her husband would have taken part in this final tribute to Champlain. Father Charles Lalemant, Champlain's friend and personal confessor, had attended him throughout his illness and led the solemn funeral rites. Father Le Jeune gave the eulogy, focusing on Champlain's character, rather than his accomplishments. He noted that Champlain had led a life of justice and piety, praising him for his loyalty to God and his King. He would later observe, "How great was [Champlain's] love for the families here, saying that they must be vigorously assisted for the good of the Country, and made comfortable in every possible way in these early stages."[2] According to historians, Champlain was initially buried in an unmarked grave. A few months later, in the spring of 1636, his body would be transferred to a chapel known as the Chapel of Monsieur le Gouverneur, or the Chapel of Champlain. This chapel was an annex to Champlain's beloved Chapel of Notre-Dame-de-la-Recouvrance and had been built under the direction of Montmagny, the man who succeeded Champlain as Governor.[3]

The death of Champlain was keenly felt in the small settlement. It was Champlain who had tirelessly championed the cause of a French colony in the New World. Certainly Hélène would have been among those who grieved his passing. Some of her earliest memories centered on this man. Champlain had known Hélène since her birth. Hélène was now fifteen years old; she had spent her first nine years living within the confines of Champlain's Habitation at the edge of the St. Lawrence River. And for most of those years, Champlain was also there. Together, they had suffered through long, cold winters, lack of food in the early spring, and threats from unfriendly natives and English invaders alike. Together they had also experienced the simple joys that life on the frontier offered: the beauty of the wilderness, the freedom, and the opportunities not available in the mother country. They had returned to find the village in ruins. It took the efforts of all to rebuild the settlement.[4] No doubt Hélène and Champlain knew each other very well.

Hélène Boullé, Champlain's young wife, had departed for France in 1624 and had never returned to the colony. There are no records to indicate that Champlain and his wife ever had children. The little group of colonists had become Champlain's family. He had a deep respect for the men and women who settled at Quebec, as well as a fondness for their children. From the earliest days of the settlement, he also welcomed the Amerindian women and children into the Habitation. In 1627, he warmly received the girls given to him by the Montagnais natives, treating them as if they were his own children and becoming their godparent. Champlain also had two French god-children: Hélène Martin and Marguerite Couillard. Hélène Desportes was his wife's godchild.[5] When Hélène returned to Quebec from France, she was an orphan. In that era, it was not uncommon for children to lose one or both parents at an early age. If one was fortunate, extended family and community leaders stepped up to provide sustenance, protection, and guidance for the child. It is not difficult to imagine that Champlain was among the men in the settlement who came forward to serve in this role. Hélène grew up around him; he must certainly have had a profound influence on her character.

Who was this man, admired by so many? Few documents have survived to yield much information on Champlain's early years. It is known that he was born in Brouage in the province of Saintonge in 1574 and was the son of the mariner Antoine de Champlain and Marguerite Le Roy.[6] The infant was baptized in nearby La Rochelle on August 13, 1574 in the Calvinist temple of Saint-Yon.[7] Champlain spent his youth in the village of Brouage, where his father owned a home. This small town was already many hundreds of years old; records of Brouage date back to the eleventh century. It was situated on low marshlands bordering an inlet of the sea on the coast of western France. Brouage boasted an excellent harbor, supposedly one of the best in France, where even large vessels could drop anchor. It was a center for the manufacture of salt which was produced in the labyrinth of salt basins which surrounded the village. This local commodity was then loaded onto the ships in the harbor to be sent to other French ports, to London, to Antwerp, and beyond.[8]

When Champlain was growing up in the late sixteenth century, Brouage was embroiled in the civil war between Roman Catholics and Protestant Huguenots. Brouage itself was situated only about thirty-five miles from La Rochelle, which was at that time a seat of Huguenot power. In the civil war which began in 1562, the village of Brouage came under the possession of first one side, then the other side, in the course of the war. This civil war lasted until 1598 and it is known that Champlain participated in the conflict, at least during the later years: he was serving as a quarter-master with the Royal Army in Brittany about 1592, employed in the struggles against the Hugue-nots. Chroniclers believe that he served until 1598.[9] The discovery of Champlain's baptism record in 2012 in the register of a Calvinist temple in La Rochelle confirms what historians have long surmised: that Champlain was born Protestant but converted to the Roman Catholic faith when he reached maturity.

Champlain followed in his father's footsteps and took to the sea. In 1599, Champlain was given command of a 500-ton French ship which had been chartered by the Spanish to go to the West Indies. This was a position of some importance, so it is reasoned that Champlain had had a few years' experience as a seaman prior to his military service in 1592. It was on this voyage of 1599 that Champlain had the opportunity to visit many cities and regions in New Spain: Hispanola, Cuba, Mexico City, the Isthmus of Panama, and the coast of South America. When he returned, he compiled an extensive report for Henry IV, King of France at the time. He described his discoveries in detail and illustrated the report with his own drawings. In this account, Champlain wrote about the appearance, the customs, and the manners of the people who populated the areas he visited. He described the geography of the landscape: its mountains, rivers, and lakes. In addition, he wrote about the plant and animal life he encountered in his travels. He also reported on the management of these new lands now under the control of the Spanish monarchy, as well as the generous income produced by the colonies for the Spanish crown. Spain had grown wealthy from its investment in the Americas. Champlain possessed an inquisitive nature and keen powers of observation. His explorations were thoroughly documented and surprisingly detailed when compared with the reports of other explorers.[10]

Champlain's report on this trip to the Spanish colonies caught the attention of Henry IV. This monarch brought Champlain to Paris and into the circle of men in power. In 1603, it was the King who directed Champlain to sail with the Pont Gravé expedition, whose mission it was to explore the coast of North America. As before, Champlain was ordered to provide a detailed report on the exploration.[11]

Judging from his writings and where he spent his time, Champlain was probably happiest when at sea or out exploring. Late in life, Champlain referred to navigation as "the art which in my early years won my love, and has induced me to expose myself all my life to the impetuous waves of the ocean."[12] It was in 1632, close to the end of his life, that Champlain wrote his lengthy treatise on "Seamanship and the Duty of a Good Seaman." In the preface to this discourse, Champlain wrote that,

> having spent thirty-eight years of my life in making many sea voyages, and been in many dangers and run many risks (from which God has preserved me), and having always been fond of making voyages into distant and unknown regions, [he had received] much enjoyment, chiefly in relation to navigation.[13]

During his lifetime, Champlain was to make twenty-seven voyages across the Atlantic Ocean.[14] He was a man of uncommon health, vigor, and industry.

Champlain wrote at length about what he encountered during his explorations of the New World. He said almost nothing about his personal life or about the lives of the French settlers in his writings. Rarely did Champlain reveal his feelings about what he observed. However, his writings do provide insight into the disposition of this man. Champlain's character was shaped by his environment and his experiences as a seaman and in the military as well as by his innate abilities. As a young man, he learned self-discipline and developed leadership skills. A love of adventure and a zest for travel were in his nature; it is suggested that he came from a long line of seaman, although nothing is known of his ancestry beyond his parents.[15]

In his document on seamanship, Champlain detailed the qualifications of a "good and finished navigator." It would appear that these were also the principles that he tried to apply in the leadership of the colony. One can only be reminded of Champlain's honorable comportment at the conquest of Quebec in 1629, when he wrote in the treatise:

But when ill-fortune brings you to [a dangerous course], there you must display manly courage, make light of death though it confronts you, and in a steady voice and with cheery resolution urge all to take courage and do what can be done to escape the danger, and thus dispel fear from the most cowardly bosoms; for when they find themselves in a hazardous situation, every-one looks to the man who is thought to have experience ...[16]

Champlain was an extraordinary gentleman, a man at home in diverse settings. He was able to conduct himself admirably in the presence of royalty and aristocracy, but also willing to spend many months among the Huron natives in order to get to know them bet-ter. He counted among his friends wealthy Parisians, sailors, settlers, and Amerindians: those with money, power, and influence as well as those without.

Again, from the "Seamanship and the Duty of a Good Seaman", one comes to understand the leadership qualities and convictions that shaped Champlain's relationship with others, both on land and sea:

[A good seaman] should be pleasant and affable in conversa-tion, authoritative in his orders, not too ready to talk with his fellows, except with those who share the command; otherwise in course of time a feeling of contempt for him might arise. He should also punish evil-doers severely, and make much of the good men, being kind to them, and at times gratifying them with some friendly demonstration, praising them, but not neglecting the others, so as not to give occasion for envy, which is often the source of bad feeling.[17]

In this discourse, Champlain also noted that a good seaman should be, above all else, an upright and God-fearing man.[18] Prayers should be said morning and night.

And if the navigator can find the means, I advise him to take with him a resourceful and competent priest or friar to give exhortations from time to time to the soldiers and sailors, so as to keep them always in the fear of God, and otherwise to help them and take their confessions when they are sick, or in other ways to comfort them during the dangers encountered in the chances of the sea.[19]

Champlain was clearly a deeply religious man. In the early seventeenth century, the French monarchy and the Roman Catholic clergy of the country saw the opportunity for spreading the faith among the native people of the New World. In every way that he could, Champlain had promoted their cause. It was at least partially due to his efforts that the trading companies allowed the Récollet missionaries to come in 1615. Champlain fully supported their labors to establish missions among the Algonquin and Huron peoples. The arrival of the Jesuit missionaries in 1625 certainly had Champlain's blessing.

Although Champlain was often at odds with French merchants and traders at Quebec, his work to establish a French colony in the New World did receive recognition and approval from the investors in France. In the spring of 1629, Champlain received a commission from the Company of One Hundred Associates to govern all of New France. The document, signed by the directors of the Company, recognized his accomplishments and abilities in establishing a French presence in the New World. It read in part:

> The experience that you have acquired in becoming acquainted with the country of New France and its inhabitants during your residence therein, together with the special knowledge that we have of your good, competence, generosity, prudence, zeal for the glory of God and affection and fidelity to the service of the King, having led us to nominate and present you to his Majesty...[20]

Over the course of his many years in the New World, Champlain worked hard to foster a good relationship between the French and the natives of North America. However, not all of his actions had the desired outcome. One decision would bring lasting enmity between the French and the natives who lived south of the St. Lawrence River. It would threaten the survival of the infant French colony. In 1609, Champlain developed alliances with various indigenous groups, in particular the Huron and Algonquin tribes, in order to develop the fur trade in the New World. In this undertaking, Champlain agreed to assist these natives in their battle against the Iroquois, their traditional enemy. At Ticonderoga, on what came to be known as Lake Champlain, an event took place that would significantly impact the lives of the French settlers for many years.[21] Algonquin and Huron natives, aided by Champlain and the French, defeated the Iroquois, largely because of the effectiveness of the French arquebus. This was an early rifle-like firing arm, fired using a slow-burning match. A similar battle occurred the following year. These military actions strengthened the alliance between the French and the indigenous tribes to the north of the St. Lawrence River. They were also the beginning of almost one hundred years of sporadic clashes between the French settlers and the Iroquois. The battles ended with the peace treaty of 1701. By that point, the population of indigenous people had been greatly reduced as a result of the casualties of war, but also by diseases, especially smallpox, introduced by the French and English.[22]

All was not business with Champlain; he was not above having fun. Like his French compatriots, he enjoyed good food and good wine. Prior to the establishment of Quebec, Champlain had spent some time in Port Royal. According to the seventeenth-century author Marc Lescarbot, who was there at the same time, Champlain organized the men into a society which he named "The Knightly Order of Good Times." There were fifteen men who dined together. Each member, in turn, became Grand Master of the Day and was responsible for hunting, collecting, cooking, and serving the food. A competition among the men resulted in dinners offering a delectable spread of game (venison, bear, grouse, ducks, geese and plover) and fresh fish accompanied by dried beans, French bread, and a generous quantity of alcohol. The colony at Port Royal had been supplied with enough wine to allow each man to imbibe three pints daily. Lescarbot boasted that meals were as good as could be had anywhere in Paris.[23] According to him, "The table was constantly furnished with the most delicate and well-seasoned game, and the sweetest as well as choicest varieties of fish. The frequent change in office and the ingenuity displayed, offered at every repast, either in the viands or mode of cooking, something new and tempting to the appetite."[24]

Champlain's Last Will and Testament was drawn up and signed on November 17, 1635, in the presence of a number of men in the settlement.[25] In this document, Champlain named the Holy Virgin Mary as his principal heiress, leaving the bulk of his estate in Quebec, namely his gold, silver, and furniture, to the chapel of Notre-Dame-de-la-Recouvance, which had been dedicated in her name. No one can doubt Champlain's deep attachment to his Catholic faith and the Blessed Virgin. The will also provides further proof that Champlain regarded the pioneers of Quebec as his family. He was generous with the distribution of his personal belongings among many of the settlers, those with rank and those without. Women in the colony received special consideration from Champlain. The only time that Champlain mentions Hélène Desportes by name in his writings is in his will. The bequests included "a pair of undershirts of white cotton" which he left to Hélène Desportes. To Marguerite, the godchild of Marguerite Lesage, he left another shirt of the same cloth. Marguerite and Hélène were also to share Champlain's ribbons of silk and hairpins. One can imagine that the governor's undershirts (the shirt worn under the doublet jacket) were of the finest material and trimmed in lace. Champlain must have intended that the material in the shirts be made into something very nice for the girls. To Madame Giffard, Champlain willed the painting of Notre-Dame, which hung in his bedroom. Champlain designated Father Lalemant, his personal confessor, to be the recipient of his painting of the crucified Lord, his compass, the copper astrolabe, and sextant. In his will, Champlain also requested that Father Lalemant send his wife, who had remained in Paris, his painting of the *Agnus Dei*, a skin of grey fox, two other furs, and a gold ring set with a diamond. Champlain's papers were also to be sent to her.[26]

Champlain's assets in France were to go to his wife if she survived him.[27] If she did not, Champlain provided instructions on how funds from his estate were to be distributed. A number of the colonists would be beneficiaries of Champlain's generosity. Among them, Hélène Desportes, "my wife's godchild," and Marguerite Couillard, "my godchild", were each to receive three hundred *livres*. Abraham Martin and his wife were to receive six hundred *livres* to be used to buy and clear land in New France. Their daughter Marguerite was also to receive a dowry of six hundred *livres* if she married and settled in the New World. Their daughter Hélène, Champlain's godchild, was to receive three hundred francs. Champlain's will was ratified in Paris in 1637. Two years later, Champlain's cousin Marie Camaret succeeded in having it annulled.[28] It is doubtful that Hélène Desportes or any of the other pioneer settlers received any of Champlain's money, but one can imagine that they did receive his personal effects as designated in his will.

Champlain does not mention his adopted Amerindian daughters Foi, Espérance and Charité in his will. The last time they are mentioned in any of Champlain's writings, or in the writings of the religious for that matter, is in accounts of the conquest of Quebec by the English in 1629. At that point, Champlain talks only of Espérance and Charité. When the girls were not allowed to go to France with the French settlers, Champlain entrusted them to the care of his good friend, Guillaume Couillard and his wife.[29] There is no mention of the girls upon the return of the French in 1632. Did they succumb to one of the European diseases that proved so deadly to the natives? Did these two girls slip back into the forest to return to their native families? History is silent on their fate.

Hélène had lost some of the most important male figures in her young life. Her father had died in France some five years earlier. Hélène had also lost Louis Hébert, her husband's father and the colony's first farmer. And now Champlain! Other community leaders would take the place of these men in Hélène's early life.

Hélène had been raised under the spiritual guidance of the Jesuits. When she married Guillaume Hébert, she moved to the Upper Town, just a short distance from the chapel of Notre-Dame-de-la-Recouvrance. One can imagine that she had daily contact with the

Jesuits who ministered to the little community of French settlers. Two Jesuit priests, in particular, must have stood out. She had known Father Charles Lalement since her childhood. He had arrived in Quebec in 1625 with the first Jesuits to come to the colony. Hélène was just five at the time. In the autumn of 1627, because of his ties to the French court, Lalemant was ordered back to Paris to plead the case of the colony.[30] Although Father Lalemant remained keenly interested and involved in the wellbeing of Quebec, he would not return to the settlement until 1634. He spent another four years in the colony before he returned to France permanently.[31]

Hélène might well have encountered Father Paul Le Jeune in Dieppe. If not, she would have met him when she returned to Quebec in 1634. Father Le Jeune spent four years at the Jesuit residence in Dieppe before coming to the New World in 1632 when Quebec was returned to the French. Le Jeune was born in July of 1591 in the French town of Chalons-sur-Marne to Huguenot parents. He converted to Catholicism as an adult and entered the Jesuit novitiate at Rouen in September of 1613, at the age of twenty-two. Le Jeune was a learned man, having studied at La Flèche, one of the premier Catholic Universities. He then taught rhetoric at Nevers and at Caën before taking a position as preacher at Dieppe. In New France, Father Le Jeune would serve as Superior of the Canadian mission until 1639 and remain in Canada another ten years.[32]

Another person who would certainly have a positive influence on Hélène in the years to come was Robert Giffard, who had served as witness to Hélène's marriage to Guillaume Hébert in 1634. Giffard and Hélène would be brought together countless times; they would share in each other's joys and sorrows. Thirty-three years her senior, deeply religious, and held in high regard in the colony, Giffard exemplified the strength of character and the commitment necessary for building a moral, as well as a thriving, society.

Hélène did not lack for examples of grit, determination, courage, and virtue. As her life unfolded, one cannot help but feel that the decisions she made and the direction her life took were influenced, in large measure, by powerful and virtuous men.

It had been just three years since the French had returned to Quebec. Champlain had seen to it that many of the structures destroyed by the English had been rebuilt. Quebec in 1635 was a beginning, but not much beyond that. It had a population of some two hundred. The settlement at Quebec consisted of a primitive fort, a trading post, a small Jesuit mission, and a scattering of simple homesteads. There were a number of good men in the settlement. But did they have Champlain's vision for New France and his leadership abilities to hold the colony together and make it grow? Would the Company of One Hundred Associates send a strong leader to replace Champlain? Certainly, in the waning hours of 1635, many of the settlers agonized over their future and the future of the infant colony. The newly married Hélène and Guillaume must have wondered and worried that they would find themselves again on a ship crossing the Atlantic.

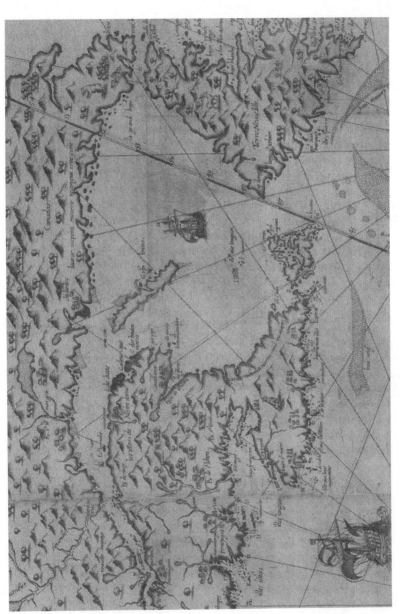

Detail from a map drawn by Samuel de Champlain in 1612 (Samuel de Champlain, 'Carte géographique de la Nouvelle France,' 1612, National Library of France, PD)

'Le Parfait Négociant,' frontispiece of the book by the same name, written by Jacques Savary in Paris in 1675 (Musée de la civilisation, bibliothèque de livres rares et anciens du Séminaire de Québec, photograph: Jacques Lessard, 165-2)

Top: Detail from a map drawn by Samuel de Champlain in 1612 (Samuel de Champlain, 'Carte géographique de la Nouvelle France,' 1612. National Library of France, PD)

Bottom: Algonquin Couple, an 18th century watercolor by an unknown artist (City of Montreal Records Management & Archives, Montreal, PD)

Le Grand Voyage du Pays des Hurons, 1632' by the Récollet Missionary Gabriel Sagard ('La Rochelle-Quebec,' PD)

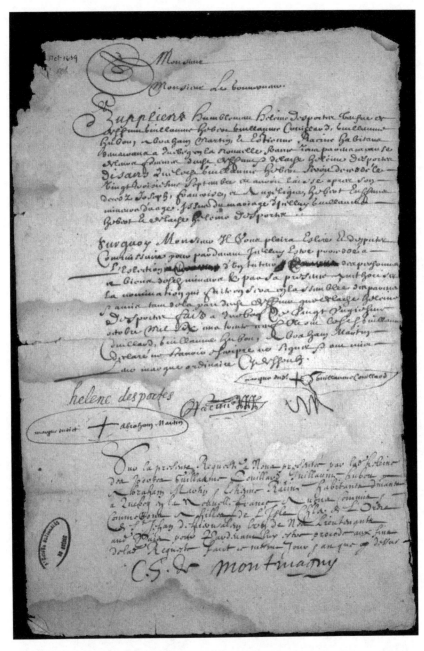

A record of the request made before Governor Montmagny on October 21, 1639
concerning guardianship of the three minor children of Hélène Desportes and
Guillaume Hébert, deceased; This is one of three documents on which Hélène's signature
appears. (Pistard Database, Bibliothèque et Archives nationales du Québec)

A View of Paris in 1607: Facsimile of a copper plate by Léonard Gaultier

(Collection of M. Guénebault, Paris, PD)

LE PORT   DE DIEPPE
Vu du   grand Quai

Top: *A view from the Grand Quai of the port of Dieppe, a seaport city in upper Normandy, France (PD)*

Bottom: *An engraving depicting a sea view of Dieppe around 1830, produced by the Scottish engraver William Miller (1796-1882) (Archiv "Deutschland und die Welt," PD)*

Le dixiesme jour de neuf de Septembre mil
Cent Cinquante neuf a esté Baptisé par moy Georges ...
mon __ par Helene Desportes sage femme de Noel Mo...
Jean Halay. Sage femme de Helene Desportes femme de Noel Mor...
Halay et Matsumi vedve sa femme ... ...
sous seyng apni par la mesme sage femme qu'il estoit
vrayement Baptisé ont Jean Forapel Thon et ...
En __ Appele nommere es sacrer Comme vu f
Baptisés et exposé le nom de Jean en presenc...
de Jean Bourdon et de Marie Magdelaine Gifthar...
femme de Nicolas Inthenau. Forapel

Baptism record for Jean Halay, dated September 10, 1659

This is the first time Hélène Desportes is listed as a sage-femme in the records of the church of Notre-Dame de Quebec. (Notre-Dame de Quebec Parish Register)

Battle of Quebec, 1690; fought between the colonies of New France and Massachusetts Bay

(National Archives of Canada; PD)

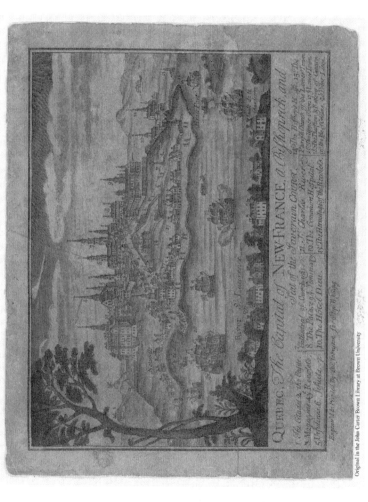

'Quebec, The Capital of New-France, a Bishoprick, and Seat of the Sovereign Court,' by

Thomas Johnston [Boston, 1759]

Painting is based on an inset on a map by Nicolas de Fer, published in 1718.

(Courtesy of the John Carter Brown Library at Brown University, Providence, Rhode Island)

"Les Premiers Colons de Québec" Plaque on the Louis Hébert Monument, Montmorency Park, Quebec City (Photo by SAM 2011)

(L) Notre-Dame-des-Victoires, founded in 1687 and located on the site of Champlain's Habitation in the Lower Town, Quebec City

(R) Samuel de Champlain, Father of New France; Sculpture on the Terrasse Dufferin near the Château Frontenac, Quebec City (Both photos by SAM, 2011)

The sculpture of Marie Rollet and her three children is found on the Louis Hébert Monument in Montmorency Park, Quebec City. The young boy is Guillaume Hébert, first husband of Hélène Desportes. (Photo by SAM 2011)

(L) Guillaume Couillard, shown with the first plow in Quebec, was the brother-in-law of Hélène Desportes; The sculpture is located on the Louis Hébert Monument in Montmorency Park, Quebec City.

(R) Sculpture of Marie de l'Incarnation and two pupils; Outside the Museum of the Ursulines, Quebec City (Photos by SAM 2011)

Entering the walled city of Old Quebec through the Saint-Louis Gate; Quebec City has the only remaining fortified city walls on the North American continent, north of Mexico. (Photo by SAM 2011)

Celebrating Seventeenth and Eighteenth-Century French-Canadian History at
Les Fêtes de la Nouvelle-France in Old Quebec (Photo by SAM 2011)

Colorful shops in Old Quebec retain the names of the colony's first settlers.

(Photo by SAM 2011)

Hotel Frontenac, historical landmark in the Upper Town of Old Quebec

(Photo by S.AM 2006)

CHAPTER NINE

NOVEMBER OF 1637

—⊗⊗⊗—

Marriage of French girls at an early age; Native courtship and marriage; Epidemics of smallpox, plague, dysentery and other infectious diseases brought by Europeans; Natives blame the Jesuits; European and native medicine in the seventeenth century

It had been a year and a half since Champlain's death. Charles Huault de Montmagny arrived in 1636 as Champlain's replacement and was now the governor of the little colony.[1] Hélène and Guillaume were busy establishing a home and starting a family. The young couple had been given 40 perches (one quarter acre) of land and a home, measuring twenty-four feet by sixteen feet, in the Upper Town by the colony's governor, Samuel de Champlain. This land was just north of the store of the Company of One Hundred Associates and near the chapel of Notre-Dame-de-la-Recouvrance.[2]

In October of 1636, Governor Montmagny granted Guillaume an additional twenty-two arpents of land (about nineteen acres) in the Upper Town of Quebec, bordering the lands of Guillaume Hubou, Abraham Martin, and Pierre Repentigny.[3] This grant of land came just in time to welcome the first-born of Hélène and Guillaume. Joseph Hébert made his appearance on November 3 of 1636. Hélène was now expecting their second child.[4]

In the fall of 1637, Hélène's nieces, the two oldest girls of Guillemette Hébert and Guillaume Couillard, were married.[5] They were still children: Louise was twelve when she married Olivier Letardif. Her sister Marguerite was even younger; she was just eleven when she married Jean Nicolet. Hélène's cousins, the six daughters of Abraham Martin and Marguerite Langlois, would also marry when they were between the ages of twelve and fourteen.[6]

It was not uncommon for the fate of young girls to be sealed long before they reached maturity. As mentioned in an earlier chapter, marriages were a business transaction between families. A daughter's future was generally determined by her parents; they would decide whom she would marry. Or, perhaps, they would determine that she should go into a convent. Often, although not always, a young woman would have little to say in the matter. In the *Ancien Regime* of France, girls were used by their parents to cement relationships, augment wealth, or to gain honor and status for the parents. Anne of Austria, wife of Louis XIII and mother of Louis XIV, was married in 1615, at the age of fourteen. In 1688, Louise-Françoise, the daughter of Louis XIV, was married two months before she turned twelve to the Duc de Bourbon, who was seventeen at the time.[7]

Many girls accepted their fate without complaint. Others rebelled and suffered the consequences. Hélène Boullé, the child bride of Samuel de Champlain and the godmother of Hélène Desportes, rebelled against her parent's wishes. Reportedly headstrong and willful, she was unhappy with her marriage to Champlain in 1610. In the fall of 1613, Champlain had returned to France from the New World and fifteen-year-old Hélène was sent to live with her husband. There are records indicating that she ran away some four months later. Hélène's parents found her and returned her to her husband. Monsieur and Madame Boullé were so angered by the incident that they filed papers to disinherit their daughter on January 10, 1614.[8]

In 1648, the beautiful Anne de La Grange, daughter of the wealthy seigneur de Trianon et de Neufville, secretly married the Comte de Frontenac, a man who would become governor-general of Quebec in the late seventeenth century. Her father had other ideas for her future and had tried everything to prevent the marriage, even imprisoning his daughter in a convent. When he learned of the marriage, he disinherited her and prevented her from receiving a separate and sizeable inheritance from her mother.[9]

In the colony of New France, there was strong pressure on girls approaching maturity to marry as soon as possible. This would encourage men, who far outnumbered women, to settle in the New World, rather than return to France. Women who bore children in New France were more likely to put down roots and to stay in the infant colony. They were key to increasing the population. At the beginning of the seventeenth century, women in France were marrying at an average age of nineteen. By 1670, the age at first marriage had risen to twenty-three. In Quebec, the age of the women at first marriage was much younger. Two out of three of the French girls born in Canada married at or before the age of puberty, before they were fifteen. Unmarried female immigrants tended to marry soon after they arrived, so that the age they married corresponded closely to their date of immigration. For them, the age of first marriage ranged from fourteen to twenty-three. The average age at which men in France married stayed at twenty-five for the century. In Quebec, men tended to marry later than their counterparts in France. In four out of five marriages in Quebec, husbands were more than ten years older than their wives. The age of marriage for the men was generally between twenty-two and thirty-two. An important reason was that there were many more men than women. Eligible women were not always available. Some men also wanted to fulfill their contract as laborer or soldier before marrying.[10]

The strict rules and regulations that governed every aspect of life for the French, including marriage, were absent among the natives. In his writings, Champlain elaborated on the courtship patterns that he had observed among the aborigines. The young men and women were free to seek the affections of the opposite sex until a favorable partnership was formed. When a native girl reached the age of eleven or twelve, she was ready for courtship. An interested male would woo her with presents of porcelain jewelry. After a period of time and with the consent of her parents, the man was allowed to spend a few nights with the girl. If she was attracted to him, she stayed with him. If not, she was free to move on to another suitor and the young man found another woman. When a woman became pregnant, there might be more than one man claiming to be the father of her child. She chose the man who pleased her the most and stayed with him. Native men were often jealous and continued to give presents to the relatives of their wives, presumably to continue in the woman's good graces. After marriage, the couple generally remained together for the rest of their lives. However, it was possible for the man to dissolve the union, alleging that his woman was worthless. Men and women might also continue to have relationships with others without recrimination. Thus, the identity of the father of children born in these more or less formal unions could not be certain.[11] There seemed to be little restraint put on individual sexual behavior among the natives; both men and women could do as they pleased. The Frenchmen, used to severe injunctions against premarital and extramarital sex in their own culture, found the native women and their relative freedom very attractive.[12]

From the beginning, it had been Champlain's practice to send young Frenchmen off to live with the natives so that they might learn the language and customs of the indigenous peoples. In 1628, twenty men who had come from France spent the winter with the Hurons, in part, because supplies in the French settlements were running low and Champlain didn't feel he could sustain the men in the colony.[13] One can only imagine the number of babies engendered by French and Amerindian liaisons that winter. The relationships that happened outside of marriage sanctioned by the Roman Catholic Church were rarely acknowledged in the records or the writings of the early French settlers. Because the natives were a matrilineal society, the infants stayed with their mothers and were raised as part of her family.

In the fall of 1637, the French colonists were, no doubt, most concerned with the harvest and having enough food to eat over the coming winter. But they could not have been unaware of the smallpox epidemic that was ravaging the native settlements along the St. Lawrence River. The first recorded disease of European origin among the Huron natives struck in 1634. It is believed to have been measles and lasted through the winter of 1634-35. It is possible that the disease came with the arrival of twenty-five French children in Quebec in the summer of 1634.[14] Now in 1637, it was smallpox which was spreading from the French to the Montagnais and Hurons. Native peoples had not been exposed to this virulent disease. They had no immunity, no resistance, and died in droves. The symptoms of the disease were terrible. The sick experienced high fever, retching, and severe pain. Ugly, oozing blisters covered their body.[15]

The Spanish first recorded an outbreak of smallpox in Hispaniola in late 1518, a century before the French settled along the St. Lawrence River. It was said to have killed one third of the natives before moving on to Puerto Rico and Cuba. Hernán Cortés brought the disease to Mexico in 1520. Once introduced into the Americas, the disease spread like wildfire across the land, following ancient trade routes. There were soon accounts of the disease throughout Central America. Then it moved on to the Inca Empire, arriving there even before Pizarro and his band of Conquistadores.[16] What the early European explorers and settlers did not understand was that it was Europeans who brought the disease to the New World.[17]

Smallpox and other diseases long known in Europe did take their toll on the French, but they were not as devastating as they were for the Native Americans. Over the centuries, Europeans had developed some natural immunity to these diseases, so that those who did become sick had more of a chance of recovering from these illnesses. Nonetheless, these diseases continued to be a problem for them as well, knowing no boundaries of age and rank in their ability to attack and kill.[18] In the spring of 1711, the Grand Dauphin, the healthy fifty-year-old son of Louis XIV, fell victim to smallpox and died on April 11. It was said that he was exposed to the disease when he knelt by the wayside to pay his respects to a priest carrying the Blessed Sacrament after a visit to an individual sick with smallpox.[19]

Europeans were also bringing pigs, horses, and cattle to the colonies. Humans in contact with these domesticated animals were exposed to the microbes carried by these creatures. Pigs, which were a mainstay of European farms, can transmit anthrax, brucellosis, leptospirosis, trichinosis and tuberculosis. Pigs were able to pass these diseases to wildlife, such as deer and turkeys. In turn, humans who ate the flesh of infected wild animals might contract the disease. Amerindians had no immunity to the diseases brought to the New World by European animals.[20]

Plague was another dreaded disease carried by ship across the sea. On September 7, 1659, the Saint André, the last ship of the season, would arrive from France with two hundred people on board. The passengers had experienced the worst of ocean voyages: intemperate weather, limited rations, poor quality food, cramped conditions, poor sanitation, danger from ships of rival nations, and disease. When they arrived in Quebec, most of the passengers were sick with purulent fevers associated with the plague. Eight had died at sea and others would die soon after their arrival. Children were among those who died on the voyage across the Atlantic. Mathurin Thibodeau and Catherine Avrard lost three of their children on board the ship. Father De Quen, superior of the Jesuits, hurried to the ship to meet Jeanne Mance and the other Hospitallers of St. Joseph from La Flèche who were en-route to Montreal. As a result of his visit to the ship, he contracted the plague and died a month later, on October 8. The disease spread to many others in Quebec, including the Hospitallers in the Upper Town who were attempting to care for the sick.[21]

Other diseases introduced by Europeans for which the natives had no immunity were hepatitis, typhus, influenza, and diphtheria. Occurrences of these diseases in the New World were recorded in European accounts in the sixteenth and early seventeenth centuries. Between 1616 and 1619, the natives of the New England coast were afflicted with a sickness previously unknown to them. Historians do not believe that the sickness that befell the natives in 1616 was small-pox, but rather a viral hepatitis, the plague, or an infectious fever of another sort.[22] It is estimated that up to ninety percent of the natives of coastal New England died. The Massachusetts and Pokanoketes tribes were almost wiped out. Previous to the epidemic, they numbered in the thousands; there were only a few hundred survivors after the disease had run its course. According to the local tradition, Frenchmen trading for beaver along the New England coast before the settlement of Plymouth may have brought the disease with them.[23]

Thomas Morton of the Massachusetts Bay colony, writing in 1634, described the epidemic of 1616-1617 thus:

> The hand of God fell heavily upon them with such a mortal stroke that they died in heaps as they lay in their houses; and the living, that were able to shift for themselves, would run away and let them die, and let their carcasses lie above the ground without burial. For in a place where many inhabited, there has been but one left alive to tell what became of the rest; the living being (as it seems) not able to bury the dead, they were left for crows, kites, and vermin to prey upon. And the bones and skulls upon the several places of their habitations made such a spectacle after my coming into those parts, that I travailed in that forest near the Massachusetts, it seemed to me a new-found Golgotha.[24]

In the early seventeenth century, the natives along the Massachusetts coast came to the conclusion that their gods had turned against them. The Pilgrims agreed. Governor Bradford ascribed the plague to the hand of God, whom he believed favored European settlement by eliminating great numbers of natives to make room for the newcomers. More than fifty colonial villages in New England were established on land previously occupied by native settlements which had been laid waste by disease and death.[25]

Now in 1637, all along the banks of the St. Lawrence River and far to the west of Quebec, death was everywhere the Jesuits went. Many of the natives attributed the disease to the missionaries. Le

Jeune described visits to the village of Angoutenc, stating that they had made two previous trips to the settlement without a problem. However, when they returned a third time, on the third of July, "We found a considerable number of sick people, but they wrapped themselves in their robes and covered their faces, for fear of speaking to us; others, upon seeing us, hastened to close the doors of their cabins."[26]

Father Le Jeune detailed these accounts of death and the native reaction to this disease in his annual report to his supervisors in Paris. In a chapter titled, "Of the Persecutions we suffered in the year 1637", the French missionary wrote:

> Some of [the natives] took occasion to spread new reports and to authorize the previous calumnies, namely, that we were causing the death of these peoples by our Images. In a few days the country was completely imbued with this opinion, that we were, without any doubt, the authors of this so universal contagion. It is very probable that those who invented these slanders did not believe them at all; yet they spoke in so positive terms that the majority no longer doubted them. The women and children looked upon us as persons who brought them misfortune. God be forever blessed, who willed that for the space of three or four months, while these persecutions were at their height, we should be deprived of nearly all human consolation. The people of our village seemed to spare us more than the others, yet these evil reports were so persistent and were such a common subject of conversation in their assemblies that suspicion began to take hold upon them, and the most prominent ones, who had loved us and had been accustomed to speak in our favor, became entirely mute, and when they were constrained to speak, they had recourse to excuses, and justified themselves as well as they could for having built us a cabin.[27]

These were difficult times for the Jesuit missionaries. The natives accused the Jesuits of witchcraft and were suspicious of anything that belonged to or came from the missionaries. According to reports, one entire village decided to toss out the kettles which had come from the French. Le Jeune had to put away his clock, for the natives believed it to be an instrument of death. The religious images likewise were considered suspect in causing this dreadful disease. The Jesuits felt very threatened by the natives who appeared at their cabins, raising their bows and arrows against them, and treating their religious ornaments with scorn and contempt.[28] Rumors circulated that the English were inciting the natives against them: "Those who commanded them maintained that the black robes were the cause of all the sickness. It was in vain that we remonstrated with them, forcibly arguing how incredible the thing seemed; they persevered in their own notions."[29]

The Jesuits could not conceive that they could be the cause of so much death and destruction among the native peoples. It was easier to ascribe causation to a supernatural power. The natives also believed that illness had a spiritual basis, that it originated with evil spirits.[30] Presumably they believed that the Jesuits brought these evil spirits. Native healers had no power against the new sicknesses. In desperation, the Montagnais and the Hurons turned to the missionaries when their herbal remedies and spiritual leaders failed to protect them. The Jesuits at least promised a good life in the next world. The missionaries continued to minister to the Hurons, even as the epidemic raged through the winter and into the spring of 1638.[31]

Dysentery from spoiled food was frequently noted in the writings of the explorers and Jesuit missionaries. It occurred on land and sea and afflicted Native Americans and Europeans alike. In 1608, Champlain noted in his journal that a sailor and a locksmith who were going to spend that first winter in Quebec died of dysentery in the fall. He noted that a number of natives died as well and attributed it to poorly cooked eels.[32] In 1629, Champlain was to observe that eleven of the Englishmen sailing with Captain Kirke died of dysentery on the voyage across the Atlantic.[33] In the mission fields, the Jesuits ate the same food as the Amerindians and in the same manner; one of the missionaries was to record that the Jesuits and their domestic servants had to get up four or five times each night due to diarrhea caused by tainted food.[34]

In addition to the infectious diseases, scurvy was another curse for Europeans traveling to the New World. The men who accompanied Jacques Cartier in his sixteenth-century travels suffered from scurvy. Supposedly Cartier learned of a Native-American remedy: a potion made by steeping the leaves and bark of the red spruce.[35] If this remedy was effective, the knowledge of it was not widely disseminated. Champlain had a number of men die of scurvy during that first winter in Quebec (1608-09). He noted in his "Voyages" that January through March were dangerous months. The men had little to eat beyond salted meat and vegetables. Champlain thought that scurvy was due to the lack of fresh meat and other foods. Champlain might have been ahead of his time when he ascribed scurvy to a poor diet. According to him, this was an equal-opportunity disease. It afflicted the fit and healthy, as well as men in poor health and in wretched shape. It attacked men who traveled to the East Indies and to various other countries in Europe, as well as men who were exploring the New World. Champlain decried the lack of a treatment for scurvy. According to him, the Flemish had found a remedy for the disease, but had failed to share their discovery with the world.[36] Scurvy continued to be a problem for travelers and explorers throughout the seventeenth century and beyond. It would be a long time before the cause of scurvy and effective treatment were completely understood.

Medicine in seventeenth-century France left much to be desired: its practice was rife with competing practitioners and controversy. Treatment was limited and viewed with distrust and skepticism. Physicians were not held in high regard: they were often ridiculed as clowns or considered no better than murderers. Perhaps a good dose of skepticism and a certain reluctance to seek the physician's services were in the best interests of the patient, considering the treatments promoted by physicians.[37]

Medicine began to be taught publicly in Paris in the twelfth century. By the seventeenth century, there were two well-established medical schools in France: one in Paris and a rival school in Marseille. To enter the medical school in Paris, one had to be a Roman Catholic in good standing. A certificate of good conduct signed by the local parish priest was required. Dr. Guy Patin, the Dean of the Faculty of the Medical School of Paris University in 1652, wrote prolifically. His writings provide insight into the medical thinking of that era. Especially at the school in Paris, age-old traditions dating to the time of Hippocrates regarding the treatment of illness and disease were to be followed, unquestioned. Among other things, physicians in seventeenth-century France were required to study astrology and were known to consult astrological charts prior to treating their patients. Any new discovery or treatment was routinely eschewed by the medical establishment of the seventeenth century. Chemists and apothecaries were lumped together with charlatans, unfrocked monks, and the like. On the streets of Paris, one could buy a potion guaranteed to cure anything and everything imaginable, and at much less cost than the physician's fees. Physicians were also suspicious of each other, as well as of surgeons (a different profession at that time).[38]

Medications recommended by physicians were few: cassia, senna, quinine, antimony and syrup of roses. For physicians, bleeding and purging were the treatments of choice in the seventeenth century. Bleeding was recommended as a remedy in a wide variety of maladies: fevers, side-pains, inflammation of the lungs, colds, coughs, and toothaches. In one case, an eighty-year-old man was bled seventy-two ounces of blood in a month and was subjected to a purging four times in the treatment of a lung disorder. Louis XIII received almost fifty bleedings, more than two hundred doses of purgatives, and two hundred enemas in one year. Powerful purgatives were used just as often as blood-letting.[39]

It must be admitted that some learned Europeans of the era found blood-letting and purging abhorrent. Phillip von Hohenheim, the son of a Swiss physician, was one who believed that these treatments did little more than maim and kill patients. In the sixteenth century, he had asserted that a compassionate God had given ordinary people the means to cure illness and protect themselves against disease.[40] He believed in an approach based on nature; toward that end, he spent a number of years in the countryside collecting information from the peasantry on folk healing and natural remedies. The secrets of nature, he believed, would offer the patient more in the way of healing than the opinions of ancient authorities. His approach to health was based on a combination of alchemy, mysticism, folk lore, and observation of nature.[41]

There were no physicians in the colony. There were, however, a number of surgeons, one of them being Hélène's good friend, Robert Giffard. Surgeons of that era attended the same schools as barbers and were members of the Society of Barber-Surgeons. Surgeons performed the blood-lettings, operations, amputations, and lancing of boils. They did not have the status of physicians; rather, they were considered to be manual laborers or craftsmen. When physicians were available, surgeons often functioned as their hired hands.[42]

There does seem to be at least some understanding of the importance of hygiene in seventeenth-century medicine, although it was not widely accepted. In 1607, one physician in Paris suggested that the epidemic of plague could be lessened if the streets and gutters were kept clean. Toward the end of his career, Dr. Patin of the Parisian School of Medicine would admit that there was nothing particularly injurious to one's health in the practice of frequently washing one's hands.[43]

Champlain, without benefit of a medical education, also appeared to understand the importance of cleanliness. In his Treatise on Good Seamanship, written in the later years of his life, he urged his fellow seamen to take care to have everything in good order on the ship, everything and everyone neat and clean. Filth "frequently causes a stench and gives rise to deadly disease" and, in a nod to the importance of good nutrition in the prevention of disease, he also advised, "take good care to have wholesome food and drink."[44]

In matters of illness, the European Christians consulted their saints: it was believed that their intercession might be as effective as the physician's cure. More than one hundred saints were known to intercede in the cases of fevers. There were saints for the animals as well. St. Ambrose was known as the protector of bees and St. Gertrude could be implored in the case of sick cats.[45]

When they first came to the New World, the French encountered a vigorous indigenous population. Those natives who were sickly did not survive in the harsh environment. When one of their own did become ill, native treatments included the use of herbal teas, poultices, fasting, purging, blood-letting, and sweating.[46] Perhaps their practices were not that different from those of the Europeans.

The leaves of a variety of plants, as well as the roots and bark of trees, were believed to have medicinal qualities. Algonquin natives used a tea made by boiling the roots of the prickly ash to treat the aches and pains of rheumatism. Indigenous peoples chewed hulls of the black walnut to treat colic and ate anise to rid the stomach of gas. Sometimes, a tea made by boiling the buckeye nut was used to treat diarrhea. Infusions made from the bark of the birch and dogwood trees were also thought to be beneficial in the treatment of illness. The Amerindians drew blood to treat fevers, inflammations, and local pain, utilizing knives made out of flint or sharp bones.[47]

The missionary LeJeune was particularly impressed with the Amerindian sweat lodges. He described them thus:

> They make a little low tent of bark, and cover it with their fur robes; then they heat five or six stones and put them into this oven, which they enter entirely naked. They sing all the time while in there, gently striking the sides of these stoves. I saw them come out all wet with perspiration; this is the best of their medicines.[48]

Before European diseases decimated the native population, the men were more likely to die from hunting accidents or in battle. The natives knew how to apply splints to treat broken arms and legs. Wounds were treated with cautery, that is, burning with an ember from the fire or hot stones. Or the wound might be stitched together, using a fiber from the tendon of a deer's leg. Natives did not use amputations in the treatment of the injured.[49]

Tobacco was particularly prized by the natives. For them, tobacco had desirable restorative qualities in addition to its ceremonial use. The herb was dried in the sun, ground into a powder, carried in a small pouch around the neck, and smoked in a pipe. Smoking tobacco kept the natives warm in winter. The leaves could also be chewed to diminish hunger and thirst. The powder could be made into a paste to be applied to wounds.[50]

The medicine man held a place of honor in the tribe, combining as he did the offices of physician and priest. When natural remedies failed, the village medicine man was depended upon to drive out the evil spirit causing the disease. Father Le Jeune described the treatment of the sick among the natives:

> They summon the sorcerer, who, without acquainting himself with the disease of the patient, sings, and shakes his tortoise shell; he gazes into the water and sometimes into the fire, to discover the nature of the disease. Having learned it, he says that the soul of the patient desires, for his recovery, to be given a present of such or such a thing,—of a canoe, for example, of a new robe, a porcelain collar, a fire-feast, a dance, etc., and the whole village straightway sets to work to carry out to the letter all the sorcerer may have ordered.[51]

Sometimes the list of items a person desired was quite long. If the village failed to provide any one of the gifts, this was considered to be the reason that the sick person died. If the illness was not cured, showering a sick person with gifts was, at the very least, a comfort measure.

In contrast to the quiet and rest advocated by the French, a lot of noise and commotion attended the sick of the native villages. The women, young and old, were summoned by the sorcerer to sing and dance; on occasion, they dressed in costumes and acted out stories. A banquet might also be ordered and all of those present compelled to prepare the prescribed feast. As often as not, the sick individual was obliged to participate in both the preparation of the food and in the dancing.[52]

Maybe it should be said, with respect to both native and French medicine, that people who survived often did so in spite of the treatment. However, when it came to smallpox and other diseases of European origin, the odds were very much stacked against the natives. The indigenous villages along the St. Lawrence River and beyond would never recover. The French settlement at Quebec would experience more than its share of death in the years to come; Hélène's household would not be spared.

CHAPTER TEN

FALL OF 1639

———— ᗞᗺᗢ ————

Arrival of the Ursulines and the Augustinian hospital nuns; Village pageantry; Establishment of the mission at Sillery; Epidemic of small-pox decimates the native population; The hospital at Quebec; Guillaume Hébert's death

Mother Marie Guyart de l'Incarnation would later write of the exhilaration she felt upon her arrival at Quebec in the summer of 1639. One wonders who felt the excitement more: the nuns who had come to establish a school and a hospital in the New World or the villagers who greeted them.[1] Certainly, they were welcome additions to the tiny community.

The new arrivals would eventually settle in the Upper Town, not far from the home of Hélène. For the rest of her life, in ways she could not yet imagine, Hélène's life would be entwined with the lives of these devout and devoted women who were every bit as strong and determined as the male leaders in the colony.

Among those who were most happy to see the new arrivals were the Jesuits. The missionaries saw the need for the education of the native girls as well as the boys. They also recognized the need for a hospital to care for the sick, French and natives alike. Father Le Jeune had written about these needs in his *Jesuit Relations*. His appeals fell on fertile ground: the Jesuits were instrumental in bringing both the Ursulines and the Augustinian nuns to Quebec in 1639.[2]

A strong missionary impulse was part of the religious renewal, or counter-reformation, of the seventeenth century. Marie-Madeleine Chauvigny de La Peltrie was a young widow in Alençon, France, inspired by what she read in the *Jesuit Relations* to devote her time and her wealth to missionary endeavors. Toward that end, she vowed to found a seminary for native girls in New France. In Tours, 150 kilometers south of Alençon, the Ursuline nun, Marie de l'Incarnation, was also familiar with the writing of the Jesuits concerning their experiences in the New World. She, too, was interested in building a convent and a school at Quebec, with the ultimate goal of winning over the souls of the native children for Christianity. Initially, the women encountered tough opposition to this undertaking that had no precedents in France. Eventually, with the strong backing of the Jesuits, they received permission from the Bishop of Tours to pursue their vision. They also gained the needed support of the Company of One Hundred Associates for these endeavors. Madame de La Peltrie became the patron and secular founder of the Ursulines of Quebec.[3] When approval was received for the venture in the New World, she personally chartered a ship, filling it with 8,000 *livres* worth of furniture and provisions for the Ursuline nuns. The Duchesse d'Aiguillon, niece of Cardinal Richelieu of the Company of One Hundred Associates, had also become enamored with the missionary efforts in the New World. She become the patroness of the Augustinian Hospitallers, giving 22,000 *livres* for the establishment of a Hôtel-Dieu in Quebec.[4]

There were similarities in the early lives of Madame de La Peltrie and Marie Guyart de l'Incarnation, the two women who would be responsible for founding a school for girls in Quebec. Marie-Madeleine Chauvigny de La Peltrie was born to a wealthy family in Alençon in 1603; the castle of the Seigneur of Vaubougon was her ancestral home. Her parents arranged for her marriage at the age of seventeen. At twenty-two, Marie-Madeleine was widowed; she had borne one child who died young. Madame de La Peltrie was not interested in remarrying, in spite of her father's efforts to find her another husband. Deeply religious, she spent her time in France visiting the sick and the poor, sharing her wealth with the less fortunate.[5]

Marie Guyart de l'Incarnation was born in 1599 in Tours, France, into a family of craftsmen and bakers. Even as a small child she was drawn to religion. However, when she was seventeen, her parents arranged for her to marry a man in whom she had no interest. Two years later, her husband died and she was left a widow with a small child. She, too, avoided remarriage and involved herself in works of charity around Tours. In 1631, with her son away at a Jesuit school, Marie entered the Ursuline Convent of Tours as a novice.[6]

So it came to be that Mother Marie de l'Incarnation, along with two Ursuline companions and Marie-Madeleine de La Peltrie, arrived at Quebec on August 1, 1639.[7] With them were three Hospitallers, prepared to establish a Hôtel-Dieu in the settlement.[8] Four Jesuit priests and a lay brother were also members of the party of religious men and women arriving in 1639. The group had left from Dieppe on May 4, 1639 on board the *Saint-Joseph*. It would be three months before the ship arrived at the colony. As with so many trans-Atlantic voyages of that era, this trip was difficult, plagued as it was with stormy weather, rough seas and, according to Marie de l'Incarnation, danger of capture by the Spanish.[9]

The new arrivals were warmly welcomed by the governor, Charles de Montmagny, and the residents of Quebec, as well as curious natives. The day had been declared a holiday in the settlement and the occasion was marked with as much pomp and ceremony as the little colony could muster. The newcomers were escorted up the hill to Fort Saint-Louis for their first meal in Quebec. Following that, they were given a tour of the village, such as it was. When the Ursuline and Augustinian nuns arrived in 1639, Quebec had a population of fewer than 300 inhabitants. There were only some half-dozen homes in the settlement itself, with other dwellings scattered in the nearby woods. The little community had not fully recovered from the destruction wrought by the English between 1629 and 1632.[10]

Everyone in the settlement must have been on hand to greet the newcomers, including Guillaume Hébert, a very pregnant Hélène, and their two small children: Joseph, who was not yet three, and Françoise, who was born the previous year, in 1638. One can imagine the young family carefully making their way down the path to the Lower Town, with babies in arms, not wanting to miss any of the excitement. Their third child would be born on August 2, 1639, the day after the arrival of the nuns, and baptized Angélique.

The sisters had successfully made it across the Atlantic and were ready to face whatever dangers and discomforts were now in store for them. A priority was to see that the newcomers were settled. Madame de La Peltrie had arrived first and rented a house for the Ursulines. It was in the Lower Town, just a few yards from the river bank. The Hospitallers had a home in the Upper Town constructed for them under the orders of their patron, the Duchesse d'Aiguillon. However, neither of these homes was ready when they arrived in August of 1639. For the first few nights, both groups of nuns stayed at a cabin belonging to the Company of One Hundred Associates.[11]

Hélène might well have become acquainted with the Augustinian sisters during her stay in Dieppe five years earlier. This religious order had operated a hospital in Dieppe since the thirteenth century. Since the Middle Ages, and likely well before then, the care of the poor and the sick, as well as the education of boys and girls, had been the role of religious institutions, in particular the Roman Catholic Church. The hospital of the Augustinians in Dieppe served as a sanctuary for those in need: the old, the disabled, the sick, the poor, abandoned children, and pilgrims. All were welcomed. The sisters of St. Augustine were poor themselves and could be found at the port, begging for fish to feed the needy.[12] It is quite possible that those returning to Dieppe from Quebec in 1629, including Hélène and her parents, had turned to the Augustinian sisters for help. It is not a stretch to imagine that Hélène's mother might have been cared for by

Augustinian sisters before her death in 1632. It is very possible that Hélène encountered the sisters at the market or on their way to the harbor seeking donations of food for those who had come to their door for help.

In the summer of 1638, the colonists had learned that the French queen was pregnant. The Dauphin, who would become Louis XIV, was born that fall, on September 5, 1638. Quebec did not get word of the birth until late in the summer of 1639, as ships had been delayed in reaching New France. When the news did arrive, it was greeted with great joy and festivity. The birth was to be celebrated in Quebec as it had been in France. Pageantry was a part of both the French and the native culture: celebrations broke the tedium of everyday life. Naturally, French pageantry was linked with religious observance. To celebrate the birth of a new French Dauphin and to honor, if not impress, the recently-arrived nuns, the Jesuits organized a day-long celebration.[13] The August feast day of the Assumption of the Blessed Virgin Mary into Heaven was chosen.[14]

The day began with a celebration of the Mass, attended by Christian natives and French settlers alike. The firing of cannons from Fort Saint-Louis on Cap Diamant announced the beginning of a formal procession and imbued the day with a sense of anticipation and excitement. At the front of the parade, two men carried the Cross and French banner. Next came one of the prominent Frenchmen, escorting the native men from the neighborhood, marching two-by-two in a solemn and dignified manner. Some of the Amerindians were clad in royal garments that had been gifts from the King. Behind the men came Madame de La Peltrie, escorting three or four native girls who had been bathed and dressed in the fashion of French children. She was followed by the rest of the natives, each in their own costume, and equally solemn and respectful. Next came the French clergy, Governor Montmagny, and finally the French men and women of the settlement.[15]

The French colonists would have been outfitted in their "Sunday best." The women were dressed as much as possible in the fashion current in France. Their dresses were long, with a fitted bodice and full skirt. Bonnets covered their hair and a fichu, or scarf, was used to cover the shoulders.[16] The Frenchmen wore their hair long and sported beards and mustaches. Their clothing consisted of loose-fitting grey or brown homespun breeches, stockings, wide-brimmed felt hats made out of beaver fur, and coats that came down to their knees. Men of distinction also wore wigs of various sizes, shapes and materials. The more affluent men and women wore lace collars and cuffs and carried lace handkerchiefs. Children's clothing was modeled on that worn by the adults.[17]

This dignified parade marched through the village to the Hôtel Dieu, which was, at the time, a plain, unassuming cabin. When they arrived, all knelt in prayer: the Amerindians on one side, the French villagers on the other, and the clergy in the center. They prayed in turn for the King and Queen of France, as well as for the young Dauphin. Then came prayers for all French people and for all native peoples. When prayers were finished at the hospital, the little group moved past the fort where cannons again roared and soldiers fired their muskets in salute. The next stop for the procession was a small cottage along the bank of the St. Lawrence River: this was to be the first home of the Ursulines. There, the Hospital nuns and the Ursulines took turns singing joyful hymns to God. The simple procession ended at the church where it had begun. Prayers were said in the native language, as well as in French. At the conclusion of this religious parade, all were invited for a feast, hosted by the governor. Certain to be on the menu were provisions of favored food and wine, fresh from the recently arrived vessels from France. The day concluded with Vespers in the chapel and more speeches, this time from leaders among the natives, who also wished the King and Queen well.[18] Father Le Jeune would comment in his annual report: "We formed a procession which would have delighted all France if it had appeared in Paris."[19]

The aborigines loved music and ceremony as much as the French. Many readily participated in the external religious observances brought by the French. The children learned the prayers and church music. They loved to dress up and participate in the processions. However, deeper participation meant rejecting their own customs and traditions. The Jesuits and the nuns would come to the realization, only much later, that few of the natives were willing to relinquish their culture and lifestyle for that brought by the French.

Before they settled into their cloistered life, the Ursulines were given a tour of the Mission of St. Joseph at Sillery, a nearby settlement established by the Jesuits in 1637 for natives who had converted to Christianity. The missionaries were hoping that conversion of the natives could be accomplished by inducing them to give up their semi-nomadic way of life and settle in one spot, with permanent homes and cultivation of crops. Financial support for the mission at Sillery was provided by Noël Brûlart de Sillery, the Prime Minister of Louis XIII. This mission, initially intended for the semi-nomadic tribes along the St. Lawrence River, was located two leagues (six miles) upriver from Quebec. It was near enough to Fort Saint-Louis to offer protection from the Iroquois. The Jesuits had supervised the construction of cottages and a chapel. Some of the natives lived in these cottages; others camped in their pole lodges. All of the natives, along with a few French, shared in the work of clearing the land and raising crops. In addition to cultivating the soil, the Amerindians continued to follow their traditional lifestyle: they still fished for eel in the late summer and autumn. In the winter, all but the weakest left for their inland hunting grounds.[20]

The Ursulines, in their long, black habits, and the Hospitallers, in grey, made a great impression on the Amerindians. More notable than their curious clothing was the great affection that they showed for the native children. Madame de La Peltrie felt particularly drawn to hug and kiss every child she met; before the day was out, she had been named godmother of one of the aborigines.[21] Mother Marie's intentions were to bring the native girls from the settlement at Sillery to their school and to educate them in the French religion, language, and culture. It was hoped that the children, in turn, would educate their families in the way of the faith. There was also the expectation that they would make good wives for the Frenchmen.[22]

In the fall of 1639, the natives were reeling from another epidemic of smallpox. It is believed that the initial outbreak of the disease that so affected the natives along the St. Lawrence River began in the English colonies to the south. In 1638, a British ship which docked at the harbor in Boston carried smallpox. The disease was then carried north by natives returning home from their visit to the English communities.[23] The settlers were not untouched. Once again, the situation in Quebec must have seemed dire to the small band of colonists. Before the nuns came, the Jesuits had constructed a simple hospital to serve the sick of Quebec.[24] Upon their arrival in 1639, the hospital was gladly entrusted to the care and management of the Hospitallers of St. Augustine, who managed the Hôtel-Dieu of Dieppe.

In his report written in 1640 and entitled "Of the Nuns Recently Arrived in New France, and of their Occupation," Father Paul Le Jeune wrote:

> The Hospital nuns arrived at Kebec on the first day of August of last year. Scarcely had they disembarked before they found themselves overwhelmed with patients. The hall of the Hospital being too small, it was necessary to erect some cabins, fashioned like those of the [natives] in their garden. Not having furniture for so many people, they had to cut in two or three pieces part of the blankets and sheets they had brought for these poor sick people. In a word, instead of taking a little rest and refreshing themselves after the great discomfort they had suffered upon the sea, they found themselves so burdened and occupied that we had fear of losing them and their hospital at its very birth. The sick came from all directions in such numbers, their stench was so insupportable, the heat so great, the fresh food so scarce and so poor in a country so new and so strange, that I do not know how these good sisters, who almost had not even leisure in which to take a little sleep, endured all these hardships.[25]

The Ursuline nuns also had no time to relax after their three-month journey over rough seas. Within a week of their arrival, the small home being prepared for the Ursulines was ready and the three religious retreated into the confines of their cloister. The cottage, which would serve both as residence and school, consisted of two main rooms, plus a cellar and an attic. The first room, which was a sixteen foot square, housed the convent choir, parlor, dormitory, and refectory. The other room housed the kitchen and, at the same time, would serve as a classroom for both the French and the native girls. The chapel and sacristy for the tiny cloistered community were housed in a lean-to. The cabin and gardens were enclosed by thick cedar logs, which took the place of the walls that surrounded cloistered communities in France. The Ursulines would remain in this tiny residence at waters' edge for three years, while a more substantial and suitable structure was being built in the Upper Town. The sisters did all of the manual work around the place as well as the teaching.[26] Mother Marie would write in 1640, "This tiny house is so poor that at night time we can see stars shining through the [roof] and can barely keep a candle alight because of the wind."[27]

The Ursulines, under the leadership of Marie de l'Incarnation, were prepared to dedicate themselves to the education of the young French and Amerindian girls living in the vicinity of Quebec. Within days, a number of the Christian natives had entrusted their daughters to the Ursulines. Also among the first students were the few French girls of school age. However, the Ursuline effort to establish a school for Amerindian girls was put on hold shortly after their arrival. During the smallpox epidemic of 1639, the house of the Ursulines also became a hospital. There were not enough beds and hands to take care of the sick at the Augustinian Hôtel-Dieu, which had became known as *"la maison de la mort."* Conditions at the Ursuline convent and school were not much better. There was no furniture; make-shift beds were arranged on the floor, with little room in between. The nuns had to step over and around the sick in their ministrations.[28]

The Jesuit missionaries took a census of the natives beginning in the spring of 1639 and extending over the winter of 1639-40. Father Jérôme Lalemant noted the results in his annual report:

> We have had the means to take the census not only of the villages, large and small, but also of the cabins, the fires, and even very nearly of the persons in all the country – there really being

no other way to preach the gospel in these regions than at each family's hearth, whereof we tried to omit not one. In these 5 missions there are thirty two hamlets and straggling villages, which comprise in all about 700 cabins, about 2,000 fires, and about 12,000 persons. These villages and cabins were much more populous formerly, but the extraordinary diseases and the wars within some years past, seem to have carried off the best portion: there remaining only very few old men, very few persons of skill and management.[29]

For the Amerindians, this epidemic would end in the spring of 1640. In his visit to Huronia in the summer of 1615, Champlain estimated the population to be about thirty thousand inhabitants.[30] The number of people had been reduced by more than half over the course of twenty-five years. It is hard to imagine the devastation. Those who survived had lost spouses, fathers, mothers, children, and siblings. Not only were families destroyed, but the political infrastructure of the villages collapsed. The other indigenous communities along the St. Lawrence River, having developed no immunity to the disease, were equally decimated.

For Hélène, the excitement of the summer was replaced with shock and grief in the autumn. On September 23, her husband, Guillaume Hébert, died.[31] The reason for Guillaume's death was not recorded. When the French pioneers died of disease, this cause was rarely mentioned in the death records.[32] It may well be that he died of smallpox. Robert Giffard, as the settlement's only surgeon, was treating patients at the hospital. Those caring for the sick were overwhelmed and exhausted. Guillaume was a friend of Robert and it is quite possible that Guillaume was helping his friend in attending the sick. The young Hébert family lived in the Upper Town, just a short distance from the hospital. Guillaume Hébert had come to Quebec as a young child in 1617. The Héberts did not return to France during the English occupation of 1629-1632. While many Europeans had acquired some immunity to smallpox, Guillaume had spent most of his years in the colony and probably had no previous exposure and no resistance to the disease.

There were no medically-trained physicians in New France, and there would be none during Hélène's lifetime. Michel Sarrazin would be the first Frenchman to practice in this capacity. He came to New France as a surgeon in 1685, but returned to France in 1694 where he obtained his doctorate of medicine at Reims. Returning to Quebec in 1697, he practiced medicine there until his death in 1734 from a fever probably associated with a case of smallpox which had recently arrived in the colony by ship.[33]

On October 21, 1639, Hélène appeared before Governor Montmagny for the purpose of establishing guardianship of Guillaume and Hélène's three minor children.[34] Guillaume Couillard, Hélène's brother-in-law, was appointed guardian in the presence of Abraham Martin and Guillaume Hubou. Hélène's signature is on this document. Guillaume Couillard and Hélène's uncle Abraham were illiterate; their signatures were marked with an "x."[35]

The same day, an inventory of Hébert's possessions was undertaken by the notary Martial Piraube, at the request of Guillaume Couillard and on behalf of the deceased's three children. In 1623, Guillaume's father had received a small fief on the outskirts of Quebec from the Duc de Montmorency, the viceroy of New France at that time. Guillaume would have received a portion of this seigneury when he came into his majority. In New France, the colonists followed the laws of inheritance in place in France at the time. These laws were a modified form of primogeniture. According to these provisions, if a seigneur died before his wife, his estate was divided between the widow and his children. The widow's half would be held in usufruct, passing to her children upon her death.[36] Thus, Hélène would have inherited one-half of the property. Guillaume Couillard would manage the other half, representing the interests of the children.

The inventory of Guillaume's estate reveals the simplicity of the lives of Hélène and Guillaume. On the list were a grill, a set of tongs, a large pot, and an old spoon, all made out of iron. There were also two small copper cauldrons, a small copper plate, and a copper lamp. Three large dishes, three smaller plates, three cups, and a silver spoon were listed. Among the items of clothing mentioned were an old gray coat, shoes in two parts, hosiery in need of repair, breeches, a few doublets (tight-fitting jackets), two white shirts, five shirts of coarser cloth, two old wool hats, and three handkerchiefs. There were two pine chests, a broken mirror, a bedstead, two red blankets, a white blanket, and a few sheets. Also among Guillaume's possessions were three arquebuses, two pistols, a rifle, and a mold to make lead bullets, as well as a hatchet and a couple of saws. A barrel filled two-thirds with salt was in the cottage. In the barn were about six bushels of corn, buckwheat, and seven barrels of peas. The inventory also noted that Hébert had a shared interest in a couple of cows.[37]

The next month, beginning on November 11, 1639, the personal property of Guillaume was sold. The Abbé Jean Le Sueur purchased one arquebus; another arquebus went to Guillaume Couillard. Guillaume Hubou and Le Sueur each bought a pistol. Olivier Letardif bought a pair of snow shoes. Abraham Martin bought the barrel of salt. Guillaume Hubou bought a long saw. Clothes were sold off as well: the hats, the shirts, etc. A horn full of powder was sold to Claude l'Archevêque. A red woolen blanket was purchased by Guillaume Couillard. The small copper lamp went to Jacques Maheu. The broken mirror was purchased by Nicolas Marsolet. And so it went until most, if not all, of Guillaume Hébert's personal property was sold. A feather bed, a white blanket, a pallet and a two pairs of sheets went to Hélène herself for forty-five *livres*. The sale of personal items amounted to a sum total of 367 *livres*. Presumably this money went for the benefit of the minor children of Guillaume Hébert.[38]

On November 12, 1639, according to a document filed in the civil records, the carpenters Nicolas and Pierre Pelletier, along with the mason Jehan Eger, judged the home in which the young Hébert family had been living at Guillaume's death as uninhabitable and not worth repairing. Guillaume Couillard moved Hélène and her children to another cottage that had been the property of Guillaume Hébert and was situated near the Couillard home.[39]

Two days after Christmas and scarcely three months after the death of Guillaume, Hélène signed a contract in a civil ceremony to marry Noël Morin. Hélène was listed as the daughter of Pierre Desportes and Françoise Langlois and a native of the parish of Notre-Dame-de-la-Recouvrance.[40] Noël was listed as the son of Claude Morin and the late Jeanne Moreau of the parish of Saint-Étienne in Brie, France. It is not known when Noël came to the colony: the first time his name appears in the notarial records of Quebec is on his contract to marry Hélène Desportes in 1639. He was a cartwright by trade and was literate to the extent that he could sign his name.[41]

Both Noël and Hélène brought property to the marriage. Hélène had the home in the Upper Town, near Notre-Dame-de-la-Recouvrance. She also had forty *perches* (one quarter of an acre) of land adjoining the property and about two arpents (about one and a half acres) of land near Mont Carmel.[42] Noël Morin had property in France that he had inherited from his mother. This was a house, distinguished by its hanging sign featuring a white horse, located in the village of Brie-Comte-Robert on the rue des Fontaines near the village gate.[43] The home was in the parish of Saint-Étienne. The marriage contract specified that if Noël died before Hélène and there were no children from their union, she would receive two hundred *livres* coming from his portion of the sale of the property inherited from his mother. If Hélène died before Noël and there were no children from their marriage, Noël would have the complete use of Hélène's home and land for a period of six years.[44]

On this winter day, the couple, along with twenty family members, friends, and neighbors had gathered in the home of Martial Piraube, the colony's notary. Robert Giffard and his wife, Marie Regnouard, were there. The Hébert family was represented by Guillaume Hubou and his wife, Marie Rollet. Marie's daughter Guillemette Hébert, son-in-law Guillaume Couillard, and their daughter Louise Couillard were present. Hélène's aunt and uncle, Abraham Martin and Marguerite Langlois, along with Hélène's cousin Marguerite Martin and her husband Étienne Racine were there as well. Others from the community attending the ceremony were Nicolas Pivert, Jean Bourdon, the

Abbé Le Sueur, Jean Jolliet, Martin Prévost, Oliver Letardif, Antoine Tabouret, and Jean Guitet.[45] Certainly this showing was an indication of the depth of feeling and the widespread support for this young couple. Attending the ceremony were some of the most distinguished men and women in the colony. Noël must have been seen as a man of good character, as evidenced by the make-up of the group that witnessed the signing of the marriage contract between Hélène and Noël. It was a tight-knit community. They worked together, they played together, and they prayed together. They were there to sustain each other in good times and in bad.

CHAPTER ELEVEN

SEPTEMBER OF 1640

—∞∞∞—

Hélène marries Noël Morin; Homesteads in Quebec; Life for the French settlers: women's work and men's work; Gathering around the family hearth in the evening

Hélène was quick to move on with her life. She and Noël recited their marriage vows before Father Nicolas Adam on January 9, 1640 in a ceremony at Notre-Dame-de-la-Recouvrance.[1] The marriage had occurred less than four months after the death of her first husband. Once again, Robert Giffard, surgeon and seigneur of Beauport, was there to stand up for the young woman. Nicolas Pivert was the other witness to the marriage.

It is possible that Hélène could have remained unmarried for a time, relying on the charity and good will of her mother-in-law, Marie Rollet. However, in this new country, where French men far outnumbered the women, a quick entry into the holy sacrament of marriage was seen as the best outcome for all concerned, not the least being the young colony itself.

Women of childbearing age who lost their husbands often remarried much more quickly in Quebec than in France, often in a matter of months. Half of those who remarried did so within a year of losing their spouse. The demands of colonial life made it almost impossible for a woman to survive alone in the young colony. A male presence was a necessity. There were young children to raise. In addition, childbearing women were needed to increase the population of the settlements. With some evident pride in the fertility of the couples in New France, Intendant Talon would note in 1670 that almost all of the women who had immigrated the previous year were either pregnant or had already delivered babies.[2]

Hélène and Noël settled in the Upper Town, on the property that originally belonged to Hélène and her first husband. The homes in New France were built by settlers who had come primarily from Normandy. As such, they were modeled on farmsteads to be found in the Norman countryside, where peasants lived in small cottages surrounded by an assortment of rustic, weather-beaten outbuildings and a dung pile in a corner of the courtyard. Stables and sheds, generally in some degree of disrepair, sheltered the few animals as well as a meager supply of grains and firewood. A kitchen garden would be established on a small plot of land nearby. Here were planted a few fruit trees, as well as beds of cabbages, turnips, broad beans and other vegetables. This garden became the woman's domain and was the source of much of the diet of the peasants. Wells for fresh water and ovens for baking bread were often communal.[3]

In the colony, *habitants*, that is, those who worked the land, might expect to live in a simple dwelling built out of the material available nearby. Initially, most homes were log cabins or of wood-framed construction, where the walls were of roughly hewn timber, placed horizontally. The roof was made of thatch or shingles. In the beginning, the floor was only packed earth. Later, wooden flooring might be added. Window openings were covered with translucent oiled skins. The fireplace hearth and chimney were made out of clay or stone with a hook for hanging pots. A clay oven might be set up outside the home, in an outbuilding or at one end of the house. The cabins were often drafty. Wind and rain, small animals and insects of every sort found their way inside. The inhabitants protected themselves against the cold by keeping a fire going in the fireplace and by wrapping themselves in cloaks and blankets.[4]

The cottages had one room, which served as a living room, kitchen, and bedroom. There was little privacy for family members. There might be a large curtained bed for parents. Children slept on straw mattresses spread on the floor. Other furniture was minimal and generally homemade: a chest for clothing and bedding, a table and benches, cooking utensils. In the seventeenth century, interiors were austere and smoke-filled. The kitchen wall might be decorated with a holy picture. If there was a book in the home, it would be a bible.[5] The property assessment conducted after Guillaume died suggests that he and Hélène had such humble lodging. From 1643 onward, there would be continuing and escalating threats from the Iroquois. Sometimes homes were constructed with a sleeping area in the loft. At night the ladder to the loft was removed as a safety measure. It was dangerous to go out after dark.[6]

Before too many years passed, a typical household in New France would have ten or more family members. There were often three generations living under one roof. As families grew and became more settled, the house might be enlarged to include two stories. The first floor would hold the kitchen, dining room, parlor, and one or two bedrooms. The second floor would provide additional sleeping and storage space. On larger homesteads, the compound grew to include a barn, stable, privy, shed, henhouse, pigpen, crib for corn or grain, and a smokehouse for meat, as well as vegetable and herb gardens. Stock grazed on open land and garden plots needed to be fenced to keep animals out.[7]

Although class distinctions were not as rigidly defined in New France as in the mother country, some individuals clearly lived better than others in the young colony. The dwellings of the French colonists reflected the economic status of the settler. The more affluent in the colony would soon live in houses constructed of fieldstone with steeply pitched roofs. Guillaume Hébert's parents were known to have had the first stone farmhouse in the colony.

One of the nicest homesteads in early Quebec was that belonging to Jean Bourdon, who had come to New France in 1634 as Engineer of New France, or Engineer to the Governor as he was also known. Champlain had allowed him to select his own property and Bourdon had chosen the highest ground on what came to be known as côteau Sainte-Geneviève, on the outskirts of the Upper Town. There he built a large stone house which was finished in stucco and painted white. The land was cleared and crops were sown. The homestead was eventually enlarged to form a block of buildings which included two barns, a mill and three granaries. Bourdon also had a chapel built for his good friend Abbé Le Sueur, a secular priest who had come to Quebec with Bourdon. With the arrival of Governor Montmagny in 1636, Jean Bourdon became one of the more prominent men in the colony. Bourdon was given responsibility for supervising building operations and settling property disputes. Among his many accomplishments, Bourdon conducted a survey of Quebec and drew up plans for future building, so that there could be some uniformity and order in the development of the city.[8] Bourdon had been one of the witnesses to the marriage contract signed by Hélène and Noël in December of 1639. In due time, the Morin family would move to the côteau Sainte-Geneviève, where they would become close neighbors, as well as life-long friends, of Jean Bourdon and Abbé Le Sueur.[9]

Hélène's life changed little with her marriage to Noël. The activities of her day-to-day existence were spelled out by time-honored French tradition and the exigencies of life in a frontier settlement. Meal preparation consumed a significant part of the day for Hélène, as it did for the other women in the settlement. Large quantities of food were needed because the men who labored outdoors had hearty appetites. Supplies from the mother country were limited. The French had to rely primarily on what they could catch, kill, gather, and grow themselves. Women generally prepared and baked their own bread; however, if they lived close enough to their neighbors, the bread might also have been baked in communal ovens. When no wheat was available, the colonists made do with boiled corn and a porridge made of a coarse cornmeal.

Most cooking took place before the hearth. The meal for the day was boiled in a cauldron, roasted on the spit, grilled over coals, or buried under the ashes. Control of temperature and evenness of heat was imprecise. Pots might be hung higher or lower over the fire; the embers might be arranged to burn hotter or colder. However, the smoke and heat from the fire would have made it difficult to check on the cooking or stir the pot. In the more affluent homes, dishes might be prepared and baked in the outdoor oven, after the bread was taken out. Eventually raised stoves were developed. These were rectangular, waist-high brick constructions. A metal plate was placed on top of the bricks. The stove was heated with coals or charcoal placed in a fireproof compartment beneath the cooking surface. The stove made it much easier to regulate the heat and to attend to the cooking pots. Raised stoves first made their appearance in the late sixteenth century. By the mid-seventeenth century, many of the bourgeois homes in France had a stove.[10] No doubt some of the wealthier settlers who would come to live in the stone homes in the Upper Town of Quebec and on the seigneuries also had a stove.[11]

Home sites were chosen for their proximity to rivers, creeks, and springs. The Morin family and others who settled in the Upper Town were fortunate to have spring water nearby. However, obtaining sufficient water to meet the demands of a large household was no easy task. Water was needed for drinking, cooking, and bathing, as well as for the washing of pots, pans, and the family's clothing. Pigs, chickens, and other animals would also need water. In the summer, some activities could be accomplished at water's edge. However, settlers would have to haul most water in a wooden bucket to their cottage. This was often the task of women and children. Water was stored in wooden barrels which might also be pressed into service to catch rain water. In winter, when all bodies of water were frozen solid, snow and ice were melted to provide for household needs. From Father LeJeune comes this description of the work required in obtaining water at this time of year:

> As we have neither a spring nor a well, we are obliged to go for water every day to the river, from which we are distant about

200 steps. But to get it, we must first break the ice with heavy blows from an axe; and after that we must wait until the sea comes up, for when the tide is low you cannot get water because of the thickness of the ice. We throw this water into a barrel, which is not far from a good fire; and yet we must be careful to break the layer of ice every morning, otherwise, in two nights, it would be one mass of ice, even if the barrel were full.[12]

In addition to the cooking, Hélène was responsible for the house-work and the care of the children. Clothes were washed by hand, hung on tree branches or a line to dry, and then ironed as required. Women in the early days of the settlement fashioned the family's clothing from cloth imported from France. They hooked rugs, made quilts, and knit woolen mittens, scarves, and stockings. Candles were made by dipping a string repeatedly into hot tallow until it was large enough to stand on its own and burn slowly. Soap was made from rendered beef fat, mixed with ashes and water. In the spring, the house was cleaned thoroughly from top to bottom. Women tended the vegetable gardens, which were planted after winter frosts, and fed the livestock. The care of the sick generally fell to women: home remedies included infusions made from various herbs, barks, leaves, and roots found in the woods. Women were also there to help their neighbors when a child was born.[13]

Noël continued to work as a wheelwright, but his trade alone did not provide enough income to support a growing family. He also engaged in agricultural pursuits, which frequently required back-breaking labor from sunrise to sunset. The farmer generally built his own house, barn, farm equipment, and furniture for the home. The typical *habitant* owned about fifty acres. The land had to be cleared of trees and rocks; stumps had to be removed. Two years were gen-erally required for a family to clear one *hectare* (approximately 2½ acres) of land.[14] Colonists worked hard to put food on the table and to store excess for the long winter months. The daily work depended on the season. From spring through fall, the ground was plowed and planted, weeded and harvested. Quebec had a short growing season. Generally there were only 115 frost-free days. Fences and outbuildings needed to be constructed and kept in good repair. Firewood was gathered, split, and corded. In the spring, newborn animals required special care. The men were also engaged in hunting and fishing. Seals, found in the St. Lawrence River estuary, were hunted and killed for their skin and their oil, used in the colony's lamps, as well as for their meat. With the fall came the harvest and preparations for winter. In the colder months, when there was less to do outdoors, men also made household furniture, carts, toboggans, and snowshoes.[15]

Wheat was the main crop once the farms were established. The colonists grew a Norwegian wheat that ripened in three months. Oats, barley, and rye, as well as a great quantity of peas, were other foodstuffs grown on the farms. Flax and hemp, grown later, produced material for clothes. Most, if not all, of the production on the farms went to supporting the family's own needs. Any excess agricultural products were sold at a local market. The settlers were never completely self-sufficient. They continued to import wine, brandy, coffee, tea, and salt, as well as cloth and clothing, copper pots and pans, iron tools, and various household furnishings. In addition to farming the land, many settlers were like Noël Morin and employed in a trade which produced additional income.[16]

Farmers' livestock might include cows, pigs, turkeys, capons, chickens, a pair of oxen, a few sheep, and in later years, a horse. Herds were small, as farmers needed to provide shelter and feed over the long winter months. Most animals were slaughtered in the fall, providing meat for the winter. The exceptions were animals needed for breeding and labor.[17] While most farms had at least a few animals, the family's supply of meat was also dependent on what the men could find in the woods and kill. Meat required preparation before consumption; both men and women participated in this process. Feathers needed to be plucked before wild turkey and other birds went into the pot. Animals, both wild and domestic, needed to be skinned and drawn and the meat cut into serviceable portions. What was not served immediately was either smoked or salted for later use. Before it was fit to eat, this meat had to be soaked and scrubbed before cooking in order to remove the salt. Pigs were often slaughtered in the fall, so that families would have smoked and salted pork for the winter. Meat that was improperly cleaned or preserved could result in inedible meat and food poisoning.

As in France, fish was an important component of the settler's diet. Cod and smoked eel were a staple on days of abstinence and during Lent. The colony depended on fishing in the summer and early fall to meet basic needs. Eels were caught in the autumn and were consumed in great numbers. The fish that was not eaten immediately was dried and packed in salt to be consumed later. In the *Jesuit Relations* report for October of 1648 it was observed, "There were few eels this year, and there was a great tendency to destitution."[18]

Noël, like the majority of other immigrants, was an amateur farmer. He was learning on the job. Hélène's former father-in-law, Louis Hébert, an apothecary-turned-farmer, was the first to till the soil and he never owned a plough. As many as three-fourths of the immigrants had no farming experience.[19] These settlers were haphazard in their approach to farming and soon exhausted the land. Contrary to Champlain's belief, the soil along the St. Lawrence was less than ideal. There were no policies in place to protect the land and the livestock. No one was required to fertilize the soil; manure was thrown into the river. Although there were policies in place to prohibit animals from roaming freely on unenclosed property, there were no policies to maintain quality of animal breeding. The quality of the livestock deteriorated rapidly. The lack of experience, coupled with poor-quality soil and the short growing season, meant that agriculture in the French colony in the seventeenth century remained at a subsistence level.[20]

The annual harvest was a family affair. Men and women, young and old, all participated in gathering the crops. As much food as possible was preserved and stored for the upcoming winter. When the supply of fresh meat, fish, summer fruits, and vegetables was exhausted, the colonists would have to rely on the preserved meat and dried grains stored in their barns, as well as the produce stored in their root cellars. More than thirty years had passed since Champlain had founded the colony. Yet the settlers still had to worry about having enough food. Hélène had, no doubt, experienced her share of winters when provisions were scarce.

One can argue that Hélène and the colonists in New France would have eaten better than many of their French countrymen in the Old World in the summer and in the fall of the year. The well-to-do of the cities and towns in France certainly dined on the freshest and highest quality of country products. However, the French peasants seldom had meat, milk, cheese, eggs, and fresh fruit on their tables. Much of what the farmers produced on their small plots of land was sold to pay royal taxes and seigneurial dues. A farmer's family lived on whatever was left over. Meat was consumed only on special occasions. The only meat eaten regularly was pork, as many families kept at least one pig. Peasants were generally forbidden to hunt in the woods, as this privilege belonged exclusively to the seigneur. During days of fasting and abstinence, fish was consumed if one lived near enough to the ocean, a lake, a stream or a pond. Theoretically, the fish on the lands of the seigneur belonged to him, as well. It is not surprising that illegal hunting and fishing were a frequent occurrence.[21]

In 1640, Hélène's children were too young to help much with the work of the household. Joseph was just four and Françoise was two. However, as they grew they would have been expected to work along with the adults, doing as much as their physical strength and development would allow. Little girls helped their mothers with cooking and cleaning. Older girls also assisted with the making of soap and candles. Younger siblings were often their charge. In the evenings, girls learned to sew at their mother's knee. Older boys helped their fathers outdoors with felling trees, clearing the land, plowing, planting, weeding, harvesting, hunting, and fishing. They helped to cut firewood and bring in the logs for the fireplace. They also helped to construct the houses and outbuildings, as well as care for any livestock the family might have. Both boys and girls hauled water from the river, hunted for berries in the woods, and brought in fresh vegetables from the family's kitchen garden.

The hearth was the heart of the home and the center of activity in every household. A fire needed to be kept going day and night, winter and summer. The fireplace provided a place for cooking and a source of warmth for the inhabitants in the cooler months. In addition, the fireplace provided a bit of light for evening activities. A large log was usually burned and the fire was maintained overnight by burying the burning log in ashes. Generally, the natives and the pioneers relied on flint and fine kindling to start fires. If a family's fire went out, it was sometimes easier to borrow fire from a neighbor, carrying the hot ember home in an iron pot.

It was around the hearth that the family gathered in the evenings. Here at the fireside, men would discuss the events of the day and would repeat stories heard from others. As one historian noted, "Much as the Parisian esteemed good eating and drinking, he loved talk even more."[22] Certainly, the Morin family, as well as the other French settlers, enjoyed these activities no less. Particularly in the winter, opportunities for other recreation were limited. One can picture Hélène and the other women in the colony sitting by the hearth at day's end, listening to the conversation and evening report as they quietly engaged in sewing, knitting, mending clothing, or embroidering a fine piece of cloth. The women might well have participated in the discussions.

In seventeenth-century France, one's ranking in society was largely determined at birth by the identity and status of one's parents. However, the French of that era were also influenced by current works of literature which suggested that one's character could be improved through the attainment of knowledge, gentility, virtue, and an appreciation for beauty. Emphasis on etiquette was another outcome of this thinking. Women's roles were changing, at least in Paris. There were bright and clever women in the city who gathered together in their salons to engage in purposeful conversation. This salon society contributed to the empowerment of aristocratic women. By 1620, salons were an integral part of the Parisian social scene, at least for the more affluent members of Parisian society.[23]

Madame de La Peltrie and Mother Marie de l'Incarnation, to a lesser extent, came from privileged backgrounds. One cannot help but believe that they introduced some of these ideas of refinement into the homes of the French settlers at Quebec. In the years ahead, Hélène would come into frequent contact with these women; her girls would attend their school. The spirited Madame de La Peltrie and the more decorous nuns would elevate life in the colony to a plane above the mere mundane; no doubt they influenced the thinking and behavior of Hélène, as well as her daughters.

CHAPTER TWELVE

DECEMBER OF 1642

———— ∘∞∘ ————

A growing colony; Painful losses; Arrival of the founders of Montreal; Hostility between the French at Quebec and the Montreal-bound; Jesuit education for the boys; Building of the Ursuline School on the hill; Education of native and French girls by the Ursulines; Update on Sillery

The colony at Quebec was beginning to grow. Between 1639 and 1642, some forty families settled within about fifteen miles of Quebec.[1] The following note, written in the *Jesuit Relations* in 1642, describes the settlement, albeit from the missionary viewpoint:

> The French colony is the chief means and only foundation for the conversion of all these tribes: there is no better or more efficacious way of procuring their salvation than by succoring this settlement, which, thanks be to God, increases little by little, and overcomes the great impediments it encounters, as the remoteness of help from Europe, the scarcity of laborers, difficulties of trade, and the long Winter which covers the earth, five and even six months, with snow. Notwithstanding all these hindrances, nearly every French household now provides its little store of wheat, rye, peas, barley, and other grains necessary to the life of man, some more, some less, some making provision for happily six months; others, for only a part of that time. Now they begin

to understand the nature of the place, and the right seasons for tilling the soil. The work is well started: it still has need of help; but, thanks be to God, it makes notable progress. Moreover, in every household you will see many children, comely and of good wit.[2]

Each year now brought new families to the colony, but there were also painful losses among the more established families. Louise Couillard, wife of Olivier Letardif and daughter of Guillaume Couillard and Guillamette Hébert, had died in November of 1641, at the age of sixteen. This was just four months after she had given birth to her first child, a son baptized Pierre.[3] It must have been a particularly sad time for Hélène. Louise and Olivier were friends of Hélène dating back to the early days of the settlement, to the years before the conquest of Quebec by the English. Letardif was one of the earliest pioneers in Quebec, a colleague of Champlain, the trading merchants, and the Jesuits. He had known Hélène since her infancy. In 1621, he had been one of the men at Champlain's Habitation who signed the petition to the King that summer, asking for more support for the colonists. In the early years, he served as an assistant clerk for the trading company of the de Caëns. He was also an interpreter, experienced in the Montagnais, Algonquin, and Huron languages. He left the colony with the other French exiles in 1629. Upon his return in 1633, he was made head clerk of the Company of One Hundred Associates. In May of 1637, he acquired a commoner's grant of 160 acres of land on the outskirts of Quebec.[4] Six months later, at the age of thirty-six, he married the twelve-year- old Louise. Hélène was four when Louise was born on the hill above the Habitation. Louise would have been one of her young playmates at a time when there were only six children in the settlement.

For the Morin family, as well as the other settlers at Quebec, the sighting of sailing craft on the river bearing the French flag brought a thrill of excitement and the promise of reinforcement and replenishment for the colony. In early August of 1641, a ship had appeared in the harbor of Quebec. Two more ships would arrive a short time later. These ships were carrying some fifty French countrymen, led by

Paul de Chomedey de Maisonneuve and Jeanne Mance. The group's intentions would soon throw the more established inhabitants of New France into great turmoil. Excitement turned to dismay.[5]

As often noted herein, there was a strong spirit of Christian renewal and religious zeal among the Roman Catholics of France in the early seventeenth century. The French would hear of the struggles, the hardships, and the courage of the missionaries in New France through the publication of the *Jesuit Relations* in France. The correspondence between the women in the religious orders of New France and the mother country also served to inspire the support of the wealthy of Paris and the French provinces for the missionary efforts in the New World.

In 1639, a new organization, the Société Notre-Dame de Montreal, was formed in Paris with the specific intention of furthering the effort to bring Roman Catholicism to the indigenous peoples in the New World. Their vision was to establish a colony to serve as a base for this endeavor on the island of Montreal in the St. Lawrence River, some fifty leagues (150 miles) southwest of Quebec. The society would be responsible for financing and supporting this venture. Cardinal Richelieu lent his support for the foundation of the society, as did the Jesuit missionary Father Charles Lalemant. The Society received a grant of the island of Montreal from the Company of One Hundred Associates in 1640. Having secured land and financial support, the Society appointed Monsieur Paul de Chomedey de Maisonneuve to organize and lead the group that would establish the colony. Jeanne Mance was selected as co-leader of the expedition. As was the case with Madame de La Peltrie and the Duchesse, they were inspired by the religious fervor of the counter-reformation.[6]

Maisonneuve was born in February of 1612 at Neuville-sur-Vanne, Champagne. As a young soldier, he had caught the attention of Father Charles Lalemant as a possible candidate to lead the Montreal expedition.[7] Jeanne Mance was also born in Champagne and baptized there, on November 12, 1606. She was the daughter of

Charles Mance, an attorney who had a practice in the French provincial town of Langres.[8] Langres, in Champagne, was the site of great misery during the French phase of the Thirty Years War. The armies on both sides of the conflict brought death and destruction, either as a direct result of battles fought or from the plagues and pestilences that also accompanied the armies. The town archives of Langres note that in 1637 alone, some 5,500 people perished in the town and surrounding countryside. The local bishop organized the upper class women of the town to assist with works of charity in the care of those caught in the clutches of war.[9] Maisonneuve and Mance were no strangers to violence and suffering.

Those who would establish a settlement at Montreal had left France on May 9, 1641, sailing on three ships departing from Dieppe and La Rochelle. Four brave women, including Jeanne Mance, were in the party. While the group intended to make the crossing in convoy, the ships eventually got separated. The crossing of the Atlantic Ocean took three months. The group from Dieppe was the first to arrive in Quebec and began the construction of a storeroom to house provisions destined for the colony at Montreal. The ship carrying Mance turned up next, on August 8, 1641. Maisonneuve's ship was the last to arrive, appearing in the harbor on August 20, after having encountered violent storms at sea. His late arrival forced the group under his leadership to spend the winter in Quebec and to postpone their departure for Montreal until the following spring. Fortunately, the seigneur of the nearby Saint-Michel and Sainte-Foi invited the newcomers to build shelter for the winter on his property, an offer they gratefully accepted.[10]

There were immediately tensions and even outright hostility between the colonists already established in Quebec and those planning to begin a new settlement farther up the river at Montreal. Those in Quebec hoped for reinforcements for their town. They feared that this new settlement, which would be at a distance from the other settlements, would further strain their limited resources.[11] Noël and Hélène Morin must have shared the view of those in Quebec who were calling the Montreal project a folly. This was certainly understandable, given the circumstances of life in the new country and mounting tensions with the natives.

The hopeful Montreal-bound settlers had arrived at a very bad time. Beginning in 1637, epidemics of smallpox had greatly weakened the Huron and Algonquin peoples north of the St. Lawrence River. These Amerindians became easy prey for the more powerful Iroquois south of the river who were bent on annihilating their traditional enemy. As allies of the Huron and Algonquin natives, the French had increasingly become targets. The French fur trade and economic security for the colony had been severely impacted. A peace conference attended by Governor Montmagny and the Iroquois in the summer of 1641 had ended with the Iroquois breaking off negotiations and declaring war. So at the end of September, just a couple of weeks after the arrival of Maisonneuve and his settlers, Jean Bourdon and Father LeJeune left the colony, bound for Paris, on the last ship of the season. They were charged with pleading the case of the French colonists before the Company and the King. The colony needed military aid: money to construct new forts and soldiers to man them. When Bourdon and LeJeune returned to Quebec in the spring of 1642, they arrived with the promise of money and men to aid in the defense of the colony. Certainly this news would have been greeted with great enthusiasm in the little settlement.[12]

For the Montreal-bound, the winter of 1641-42 must have seemed extra long, in light of the opposition to their plan expressed by those in Quebec. The new group, in need of diversion, decided that a celebration of the thirtieth birthday of their leader was in order. Paul Maisonneuve's patron saint was St. Paul. Accordingly, the festivities were scheduled for January 25, the feast day of the conversion of St. Paul to Christianity. The day began with a pre-dawn gun salute by the Montreal group wintering on the seigneury of Saint-Michel. Maisonneuve acknowledged the tribute and, in turn, ordered a holiday for his colonists. The celebration of Holy Mass was followed by a banquet of the best fare that could be cobbled together, given the time of year. The salute to Maisonneuve was heard in Quebec and, unfortunately, interpreted as an affront to the powers of Governor

Montmagny. The poor fellow who had fired the cannon was hauled away in chains and imprisoned in Quebec. Happily, he was released a short time later. Maisonneuve's group celebrated his return with another holiday, which included more feasting and drinking of good French wine.[13]

Given the icy treatment received at the hands of those settled at Quebec, it is no wonder that the colonists under Maisonneuve and Mance were anxious to leave. In the spring, as soon as the weather turned warmer and the river flowed free of ice, the group left Quebec and traveled upriver. On May 18, 1642, Paul de Chomedey de Maisonneuve and his band of settlers founded the city of Ville Marie on the island of Montreal, located at the convergence of the St. Lawrence and Ottawa Rivers. Later, the city itself became known as Montreal. Maisonneuve was appointed its first governor.[14]

Over that winter, Marie de La Peltrie had become friends with Jeanne Mance. At the time, Madame de La Peltrie was living in a little bark cabin with native converts. She had become quite enamored with the intentions of the Montreal-bound settlers. In what might have been an impetuous moment, Madame decided to join the group. She left with them in the spring, taking her furniture and, more importantly, her financial resources with her. However, this wealthy benefactress would return to the Ursulines eighteen months later, much to the relief of Marie de l'Incarnation.[15]

Life in Quebec had its share of joy as well as hardship and sadness. Otherwise it would have been intolerable. As the year 1642 drew to a close, there was a good kind of excitement in the Upper Town. The Morin family and others on the hill had new neighbors. The Governor, in the name of the Company of One Hundred Associates, had donated six *arpents* (about five acres) of land in the Upper Town for a convent for the Ursulines. The site chosen for the Ursuline monastery was on a beautiful piece of property overlooking the St. Lawrence River. The first school building was begun in 1641. A year later, and three years after their arrival in the colony, the Ursulines, with the aid of carpenters and other workmen, had constructed a proper school for their pupils. The Ursuline monastery was an impressive stone structure: a three-story building measuring ninety-two feet by twenty-eight feet, featuring four chimneys and constructed of a dark-colored limestone quarried locally. It opened on November 21, 1642.[16]

Unfortunately, the builders of the Ursuline monastery had underestimated the severity of winters in Quebec. It was impossible to heat the building adequately. Even though 175 cords of wood were burned in a winter, the nuns and their resident students suffered from numbing cold. When the Ursulines and girls first moved in, the building was like a barn. As soon as possible, the interior was finished. Each nun had a cell or cubicle; this was as much to protect against the cold as to provide each nun with a degree of privacy. Her bedstead was enclosed like a box and entered through doors which swung open like a cupboard.[17]

Marie Morin, Hélène and Noël's daughter, would later provide a description of winter in seventeenth-century Montreal that was apt for Quebec as well:

> You must know that the cold of this country can be understood only by those who are subjected to it. Their house [Hôtel-Dieu of Montreal] having holes in more than 200 places, the wind and snow easily passed through them ... so that when there had been wind and snow during the night, one of the first things to be done in the morning was to take wooden shovels and the broom to throw out the snow around the doors and windows ... and the water that was put on the table for drinking froze within a quarter of an hour.[18]

Now in the Upper Town, in addition to Fort Saint-Louis, there were three large stone buildings set among the trees: the Ursuline Monastery, the College of the Jesuits, and the Hôtel-Dieu of the Augustinian Hospitallers. The social institutions which would provide for the education, health and spiritual wellbeing of the French colonists were in place. As a writer was later to put it: "The colonists, if yet few in number, were provided with means of perpetuating the civilization they had brought to these northern wilds."[19]

One can imagine that Hélène and Noël were as happy as any to be living in close proximity to the schools. They were busy parents of a rapidly growing family. On January 21 of 1641, Hélène and Noël had become the parents of Agnés. A year later, in January of 1642, a son Germaine was born to the couple. By the age of twenty-two, Hélène had borne five children, of whom four were living.[20] Joseph Hébert was now six years old and ready for the classroom.

In the French colony, as it was in France, the education of children was entrusted to the religious orders. In general, girls and boys who received an education started school at the age of six or seven. This education might continue for three or four years, although many children attended school for less time. The school founded by the Jesuits was growing, even if slowly. The number of students fluctuated with each year and each season. In 1637, Le Jeune was to remark that the Seminary had six Huron students, although two of them were to die within a short time. Here, the students were taught the Christian catechism, reading, writing, and counting skills, all within a framework of strict discipline. In France, the aristocratic families and the bourgeois nobles arranged for their boys to continue their education in Jesuit and Oratorian colleges. Many French towns had a university for the boys. Following suit, the Jesuits had founded a college at Quebec in 1635. It was the first institution of higher learning to be established in America north of Mexico.[21]

A formal education for girls was not considered necessary in seventeenth-century France. According to various records, the number of French women of this era who were literate enough to be able to sign their own name ranged from fourteen to thirty-four percent.[22] Hélène had received some education; at least she could sign her name. She would want the same, or more, for her daughters. For the French settlers at Quebec, it was a true advantage living so close to the Ursuline School.

In France, girls who received an education did so at the hands of a governess or in a convent. The quality of that education varied; often children were taught by teachers who were not well-educated themselves. Generally, the girls learned basic reading, writing, and arithmetic, as well as fancy needlework. Young charges were also instructed in the rules of etiquette: they learned proper conduct for any and all social situations which they might encounter. In the convents and seminaries of New France as well as in Europe, a primary purpose of education was the preparation of children for their First Communion, which they made at about the age of eight. This was considered a significant religious right of passage. Religion was not a separate subject; it permeated all aspects of education.[23]

By 1642, there were five Ursuline nuns laboring under the leadership of Marie de l'Incarnation. Two other nuns had come to join the original three. No doubt Hélène's daughters were enrolled as soon as they were old enough to attend the school, as were the daughters of the other French colonists who lived nearby. However, the intention of the Ursulines in coming to Quebec was to bring the Christian religion to the natives. Toward this end, these cloistered nuns taught the Amerindian girls and women who came to them their prayers and catechism. The little girls would also be taught how to be French. Mother Marie was to write that the indigenous children who appeared at the convent door to be educated were dirty, infested with vermin, and scantily clad in rags, if clothed at all. They were covered with bear grease and smelled of smoke. The first task was to get them scrubbed and dressed in the French manner. In a letter to her son in September of 1641, Marie de l'Incarnation reported that there were more than fifty pupils in their little school and there had been more than 700 visits from the native men, women and children.[24]

During the first few years, a large number of natives, both permanent and transient, received help from the Ursulines. The nuns found themselves providing both material as well as spiritual sustenance.[25] It was a breach of hospitality to turn guests away without feeding them. So the sisters kept a pot of *sagamité* at the hearth to feed the natives who came for religious lessons. From time to time, a more substantial banquet was prepared for the Amerindian guests of the Ursulines. There might well be sixty or more natives to feed at a time. One such dinner called for "a bushel of black plums, twenty-four pounds of bread, a due quantity of Indian-meal or ground peas, a dozen of tallow candles melted, two or three pounds of fat pork", all thrown into a pot and boiled.[26] One suspects that the food was more important to the natives than the education.

The mission at nearby Sillery, established by the Jesuits for the Native Americans, was also beginning to grow. By 1642, between thirty-five and forty Algonquin and Montagnais families had settled in the village of St. Joseph, as it was also called. The hospital nuns had established a small hospital, just over the hill and about sixty steps from the Jesuit chapel and cottages. At this point, there were only four little houses built in the French fashion and the most important aborigine families lived in these homes. The other natives lodged in their bark huts until such time as additional homes could be built. Progress on building at the mission had been hampered by lack of laborers. In addition to building the cabins, the land had to be cleared and this was slow and painstaking work. In 1637, the Jesuits had the means to support eight workmen at Sillery; now they could keep just four. They were waiting to receive from France the funds promised for the maintenance of the mission from the estate of their benefactor, the deceased Monsieur de Sillery.[27]

Those indigenous families settled at the mission were often joined by other natives who continued to live in the semi-nomadic style. They came to be instructed in the mysteries of Christianity, but also to receive other assistance. The routine established at the mission was detailed in the *Jesuit Relations* of 1642:

> Father Dequen [De Quen] went every morning to the hospital, in the Algonquin quarter, to say Mass: men, women, and children all were there. The Chapel and the ward of the sick were often filled. Before Mass, the Father pronounced aloud in their language the prayers, which each one also repeated aloud. Afterward he explained to them, at length, one of the mysteries of our holy Faith. Mass being said, the Father went through the cabins to teach in private those who were to be baptized, or who were preparing to receive Communion. After noon, I assumed the charge of teaching the catechism to the Algonquin children. They assembled in the ward of the sick, with as

much diligence and fervor as those of our France. If their stability were equally firm, they would yield to them in nothing. The reward for catechism was a knife, or a piece of bread, at other times a chaplet, sometimes a cap, or an axe, for the tallest and the most intelligent; it is an excellent opportunity for relieving the misery of these poor peoples. The parents were charmed to see the fervor of their children, who went through the cabins to show their prizes. At evening, Father Dequen returned to the Chapel, where they again assembled for prayers. The Father, approaching the Hospital, cried aloud, "Come, all, to prayers; "at this cry each went forth in silence, and ran to the Chapel, where the prayers lasted about a quarter of an hour, and the instruction likewise. . . . The Hospital Nuns often intoned, at prayers and at catechism, some hymn in Algonquin speech. The [natives] take much pleasure in singing, and succeed in it very well. Usually, too, they took the girls aside to hear them in the catechism, in the ward of the sick, or at their grating, while the boys were instructed separately.[28]

All was peaceful as the year 1642 drew to a close. Those participating in the Montreal "madness" had left in the spring. The French settlers at Quebec, as well as their Algonquin and Huron allies, remembered the good news brought from Paris by Bourdon and Le Jeune some months earlier. They would have been looking ahead with great anticipation to the following year, to the arrival of promised military help from the mother country. Unfortunately, Louis XIII would die in the spring of 1643. The colonists would also learn that Cardinal Richelieu, founder of the Company of One Hundred Associates, had died five months earlier, in December of 1642.[29] There would be no assistance: no money and no men coming from France to aid the beleaguered colony. At the same time, the Iroquois would discover the presence of the colonists at Montreal in the spring of 1643. The first confrontation between Montreal settlers and Iroquois occurred that June.[30] Sporadic attacks against the colonists would only escalate in the coming years. The French pioneers would be left to wondering how the colony could survive with limited military resources in what seemed to be an increasingly hostile world.

CHAPTER THIRTEEN

DECEMBER OF 1650

⸺⸻⸺

Fire destroys the Ursuline Monastery; Religious practice among the seventeenth-century French; Persecution by the Iroquois; Poverty of Quebec; Declining Amerindian population

The routines of everyday life continued over the years, in spite of the ongoing threat from the Iroquois. It just so happened that on the twelfth day of the twelfth month of 1650, Hélène gave birth to her twelfth child. Since marrying Noël in 1640, a child had been born to the couple almost every year. The household now included ten living children: Joseph and Françoise from Hélène's first marriage and Agnés, Germain, Louise, Nicolas, Jean-Baptiste, Hélène, Marie, and the newborn Alphonse from the second marriage. Marguerite, the daughter born in the fall of 1646, lived only a couple of weeks. As noted previously, Angélique, a daughter from Hélène's first marriage, had also died in early childhood.[1]

Five years earlier, on April 26, 1645, Noël Morin had been granted forty *arpents* (about thirty-four acres) of land on the outskirts of the Upper Town, in a place called côteau Sainte-Geneviève. This property bordered that of their friend Jean Bourdon and was located behind that of Mathieu Amiot which faced the Grande-Allée. Louis Sedillot was another neighbor of Hélène and Noël on the côteau

Sainte-Geneviève.[2] In 1648, the Morin homestead in the Upper Town that had originally been the property of Guillaume Hébert had been sold to the Fabrique of the Church for a sum of eight hundred *livres* to serve as a rectory for the Church.[3] It is likely that the Morin family moved to their new property at that time. Apparently, Noël was now ready to build a more substantial home on the côteau Sainte-Geneviève. On February 6, 1650, Noël Morin arranged to have a carpenter build the framing for a two-room house. The dwelling would be twenty by thirty feet long. In the contract, Noël agreed to pay the carpenter 225 *livres* and a bushel of peas.[4] Eventually the property would include a house, barn, stable, garden and fifty-eight *arpents* (about fifty acres) of land under cultivation.[5]

Now in the final days of 1650, the Morin family, along with the rest of the colonists, would have been preparing for New Year's Day. The settlers at Quebec celebrated the holiday as they had in France. Father Jérôme Lalemant, writing in his journal for January 1, 1646, gave details of the custom as celebrated by the Jesuits that year. The day began with the soldiers at the fort firing their arquebuses in a salute to the governor. A solemn High Mass was offered by the Jesuits. The remainder of the day was spent in visiting friends and exchanging gifts. The governor paid a visit to the Jesuits early that morning, greeting each one personally and inquiring about their wellbeing. Monsieur Giffard also paid a visit to the Jesuits. The Ursulines sent letters paying their compliments along with a variety of gifts, including candles, rosaries, a crucifix and, for the Jesuits' dinner, "two handsome pieces of pastry."[6] In return, the Jesuits sent the Ursulines enamel images of St. Ignace and St. François Xavier. For Monsieur Giffard, the Jesuits had a book on Christ's life. Monsieur Bourdon was the recipient of a Galilean telescope, which also featured a compass. The woman who washed the church linen received a crucifix. Abraham Martin received a bottle of brandy and his wife, Marguerite, was given four handkerchiefs. There were also gifts for Father De Quen at Sillery: "everything that he judged suitable" (presumably gifts that would be given to the natives). Before day's end, Father Lalemant also managed to visit Monsieur Couillard, Mademoiselle de Repentigny, Madame de La Peltrie, and the Ursulines at their convent.[7] One can picture the comings and goings on paths through the woods.

On December 30, 1650, the young charges at the Ursuline Monastery had gone to bed, wondering excitedly what New Year's treats they might soon receive. Two hours after midnight, the Ursuline Monastery, completed in the Upper Town of Quebec only a few years earlier, burned to the ground.[8] Maybe it was the roar of the fire, the sound of falling timbers, or the cries of frightened children. Maybe it was the smoke that soon filled the air or the brightness of the night, lit up as if it were mid-day. All in the Upper Town were suddenly awakened in the middle of the night in the middle of winter: the Ursuline Monastery was on fire. Mother Marie de l'Incarnation described the unfortunate accident in her *Relation of 1654*. She noted that one of the novice nuns was in charge of making bread for the community. The bakery was in the cellar. As the monastery foundation and walls did little to keep out the bitter cold, this sister feared that the dough might freeze. So she put a few hot coals in a pinewood trough, along with the bread dough, and covered the assembly. The sleepy girl forgot to remove the coals later, as was her intention. As this manner of keeping bread warm was not the custom in the monastery, no one else checked on the bread. At around midnight the coals kindled the wood in the trough. Pinewood was highly flammable, and the fire spread quickly from the cellar to the rest of the convent. Mother Marie described the situation thus:

> Our provisions for the whole year were down there, both those which had come from France – lard, oil, butter, brandy for our servants - and domestic products such as fish, etc. When the fire had consumed everything down there, it rose to the ceilings which were double with earth packed between them. Had not one of the mistresses of the children been sleeping in this area and heard the crackling and noise of the fire, we would all have been destroyed by fire within half an hour. The fire had already broken through and the place was collapsing and about to fall.[9]

This mistress quickly roused the sleeping children and then raced to alert the sisters in their dormitory. The nuns, not stopping to dress, immediately returned to rescue the children, of whom there were quite a few. Within minutes, the corridors were engulfed in flames. Mother Marie had just left her room when the convent bell hanging above her alcove came crashing down. As she was leaving through the broken wooden grille which separated the nuns from their visitors, she turned to see the entire length of roof, also made of pine, on fire. The nuns, many barefoot, stood praying quietly in the snow with the stunned children huddled around them. Those witnessing the conflagration on the hill believed that it was a miracle that not a one of the sisters or students asleep in the monastery that night perished in the fire.[10]

Neighbors in the Upper Town saw the flames shooting skyward and rushed to render aid, but the fire was too advanced. The côteau Sainte-Geneviève was a short distance away; surely Noël would have been among these good neighbors. Noël and Hélène had school-age daughters; Françoise, Agnés or Louise might well have been boarding at the school. The Jesuit fathers and brothers in the nearby monastery risked their lives to rescue furnishings from the convent sacristy, but just about everything else was lost in the flames. The Quebec community offered as much support as possible. In one of her letters, Marie noted that they spent the night in the Jesuit parlor. The next day they went to the Hôtel-Dieu where they were welcomed kindly by the Hospital Sisters. They gratefully accepted the hospitality of these nuns and stayed with them for close to a month. Then they returned to the monastery grounds and moved into the small house of Madame de La Peltrie, which had been built in 1644 and had been far enough removed from the monastery that it escaped the fire.[11] It was reported in the *Jesuit Relations* that Madame's home had

> but two rooms, which serve as dormitory, refectory, kitchen, hall, infirmary, and everything, for their community of thirteen persons. Besides these, [the Ursulines] have some boarders, whom their charity would not allow them to send away, in spite of the almost unbearable inconveniences that they had to undergo, especially during the stifling heat of Summer and in a state of poverty which reduced them to being in need of everything.[12]

Mother Marie, at the age of fifty, set out to rebuild the Ursuline Monastery and School; the alternative was to return to France.[13]

She would write, "Our courage has not yet fallen as low as to admit defeat. We have not been beaten to the point of flight."[14] All rallied to the support of the Ursulines and were committed to their rebuilding. As the Jesuits would note, "experience teaches us that the girls who have been with the Ursulines feel the benefit of their stay there throughout their lives, and that in their households the fear of God reigns more than elsewhere, and they bring up their children much better therein."[15]

The Governor and his wife gave a loan of eight thousand *livres* for the reconstruction. The Ursulines received an additional eight thousand *livres* from the Jesuits. As the nuns had escaped with only their night dress, the Hospitallers loaned them their grey habits. The Jesuits sent over linens and their store of black cloth, held in reserve for their cassocks, so that the nuns could make new habits and return the grey garments to the Hospital nuns. Men from the neighborhood helped to cultivate the Ursuline land and manage their livestock. Their efforts produced enough wheat, peas, and barley to sustain the Ursuline family that year. Six cows provided the group with milk and cheese. Even the poorest of villagers offered something. Mother Marie would write, "Every day we receive gifts: a stove, a cloak, a towel, a newly stitched chemise, a few eggs. You know what the country is like, but its charity is greater than its poverty, and Heaven helps us all."[16]

By summertime of the following year, the construction of the new monastery was well under way. Mother Marie de l'Incarnation would write in 1651 "We had to build again from the ground up – a structure 108 feet long and 28 feet wide."[17] The Ursulines would move into their new building in the spring of 1654.[18]

The poverty of the Ursuline Monastery was an ongoing issue. In letters written in 1645, Mother Marie wrote of the difficulties in establishing a presence in the New World. They were completely dependent upon receiving supplies from France. She would echo this sentiment many times in many letters over the years. In her letters, Mother Marie pleaded that France help the colony. The Company

of One Hundred Associates was neglecting the needs of the settlements in their pursuit of profits from the fur trade. In letters written
in 1650 and 1652, she advised that the Ursuline School would not
be able to continue without significant assistance from the mother
country.[19] Without help, they had the choice of dying or returning
to France. Mother Marie noted that they were dependent on France
for cloth and linens, as well as for much of their foodstuffs. She
added that people in New France worked hard, and they did produce
some food but just not enough. Vegetables were abundant and the
bread made in Quebec tasted better than that in France, according
to Mother Marie. She would argue that the Ursulines were suffering
more from poverty than at the hands of the Iroquois natives.[20]

Certainly the nuns were not the only ones in the settlement suffering from want and deprivation. Marguerite Bourgeoys of Troyes
came to New France in June of 1653 to establish a school for girls
in Montreal. She would become the founder of the Congregation of
Notre-Dame in that city. Marguerite spent a winter in Quebec before
traveling on to Montreal. She declined the invitation to stay with the
Ursulines and chose, instead, to share the quarters of poor settlers.
Marguerite was to remark about her stay in Quebec that "everything
was so poor it was pitiful."[21]

In the years following Champlain's death in 1635, Quebec suffered from a lack of strong secular leadership under the Company
of One Hundred Associates. As the native population along the St.
Lawrence River diminished, the Jesuits had increasingly turned their
attention to the spiritual needs of the French settlers. The clergy
would come to hold pre-eminent power in the French colony.[22] The
policies, as well as the customs and traditions, promulgated by the
religious institutions would shape the culture of New France. The
colonists were generally devoted to the practice of their religion. It
is hard to imagine that it would have been any different for Noël and
Hélène. Samuel de Champlain, the colony's founder, was a deeply
religious man. Hélène had spent many hours in his company. She
had grown up with the missionaries. The Church of Notre-Dame
de Quebec had been built in the Upper Town of Quebec in 1647 to

replace Notre-Dame-de-la-Recouvrance, which had burned to the ground in 1640.[23] The Morin homestead was a short distance from the Church of Notre-Dame. The Morin children were taught by the Jesuits and the Ursulines. Hélène was chosen to be godmother to a number of infants born in the colony. If surviving records may be used as a guide, this family fully embraced the tenets and traditions of Roman Catholicism.

It was common among the families to gather together to say prayers, morning and evening. The Blessed Virgin and patron saints had places of honor in their homes and hearts. Many individuals made a public commitment to receive the sacraments of Penance and Communion once a month. This religious practice was nourished by the Jesuits who made regular visits to the homes of the settlers. Father Ragueneau, as Superior of the Jesuit Missions, would note, "Most of those who are in this country admit that nowhere else in the world have they found more instruction, more assistance for their salvation, or a more tender and more ready care for their consciences."[24] The study of the catechism and confirmation of adults of their baptismal vows were very much a part of seventeenth-century religion. Noël and Hélène would be confirmed in Quebec on August 10, 1659, along with many of their neighbors.[25]

Religious practice in the colony, as well as in France, included the observance of thirty-seven Holy Days of Obligation in the year. The addition of fifty-two Sundays brought the number of days devoted to prayer and works of mercy to eighty-nine days, that is, one fourth of the year. Attendance at Mass and the other religious celebrations was obligatory. On these days, people were expected to refrain from their normal labor. The requirements for abstaining from work often imposed a burden on farmers and other laborers. For this reason, people could be given dispensations from this requirement when their work was necessary for the welfare of the community. In the colony, the building and fishing seasons were short. Men received dispensations for building fortifications and for fishing in the fall, when extra food was needed to meet the colony's needs over the winter.[26]

Fasting was a compulsory part of religious observance. There were some fifty-seven fast days in the year, including all of Lent except Sundays. Days of fasting meant that no meat, eggs, cheese or milk were allowed, although the last three were tolerated in the French colony. There was one meal taken at mid-day, with a snack in the evening. In addition, in the seventeenth century, all Fridays and Saturdays were days of abstinence, where no meat could be consumed. Altogether, the number of days where an adult could not eat meat amounted to five months of the year.[27] One of the responsibilities of the police in seventeenth-century France was to enforce the Church requirements for fasting and abstinence during Lent. In Paris, there were only five shops licensed to sell meat during the Lenten season. Public houses and taverns in France were forbidden to serve meat on days of fasting and abstinence.[28]

Mass on Sundays, Holy Days, weddings, funerals, and christenings offered people an opportunity to socialize with neighbors and get the latest news. While most celebrations had their roots in religious observances, all was not prayer, sacrifice, and solemnity. Celebrations often included laughter and lively conversation, food and free-flowing wine, dancing and games. The festivities might last well into the night. They broke the tedium of everyday life.[29]

Celebrations of the various Holy Days, or Feast Days as they were also known, often began at dawn with the firing of the cannons. In the course of the day, there would be other gun salutes to honor the King and the Royal Family. Chapel bells sounded through the woods, calling people to prayer or assembly. The day usually ended with the Te Deum or thanksgiving service in the chapels. Processions and pageants, as well as special banquets, might also be a part of the day's festivity.[30]

Not all individuals were particularly devout. Licentiousness co-existed with piety and religious commitment. In France, taverns were filled with drinking peasants on Sundays and Feast Days.[31] Holy Days became opportunities for drunkenness and debauchery in New France, as well as in the Old World. In 1663, the Jesuit missionary

Father Charles Simon, in referring to Shrove Tuesday, wrote that, "Our French were intent on nothing but spending the time of the Carnival in festive pleasures, orgies, drinking bouts, and dances — not to speak of some things more serious, which may offend chaste ears and are better passed over in silence than mentioned."[32]

Religious observance was expected of the King of France and his Royal Court just as it was expected of the common man. For Louis XIV and many of his mistresses, the practice of their religion was as much a part of their life as the illicit affairs. Louis XIV was raised by a pious mother, Anne of Austria, who told him that kings, no matter how powerful, would one day have to answer to God. Louis XIV made a practice of attending daily Mass throughout his life; he rarely missed. The reception of Holy Communion posed a particular problem for the King. It was required by the Church at least once a year, at Easter. The Church considered sex outside of marriage a grievous sin; receiving Communion in this state of sin added to the gravity of this offense. However, this predicament was remedied by a visit to a priest in the confessional and the resolve, at least at the time, to amend one's sinful ways. Absolution was granted and the individual was free to receive Communion. In this manner, the King managed to reconcile virtue and vice.[33]

Although the number of Native Americans in and around Quebec had diminished significantly, they had not disappeared completely. Some had converted to the Christian faith and were integrated into the French community. In 1644, the first Christian marriage between a Frenchman and a native woman was celebrated.[34] Martin Prévost married Marie Olivier Manitouabewich, a young Algonquin native who had been given by her parents to Olivier LeTardiff, an early pioneer and interpreter in the colony. She was baptized Marie Olivier, taking the name of the man who became her godfather.[35] LeTardiff then gave the child to Guillaume Hubou and Marie Rollet to raise in the manner of a young French girl. Both the Hubou family and Martin Prévost were neighbors of Hélène and Noël in the Upper Town. It is unknown when the child was given to LeTardiff; however, Hélène would certainly have known the girl. Like so many marriages in the colony, the groom was much older than the bride. Martin Prévost was born near Paris about 1611. He would have been about thirty-three years old at the time of his marriage. Marie's age at marriage is unknown, but it is likely that she was between the age of twelve and fourteen. Martin and Marie had eight children, all baptized at Notre-Dame in Quebec. Although Martin Prévost would keep his property and house in Quebec's Upper Town, the couple would eventually move to Beauport to establish a farm and raise their family.[36]

The French had managed to remain on friendly terms with the Algonquin and Huron peoples, in spite of the bitter feelings generated by the smallpox epidemic. However, the French colonists, along with their Amerindian allies, were coming under increasing assault by the Iroquois. In her letters to superiors and friends in France, Mother Marie de l'Incarnation provided vivid accounts of attacks by Iroquois raiding parties. In one of her letters, she spoke of the recent death of six Frenchmen, two having been struck down with an ax, burned, and then required to consume their own flesh before death brought a merciful end to their suffering. She expressed great sympathy for the poor Huron and Algonquin natives, who also suffered greatly at the hands of the Iroquois.[37]

In 1649, the Jesuits Jean de Brébeuf, Charles Garnier and Gabriel Lalemant, along with a large number of Hurons, were tortured and killed by warring Iroquois.[38] The Christianized natives who were not massacred at the missions in the Huron country were brought to Quebec by the surviving Jesuit missionaries. Mother Marie de l'Incarnation would write:

> We had a fairly large family which we all helped to feed. Although many devoted people helped these poor exiles as much as they could, it was the religious houses and Madame de La Peltrie who did the most. The priests alone fed and instructed three to four hundred.[39]

In the convent of the Ursulines, Mother Marie de l'Incarnation dedicated herself to finding ways to minister to her native charges. She had already made progress in learning the Montagnais and Algonquin languages. Now, in order to better minister to these refugees, Mother Marie was attempting to learn the Huron language as well. She also set to work composing a catechism in Huron. Eventually she would work on a dictionary in the Algonquin and Iroquois languages, a catechism in Iroquois, and a sacred history in Algonquin.[40]

The Jesuits were amazed that the little colony at Montreal survived, noting that there were still only about fifty settlers in that settlement in 1650-51. "It is a wonder that they have not been exterminated by the frequent surprises of the Iroquois bands, which have many times been stoutly resisted and repelled. Monsieur de Maisonneuve has maintained that settlement by his good management."[41]

In 1650, the Iroquois came within three leagues (nine miles) of Quebec, when prior to this they never ventured closer than forty leagues. The Jesuits had fortified their seminary and it provided sanctuary for the natives fleeing the Iroquois, as well as for the priests and religious brothers. The Ursuline Monastery and School had been built next to the fort which provided the nuns with a measure of protection.[42]

At this point there were more French settlers living along the St. Lawrence River than natives; the semi-nomadic Amerindians who had traditionally made this their home had died or fled inland. As one historian put it: "Ravaged by disease, divided by missionary propaganda, unable to obtain firearms unless they turned their backs on traditional customs . . . the aboriginal allies of the French fell victim to the numerically and militarily superior Iroquois."[43]

As a child, Hélène and the other early French pioneers had stood on the riverbank of the St. Lawrence in the late spring of each year, excitedly watching the arrival of hundreds of canoes gliding over the water's surface, bringing natives and furs for the annual trade. Perhaps Hélène's older children would have witnessed the event. However, it would be a scene that her younger children and grandchildren would never have the privilege of viewing. Those days were gone forever.

CHAPTER FOURTEEN

FALL OF 1659

———— ❧ ————

Childbirth and midwifery in France and in the colony; Hélène serves as a
midwife; Contribution of the apothecaries; Childbirth among the natives;
Convent life in seventeenth-century France; Canadian-born girls enter the
Convent; Life at the Ursuline School in Quebec

Periodic disease outbreaks, as well as accidents and attacks from
the natives, took many lives in the colony. However, these
weren't the only risks to life and health. Childbirth was dangerous for both mothers and infants, particularly the first birth. In
the south of Paris in the early 1600s, one woman in eight died during
or soon after the birth of her first child.[1] In Quebec, as in France,
many infants died at birth or did not survive their first few months
of life.[2] In the French colony, women had two options when they
gave birth: they labored and birthed alone or they did so with the
assistance of another woman or women, often related or at least a
neighbor.

From earliest days, women have aided other women in giving
birth. For most of that time and in most places, training for this role
was accomplished by an informal apprenticeship: learning to support
women in childbirth through observing another, more experienced

woman. In France, this knowledgeable woman was known as a *sage-femme* or a wise woman.[3]

In the sixteenth century, both the Church and the civil authorities of France had moved to control the process of birth and midwifery. In 1556, Henry II decreed that single women who were pregnant should declare their condition publicly or face execution. He made this decree under the assumption that unwed mothers might want to kill their infant and that the dead infant would not have the opportunity for baptism. As early as the sixteenth century some municipalities in France had begun to license midwives. Following the Council of Trent in the mid-sixteenth century, the Roman Catholic Church sought to ban Protestant women from the practice of midwifery; to that end, midwives were required to go before the local priest or bishop, who would ascertain their moral fitness to baptize dying infants. Women were required to foreswear "not to use sorcery, not to take advantage of a woman in labor whom one did not like, not to reveal secrets of the household, not to deliver an unmarried woman without notifying the authorities, and not to help a woman to abort a fetus."[4] Eventually, the French woman officially designated as a *sage-femme* came to be elected for this position by the women of the village. In addition to approval by the local priest, her selection would be based on her experience and skills, which included a knowledge of both herbs and amulets which might be useful in a difficult pregnancy and birth.[5]

By the seventeenth century, efforts were under way to improve the training and the practice of midwifery in France. In 1635, midwives petitioned the University of Paris for public courses on the subject, but to no avail. Some thirty years later, their efforts would be met with success. The government established a three-month course in Paris, followed by an examination, to prepare for midwifery. The first person to teach the course was Marguerite du Tertre de la Marche, a student of Louyse Bourgeois, the queen's midwife.[6] By the end of the century, women who wanted to practice midwifery needed to be a practicing Catholic and have three months' hospital experi-

ence or have been apprenticed to a midwife. Or, they might receive
a diploma from the school of midwifery in Paris. In the midwifery
training programs, there was some understanding of the importance
of hygiene. Before touching a patient, midwives were instructed to
remove their rings and wash their hands.[7]

The more or less formal recognition of midwifery in the church
records of Quebec in the mid-seventeenth century reflected changes
in the practice occurring in France at the time. On September 9,
1655, Hélène's aunt Marguerite Langlois was listed as a *sage-femme*
on the baptism record of Marguerite Blondeau. It is the first time
that a midwife was recognized in the Church records of Quebec.
Four years later, on the baptism record of Jean Halay on September 10, 1659, Hélène was also given this title. No doubt, she would
have had many opportunities over the years to observe her aunt and
other experienced women assist with childbirth. Between 1659 and
1672, Hélène would be listed as the *sage-femme* on a number of baptism records in the Quebec diocesan archives.[8] Often there is the
note *"ondoyé par Hélène Desportes"* (baptized by Hélène). This would
have occurred when the infant was near death and baptism could not
wait for the services of a priest.[9] For Hélène to be identified as *"sage
femme"* meant that the Church recognized her skill in assisting women
in childbirth and acknowledged her high moral character.

Two daughters, a daughter-in-law, and three granddaughters would
follow in Hélène's footsteps. Her daughter Louise is listed as a *sage-
femme* on the death record of the infant of Jean Gagnon in Château-
Richer, dated February 20, 1691. Louise's three daughters (Hélène's
granddaughters) Jeanne, Hélène, and Louise Cloutier would also
be identified as *sage-femmes* practicing in Château-Richer in the early
eighteenth century.[10] Another daughter of Hélène, Françoise Hébert,
would serve as midwife in Cap-St-Ignace and Montmagny. Although
the records don't specifically state that she is a midwife, Françoise is
listed on several baptism and burial records between 1695 and 1714
as having baptized the infant. Marie Charlotte Depoitiers, the wife
of Hélène's son Joseph, is also listed as a *sage-femme* on the baptism
record of Pierre Peletier, dated July 25, 1705.[11]

The practice of midwifery in Quebec would receive more recognition and regulation as the years went by. In 1703, Bishop de Saint-Vallier published *Le Rituel du diocèse de Quebec*, in which he recommended the election of midwives by an assembly of the most virtuous and honest women in the parish.[12] In 1714, Simone Buisson was nominated *"sage-femme jurée et approuvée"* of Quebec and received a salary for her work. At the recommendation of Michel Sarrazin, the colony's first physician, Buisson was also allowed to instruct other women in the office, both in an effort to improve skills and to encourage others to formally enter the practice. Midwifery had entered a new era in the colony. By 1740, the infrastructure for midwifery as a distinct profession was in place in New France. Madeleine Bouchette came to Quebec as a *entretenue* midwife; she had trained at the Hôtel-Dieu in Paris, which at the time had the best maternity school in Europe. Paid 400 *livres* a year, Madame Bouchette was obliged to remain available to serve the poor of the city. In turn, this specially trained woman could train others in the art of midwifery. Midwifery had evolved as a separate profession; specific rights, privileges, and responsibilities were defined by the French court and the clergy and taught in the schools..[13]

Although the practice of midwifery was a time-honored and generally respected role for women, it was not without its perils. While childbearing was considered a sacred act, it was also associated with sex, blood, and evil in the form of abortion and infanticide. A midwife was sometimes the object of a witch-hunt which began with neighbors accusing her of killing a newborn, assisting in an abortion, or sorcery to induce sterility.[14] There were occasions when the midwife was sought out for the prescription of medications for conditions other than pregnancy and childbirth. This put her at risk for being seen as an unsavory or disruptive element in society.[15] Fortunately, there appears to have been no scandal involving midwives in seventeenth-century Quebec.

In her practice of midwifery, it is not hard to imagine that Hélène benefited from the expertise of her former in-laws, the apothecary Louis Hébert, and his wife Marie Rollet. Louis had died on January

25, 1627, when Hélène was a child of seven.[16] It is doubtful that she had many memories of him. Marie Rollet died May 27, 1649.[17] Hélène's mother- in-law had spent more than thirty years in Quebec. Surely she would have passed on some of the wisdom she had gained from her husband and from experience concerning the use of herbs and medicines in childbirth and in the treatment of the sick.

Apothecaries, like midwives, were expected to live an exemplary life and to be morally upright in the practice of their profession. And like the midwives, their practice was strictly regulated by the authorities of France. Three hundred years earlier, in fourteenth-century Paris, apothecaries were required to take the following oath before God:

> "To do all I can for the honor, glory and adornment of medicine, not to teach its secrets and curiosities to idiots and ungrateful persons, to do nothing rashly without the advice of physicians and only in the hope of gain. To give no medicament or purge to those laboring under any disease, without taking counsel of some learned doctor, not in any way to touch the shameful and forbidden parts of women, unless in case of urgent necessity, that is to say when some remedy has to be applied to them. To disclose to no one any secret entrusted to me, never to give anyone any kind of poison to drink, nor to advise anyone to give such a potion even to his greatest enemies; never to give any abortive potion; never in any way to attempt to induce the expulsion of the fetus from the belly of the mother, unless acting on the advice of the doctor. To dispense exactly, without adding or leaving out anything in the prescriptions of the doctors, as far as they are in accordance with the rules of the art. To use no succedaneum or substitute without taking counsel of someone of greater knowledge than myself, to repudiate and avoid like the plague, the scandalous and utterly pernicious methods of practice now employed by empirical charlatans and alchemists, to the great shame of the magistrates who tolerate them; to give help and succor alike to all who shall employ me, and lastly to keep no bad or old drug in my shop. May the Lord bless me always, as I shall observe these things."[18]

A body of folklore had developed concerning ways to ensure a healthy pregnancy and a healthy infant. If a women suffered a fall during pregnancy, one measure to protect the unborn child from any subsequent harm was to cut a short strand of red silk into small pieces and consume them with an egg. It was also believed that the pain of childbirth could be alleviated by placing the husband's hat on the belly of the laboring woman.[19] Mother, sisters, friends, and neighbors "were more than ready to offer her advice of varying usefulness about what she should eat, the cravings she should satisfy, and the fears she should avoid in case they afflicted a newborn baby; what talismans, amulets, or medallions she should wear."[20] Pregnant women in the New World as well as in France continued with their daily tasks in the home and in the garden. However, then as now, women did worry about the wellbeing of their unborn child, as well as their own health. They were anxious to avoid hidden evils and other, more apparent, dangers.

Native women received little care or extra attention during their pregnancies and birthing. Childbirth did not relieve a woman of her responsibilities: she was often on her feet and collecting logs to keep the home fires burning two hours after having given birth. However, the Amerindians had their own superstitions about pregnancy:

> Pregnant women among them cause, they say, many misfortunes; for they cause the husband not to take anything in the hunt; if one of them enters a cabin where there is a sick person, he grows worse; if she looks at the animal that is being pursued, it can no longer be captured; if people eat with her, those who eat thus fall sick. A pregnant woman, by her presence and the application of a certain root, extracts an arrow from a man's body. Moreover, they rejoice more in the birth of a daughter than of a son, for the sake of the multiplication of the country's inhabitants. The women here are mistresses and servants.[21]

There were many large families in New France by this time. In 1659, Hélène Desportes was thirty-nine years old and the mother of fifteen children. Her last child, Marie-Madeleine, had been born three years earlier, in December of 1656. Three of Hélène's daughters were married. Françoise had married Guillaume Fournier in 1651, at the age of thirteen. Agnés married Nicolas Gaudry Bourbonniere in 1653 at the age of twelve. Louise was sixteen when she married Charles Cloutier in 1659.

It is likely that Noël and Hélène had arranged the marriage of their daughter Louise to Charles Cloutier. This was accepted practice in the seventeenth century. Finding a suitable mate for a daughter and providing a dowry was considered a parental responsibility. Charles' father was Zacharie Cloutier, a long-time friend of Hélène and Noël. He had arrived in New France in 1634, along with many other families recruited by Robert Giffard. Zacharie came from Mortagne in Perche, a region that was, at the time, a part of Normandy. Zacharie, a carpenter by profession, emigrated with his wife Sainte Dupont and five children: Zacharie, Jean, Anne, Charles and Louise. As part of his agreement with Giffard, signed in March of 1634, Zacharie received an arriere-fief at the seigneurie of Beauport. After some years, Zacharie Cloutier had a falling out with his seigneur Robert Giffard. On July 15, 1652, Cloutier received a grant of land at Château-Richer from Governor Jean de Lauson. Zacharie eventually sold the fief at Beauport and moved with his family to settle at Château-Richer.[22]

Abraham Martin and Marguerite Langlois had produced at least ten children, including six daughters. By 1658, the six girls had married. Marguerite had married Etienne Racine in 1638 at the age of fourteen, thus fulfilling Champlain's desire, as stated in his will, that she marry and settle in Quebec. Anne, the last of the girls, had married in 1658, at the age of thirteen. Three of the sons, Eustache, Adrien, and Pierre (born in France in 1630) disappeared from history. The only existing records are of their baptisms and, as with so many other children of that era, these boys probably did not live beyond childhood. Charles Amador, the youngest child, would be ordained a priest by Bishop Laval in 1671. None of the progeny of Abraham Martin would carry his surname.[23]

Parents wanted to ensure the welfare of all of their children, but they often lacked the resources to give each of their daughters the required dowry for marriage. Convents were considered a good way to take care of extra daughters. Convents required a dowry, but this was often less than that required for a good match in marriage. Although some young women certainly entered the convent for religious reasons, it was often out of economic necessity. Parents decided who would enter a convent and who would not.[24]

Convents of that time in France were, as a rule, cloistered or enclosed and they could be quite fashionable and comfortable. Many housed the daughters of the nobility. These convents were more like residential clubs or boarding houses for women. The parlor, rather than the chapel, was the center of life. Conversations centered on court affairs rather than spiritual matters. The sisters were required to attend daily Mass, regular Confession, and Communion. There were additional prayer services two or three times a day. Works of mercy might be required, or teaching when there were girls' boarding schools associated with the convent. Beyond that, the sisters could engage in gardening, light reading, and letter writing. Servants or sisters of a lower order (those without a dowry) took care of the more mundane affairs. While the vows of poverty and obedience were not always strictly followed, seriously scandalous behavior was rare. Convent sins were most often pettiness and quarreling. A young woman, safely ensconced behind the convent's walls, might well have had an easier life and more freedom to pursue her own interests than a married woman of her era.[25]

In the religious climate of seventeenth-century France, it was not unusual for some women to prefer the spiritual life of a convent over life in the secular world. Louise de La Vallière, one of the mistresses of Louis XIV and the mother of four of his children, was allowed to leave the court and take the veil in the summer of 1674. A member of the minor nobility from Touraine, Louise grew up next door to a Carmelite monastery and had exhibited unusual piety since childhood. At some point, she had been sent to live in the wealthier household of three princesses and was eventually chosen as a lady's maid in the royal court. There, she was pursued by the King for amorous favors. In 1661, Louise, with some reluctance, became his mistress. The desire to enter a convent was a wish she had entertained off and on for a number of years. Increasingly burdened by a sense of her wrongdoing, she had begun to wear a hair shirt under her court robes as a penance. Louise was nearly thirty when she was finally allowed to join the Carmelite convent on the rue d'Enfer in Paris. There she took the name of Sister Louise de La Miséricorde. Following the entrance rite required of all novices, her beautiful, golden locks were shorn, symbolic of leaving the vanities of the world behind.[26]

The religious women who entered the convents at Quebec and Montreal did not encounter a life of leisure and comfort. The work of the Ursulines and Hospital nuns in the colony was demanding, and the living conditions were not much better than those of poor settlers. The sisters might have chosen the convent on their own, or the decision might have been made by their parents. Regardless, these women lived a life devoted to the tenets of their religion and to their vows of poverty, chastity, and obedience.

There would be a number of young French women living in Quebec who would enter the convents in the second half of the seventeenth century. Marie-Françoise, daughter of Robert Giffard, entered the convent of the Augustinian Hospitallers of Quebec in 1648 at the age of fourteen. The religious community was very poor and the dowry was essential, so Giffard gave the convent one-fourth of the seigneury of Saint-Gabriel (later known as the fief of Saint-Ignace). Devoutly religious and a good friend of the Jesuits, Giffard gave the rest of this seigneury to the missionaries to extend the lands of their seigneury at Sillery.[27] Marie-Françoise, who took the name of Marie de Saint-Ignace, died on March 15, 1657. She was just 23 years old when she died, having been in the convent for nine years.[28]

Hélène and Noël's neighbor and long-time friend Jean Bourdon gave four daughters to the religious community. Geneviève Bourdon, the eldest daughter, entered the novitiate of the Ursulines in 1652, becoming the first Canadian-born Ursuline.[29] Her sister Anne also joined these nuns, eventually becoming mother superior of the Ursulines. Two other daughters, Marguerite and Marie, joined the Augustinian hospital nuns of Quebec.[30]

In 1659, Hélène and Noël's daughter Marie was a ten-year-old boarding student at the Ursuline Convent. Two years, later she would decide to become a nun. First, she had to convince her parents that she was ready to undertake the privations and hard work of the nuns. In 1662, at the age of thirteen, she would leave her native Quebec to join the Hospitallers of Montreal.[31] Many years later, Marie would write her *Annales de l'Hôtel-Dieu de Montreal,* describing life in Montreal as well as life at the hospital. She spoke of the dangers those at Montreal faced from the Iroquois, the martyrdom of the missionaries, and the heroic acts of the French colonists.[32]

Life at the school of the Ursulines in Quebec was modeled on cloister rules established in France. Students as well as nuns were expected to follow the discipline outlined in the book, *Réglement pour les religieuses de Sainte-Ursule de la Congregation de Paris,* published in 1652.[33] These rules governed their life from morning to night and were described in great detail. The book decreed how each portion of the day was to be spent and what sort of behavior was expected. There were two study periods daily: morning and evening. The girls studied alone and in silence. All of the girls' activities were rigorously supervised by one of the nuns. Students who did not meet standards of conduct were disciplined.[34]

The students at the Ursuline School were immersed in religion. Everywhere one looked, there were objects to encourage religious devotion: paintings, images, sculptures, and maxims adorned the walls of the corridors and rooms. Boarders attended Mass and visited the Blessed Sacrament in the chapel daily. Prayers were recited, in private or as a group, upon arising, before retiring, and at intervals throughout the day. "Being a boarder at the Ursuline Convent meant adopting a culture, spirit, traditions, knowledge, and know-how that were centuries old. Raised behind closed doors, young girls were all the more receptive to the teachings of the nuns."[35]

The effort to educate native children was met with varying
degrees of success. Mother Marie de l'Incarnation would observe
that Amerindian girls stayed for different lengths of time. Some of
the girls were

> like birds on the wing, staying with us only until they become
> sad, a condition which the character of the [aborigines] can-
> not endure. As soon as they grow sad their parents will take
> them away, fearful they will die. . . . There are others who take
> off by whim or caprice. Like squirrels, they climb up our pali-
> sade (which is as high as a wall) and go running in the woods.
> There are also those who persevere and whom we raise in the
> French manner. Then marriages are arranged for them and they
> do very well. . . . Others return to their [native] parents. They
> speak French well and are knowledgeable in both reading and
> writing.[36]

Mother Marie noted with regret that there were now only a small
number of Amerindians at the school: this mirrored the decline of
the native population living along the St. Lawrence River. By 1659, a
majority of the students at the Ursuline School were French. In a letter written in 1652, Mother Marie argued that the reason for staying
in New France was the education of French girls.[37] She would note
that "The French children would be real brutes without the education we provide to them."[38] In 1664, Mother Marie would write again
on this theme:

> Our monastery is the refuge of those in danger of being ship-
> wrecked in their faith . . . Our work is mostly on behalf of
> French girls, for it is certain that if God had not led the Ursu-
> lines into this country they would also be wild . . .[39]

CHAPTER FIFTEEN

FALL OF 1662

Growing up in Quebec; Juvenile delinquency and punishment of juveniles; Rape in the colony; Popularity of wine and brandy; Controversy over the sale of alcohol to the natives; Torture and death of Hélène's son Joseph

Mother Marie de l'Incarnation had good reason to fear for the wellbeing of the children of Quebec. The settlement was a frontier town. In spite of a strong religious presence, it had its raucous side.

In addition to the hardy emigrants from France, there were now a growing number of young men in Quebec born of these pioneers. Included in this group were three sons of Noël and Hélène. Germain was twenty, Nicolas, eighteen, and Jean-Baptiste, seventeen. More will be said later of Joseph who was born in 1636 to Hélène and her first husband, Guillaume Hébert. These men had grown up in the rough and tumble world of the early settlement. While little girls learned women's work at the knees of their mother, young boys learned what it was to be a man from their fathers. They were taught to use firearms at an early age, both in the protection of their families and in bringing home provisions for the table. They accompanied their fathers and other males in the colony on hunting and fishing trips. These endeavors must have seemed more exciting than the grueling and back-breaking toil demanded in the fields of the family farm.

Some lads were more adventurous than others. One such person was Hélène's nephew Louis Couillard, the eldest son of Guillaume Couillard and Guillemette Hébert. He, along with the sons of Monsieur Pierre Repentigny, Monsieur Robert Giffard, and the nephews of Monsieur Noël Juchereau Des Chatelets were referred to as "rogues" by Father Jérôme Lalemant in the *Jesuit Relations* of 1646.[1] Louis and his friends were known for their tricks and fearless escapades in the woods and on the river. Although no evidence exists, one wonders if Louis Couillard did not occasionally bring his younger cousins, the sons of Noël and Hélène, with him on these excursions. There is no doubt that Louis was a brave and hardy young man. When he was twenty-one, he and a half dozen other men formed a seal-hunting association. Each year, they would endure months of danger and adversity on their hunting and fishing expeditions in the Gulf of St. Lawrence. In 1656, Couillard caught one thousand codfish in one day. In 1659, he caught 220 seals on Île Rouge, a flat and rocky island near Tadoussac. Seal oil was particularly important to Quebec because of its export potential. Although Louis Couillard eventually settled into a more conventional lifestyle, it appears that he was not above some hell raising in his earlier years.[2]

In his *Jesuit Relations* of 1646, Father Jérôme Lalemant referred to a number of occasions of unruly and violent behavior on the part of the citizens of Quebec. Often the incident involved petty arguments between neighbors. On Shrove Tuesday in February of 1646, a man from the hospital got into a fight with a man under the employ of Guillaume Couillard. After some scuffling, one chased the other and came close to beating the man to death with a club. In May of that year, a sword fight broke out between two men under contract with the Ursulines. That same month, two soldiers were also involved in a sword fight.[3] Father Lalemant did not bother to record the cause of the disputes. One can easily imagine that alcohol was involved.

Also in the *Jesuit Relations* of 1646, there is a report of a sailor who confessed to a number of instances of illicit sexual relations with a woman at the fort at Tadoussac. The commander of the fort confined both the man and woman, but thought it his duty to put the woman to death. The governor of New France and the Jesuit priests were consulted about the matter. The sailor later confessed to being in a state of despair and fabricating the story. Apparently the case was resolved without dire consequences to either party, but it does reveal the double standard for men and women accused of unlawful sexual affairs.[4]

Marie de l'Incarnation would attest to the rough edges of life in the colony. In a letter to her son in 1668, she wrote,

> I can assure you that were it not for the Ursulines, [girls'] salvation would be in constant danger. The reason is that there is a large number of men here, and a mother and father . . . will leave their children at home with several men to watch over them. If they are girls, they would be in clear danger no matter what their age; and experience has shown that they must be put in a safe place. Finally, I can avow that the girls of this country are, for the most part, more knowledgeable in many dangerous ways than those of France.[5]

In 1649, a young girl was convicted of theft and hanged in Quebec.[6] Hélène's uncle Abraham Martin apparently had some role in the incident, described thus in the *Jesuit Relations*: On January 19, 1649, "occurred the first execution by the hand of the hangman, in the case of a Creature of 15 or 16 years, a thief. At the same time, they accused Monsieur Abraham of having violated her; he was imprisoned for this. . ."[7] Apparently, Martin's standing in the community wasn't too diminished. He received a bottle of brandy as a gift from the Jesuits on New Year's Day of 1650.[8] Later in the year, on November 22, Abraham stood as witness at the wedding of Mathieu Amiot Villeneuve and Marie Miville.[9]

In 1657, Louis de la Saudraye was found guilty of attempting to rape Marie-Marthe Pinson, a young woman in Montreal. The consequence of his conduct was the confiscation of his land. It was stipulated by Governor Maisonneuve that half was to go for the benefit of the Church and half to Marie-Marthe's children.[10]

The justice system in the colony was based on the attitudes and laws of the mother country. These, in turn, were greatly influenced by the precepts of the Roman Catholic Church regarding morality and wrongdoing. Punishments were freely handed out for a variety of offenses. There was little uniformity: seemingly minor crimes could receive serious punishment. Swearing in public could result in fines and detention. The most common punishment was a public whipping.[11]

Life was often cruel for the colonists who were trying to eke out an existence in the unforgiving environment along the St. Lawrence River. Childhood came to an end at an early age. Young people were judged by strict standards. As mentioned previously, they were considered miniature adults and were expected to assume adult responsibilities as soon as they were able to do the work. Family survival depended upon help from children. Many in the settlement lived in impoverished conditions. Children in these situations, in particular, were at increased risk for abuse and neglect from overworked and sometimes drunken parents.[12]

Children over seven were often treated as adults when it came to morally offensive behavior or infractions of the law. According to the Church's teaching, a child had reached the age of reasoning at the age of seven. A child under this age was considered incapable of criminal acts. Between the age of seven and thirteen, culpability depended upon whether or not the child had the knowledge and experience to know right from wrong and to understand the seriousness of the offense. Children convicted of a crime faced the same consequences as adults, although sometimes courts did show mercy toward young offenders.[13]

The colony had a large number of children who were without any parental supervision. There were instances where children left France in the company of their parents, but were orphaned before they reached the New World as a result of sickness and other dangerous situations which arose on the long trip across the Atlantic. Some were the younger sons of aristocratic families, without hope of an inheritance and seeking their fame and fortune in the New World. Other children were sent to the colony on their own, turned out by courts, orphanages, jails, and poor houses of France. In Quebec in 1684, according to one record from the archives, there were sixty individuals who arrived that year as indentured servants. The oldest in the group was sixteen; most were between the ages of twelve and fifteen.[14]

Indentured servants were at the mercy of those who employed them; they often lived in the meanest of circumstances. It is not surprising that a number of servants broke their contracts; this was the case, in particular, for young girls. In 1676, the authorities in Quebec decided that those who broke their contracts would be made to wear an iron collar and to suffer the public humiliation associated with it. For a second offense, the offender would receive a beating and branding. Sometimes young girls working as servants found themselves pregnant. If there was not a man willing to marry them, they suffered terrible consequences. Once the pregnancy was discovered, they faced social stigma and a life of poverty. They were usually dismissed and found it difficult to find other employment. Girls in these circumstances sometimes resorted to abortion and infanticide, but these were considered serious crimes, punishable by death.[15]

Although the level of juvenile delinquency was generally low in seventeenth-century Quebec, youthful offenders were responsible for a variety of crimes. These ranged from relatively minor offenses, such as theft and petty vandalism, up to more serious crimes, including murder. In Trois-Rivières in 1672, Isabelle Bertault, a thirteen-year-old girl, and her parents would murder Julien Latouche, the girl's husband. She had been married to him at the age of twelve. When he turned out to be a violent man, she was able to convince her parents to assist her in getting rid of him. After a failed poisoning attempt, the husband was beaten to death.[16]

In June of that year, justice would be duly served in Quebec and recorded in the registers of the Sovereign Council. The couple and their daughter, all convicted of a capital offense, were conducted by their executioner to the front steps of the parish church in the Upper Town. There they were required to beg pardon of God and the King for their offenses. Jacques Bertault, Isabelle's father, was then bound to the *croix Saint André* (two sturdy beams nailed together in the shape of an x). This was placed on scaffolding especially constructed for the purpose of the public execution. After death by strangulation, Bertault's body was lashed to a cartwheel. His arms and legs were smashed with a bar and the broken body then displayed in a prominent place on Cap Diamant. In seventeenth-century France, breaking on the wheel was used only for the most heinous crimes. In this instance, the punishment was symbolic: the convicted murderer was already dead. In other cases, the person was alive when strapped to the wheel and was tortured to death by the repeated blows to his limbs. Gilette Baune, Bertault's wife also suffered death by strangulation. The couple's property was confiscated. Sixty pounds went to the Récollets for their prayers for the repose of the soul of the victim Julien Latouche. Isabelle, shown mercy because of her age and the circumstances, was allowed to live but made to watch the execution of her parents.[17] One can imagine that a majority of those who lived in Quebec would be witnesses to the event. Executions were public spectacles. At the very least, the activities of their daily life would take them past the display of the lifeless body on Cap Diamant.[18]

The French colony had its share of drunk and disorderly conduct, not infrequently leading to brawls and other, more serious, crimes. Wine was consumed in great quantities in France, as in much of Europe. It was the drink of choice for both men and women and for all classes of people. Although people drank water, it was to be avoided as it was often contaminated with human and animal waste, especially in the towns and cities. It was better to drink wine or beer. Wine was served at all hours of the day: for breakfast, at the noonday meal, and in the evening. It was often watered down, but not always. Those who could not afford even the cheapest of wine drank piquette, a bitter, low-alcohol drink that was produced from the final pressing of the grapes.[19]

In the seventeenth century, brandy was added to the list of beverages regularly consumed by the French. Muslim physicians had learned to distill alcohol in the preparation of their medicines and had introduced the technique to Europeans in the Middle Ages. In Europe, distillation was largely the business of apothecaries and alchemists until the early seventeenth century. At that time, brandy began to be produced by distilling certain French wines that were light and otherwise lacking in character. Dutch merchants had long been involved in commercial interests in France. They took the lead in organizing the manufacture of brandy in the French cities along the Atlantic coast and exporting the commodity to other areas of France, as well as to the network of countries with which the Dutch traded. It soon became readily available in a range of quality and price.[20] Large quantities of brandy as well as wine were shipped to New France every year. By the mid 1660s the colony was spending 100,000 *livres* annually on the importation of alcoholic drink.[21]

Brandy had a number of attributes that made it a popular beverage. It was concentrated, having up to eight times the alcohol content as the same amount of wine. Less was needed to feel its intoxicating effects. Those who drank straight brandy experienced an immediate warming sensation, a most desirable quality for those sailors caught in cold winds and stormy seas. One can understand, too, its appeal for settlers suffering through the long winters in New France. On ocean voyages it was added to barrels of drinking water to improve its taste. It did not spoil; small quantities were sometimes used to stabilize wine to prevent the latter's conversion to vinegar.[22]

In the colony, missionaries and settlers brewed beer from their harvest of wheat, oats, and barley. Father Jérôme Lalemant mentions in 1646 that Brother Ambroise was employed in making beer for the community and that the Jesuits were constructing a brewery at Sillery.[23] Intendant Talon, who arrived in Quebec in 1665, established the first commercial brewery in the colony. It began production in 1670, but ceased operation in 1675.[24] Beer was cheaper and could be produced in the colony; water was generally safe to drink. But the early French colonists much preferred the alcoholic beverages imported from the mother country.

Wine and brandy, so much enjoyed by the French, became a particular problem for the Native Americans. There are many references to the drunken behavior of the Amerindians in the *Jesuit Relations*. It was soon abundantly clear that the natives were unduly susceptible to the intoxicating effects of the beverage and that their behavior under its influence was dangerous. In their state of drunkenness, the natives quarreled and killed indiscriminately. Father Le Jeune would declare that it was not safe to visit the Amerindians after 8 o'clock in the morning. The aborigines blamed their bad behavior on alcohol given them by the French and other Europeans, asserting that "if thou hadst not given us brandy or wine, we would not have done it."[25]

Mother Marie de l'Incarnation addressed the issue as well. She wrote to her son in August of 1662:

> This drink ruins all these people – men, women, boys, and even girls. . . . They are immediately overcome and become like mad people. They run naked with swords and other weapons and force everyone to flee, be it day or night. They rampage throughout Quebec without anyone being able to stop them. As a consequence there are rapes, murders, horrible and unheard of brutalities.[26]

Because of its effect on the indigenous population, the sale of alcohol to the natives was the subject of much debate in the seventeenth century. Trafficking in spirits had been prohibited in the colony since the days of Champlain, although this policy was routinely ignored. Sale of wine and brandy to the Native Americans was opposed by all of the religious elements of the colony. Alcohol exploited native weakness and interfered with missionary attempts at conversion. In 1657, the King in France confirmed this prohibition of trade in spirits. However, his stance was strongly opposed by the merchants and civil authorities of Quebec, as well as a majority of the colonists. Business interests argued that if the Amerindians couldn't get brandy from the French, they would trade with the English and the Dutch who had no such qualms about selling alcohol to the natives. In 1663, Bishop Laval and the Governor of the colony would jointly forbid trafficking in alcohol. This agreement between church and state officials lasted until 1668. In October of that year, the Sovereign Council, with the support of the Intendant Jean Talon, reversed its stand and voted to allow trade in spirits, adding the stipulation forbidding Amerindians to get drunk. Bishop Laval responded to this action by imposing excommunication from the Church for those caught providing alcohol to the natives. Thus, while the brandy trade was forbidden by the state at times, it was generally allowed in order to maintain the fur trade. Unfortunately, when Amerindians did get the alcohol they desired, they were unable to work. No one truly benefited from the sale of alcoholic beverages to the natives.[27]

In 1662, New France had a population of about 2,500, with most colonists living in Quebec, Trois-Rivières, and Montreal. The area between towns was sparsely settled; very few French had established homesteads south of the St. Lawrence River due to fear of the natives. The settlements were suffering from increasing attacks by Iroquois; these were most frequent between 1642 and 1652. However, new conflicts erupted in the 1660s. It was dangerous to be far from the forts and difficult to carry on the business of the settlements. As a result, few furs were able to reach the French trading posts. The fur trade declined significantly. Animal pelts were the only real export from New France, and this resource was in jeopardy. Meanwhile, New Netherland had a population of 10,000 in 1663 and Virginia had grown to 30,000 inhabitants. More than fifty years after their establishment, there was still talk about abandoning the settlements on the St. Lawrence River.[28]

Hélène's family would not escape the brutality of the Iroquois. In 1662, Joseph Hébert, the oldest child of Hélène and Guillaume, was captured by the Iroquois at the end of October. It was not immediately known what had happened to this young man, who would have been about twenty-five years old. His death was confirmed by another Frenchman, also held in captivity by the Iroquois: "As for

Monsieur Hébert, who was wounded with a musket-ball in the shoulder and arm, he was given to the Iroquois of Onneiout, and was there stabbed with knives by some drunken men of the country."[29] The Couillard family was also grieving losses to the Iroquois. Guillaume and Guillemette's son Guillaume was massacred by the Iroquois near Tadoussac about the same time that Joseph Hébert was captured. In June of the preceding year, their twenty-year-old son Nicolas was one of three young Frenchmen who were killed by the Iroquois and buried in Quebec two days later, on June 24, 1661.[30]

CHAPTER SIXTEEN

LATE SUMMER OF 1663

———◦◦◦———

Earthquake in Quebec; Arrival of filles du roi in the summer of 1663;
Origins of new arrivals; Paris in mid-century

In the summer of 1663, everyone in Quebec could have told you where they were and what they were doing on the previous February 5. That was the day the big earthquake struck. The temblor occurred in the evening. Snow was on the ground. The sun had set and families were gathered around the hearth preparing for the evening meal. It was also "Shrove Monday," the day before Mardi Gras. A good number of villagers were undoubtedly planning their celebrations for the next day.

From the Ursuline Convent, Mother Marie de l'Incarnation described the event in a letter to her son. She noted that

> The day was absolutely serene when of a sudden we heard a loud rumbling as if hundreds of carts were rolling with mad speed through the streets. Yet this sound seemed to come at once from the earth and from the air, a strange and terrifying thing. A roaring as of winds and waters was in our ears. A shower of stones came rattling on the roof, as though the rocks on which Quebec is built had been torn from the soil, and tossed down on us from the sky. A thick dust filled the air. Doors opened

and shut of their own accord. The church bells clanged, and all the clocks in the convent struck at once. The floors heaved, the walls swayed. Chairs and tables were overturned. Amid the confusion we could hear the barking of dogs and the distressful bellowing of cattle. We ran out of the house and felt the earth tremble under our feet. It was as sickening as though we stood on the unquiet deck of a ship. Men and women flung their arms for protection around the trunks of trees which seemed to give way under their grasp, while the branches sweeping downward struck at them angrily. The terrified [natives], possessed by the belief that the souls of the dead were responsible for all this uproar, fired their guns in the air to frighten them away, thus adding to the indescribable tumult and commotion."[1]

Father Jérôme Lalemant also experienced the earthquake and described it thus in his journal:

This noise, which gave one the impression that the house was on fire, made all rush outdoors to escape so unexpected a conflagration; but, instead of smoke and flames, people were much surprised to behold the walls tottering, and all the stones in motion, as if they had been detached. Roofs seemed to bend down in one direction, and then back again in the other; bells rang of their own accord; beams, joists, and boards creaked; and the earth leaped up, and made the palisade stakes dance in a way that would have seemed incredible, had we not witnessed it in different places. Then all left their houses, animals took flight, children cried in the streets, and men and women, seized with terror, knew not where to take refuge, — expecting every moment to be either overwhelmed under the ruins of the houses, or swallowed up in some abyss that was to open beneath their feet. Some knelt in the snow and cried for mercy, while others passed the rest of the night in prayer; for the Earthquake continued without ceasing, maintaining a certain swaying motion much like that of Ships at sea, so that some experienced from this tossing the same heaving of the stomach that one suffers on the water.[2]

In the report submitted by Father Lalemant to his superiors in September of 1663, he noted that this earthquake was different from others that had struck the area. The aftershocks continued for six months, into the month of August, with the aftershocks varying in number and in intensity from one region to another. The earthquake was felt in all of New France, from Gaspé at the mouth of the St. Lawrence River west to Montreal and the country beyond. It was also felt in New England.[3] That the extent of the earthquake was known attests to the fact that the colonists in the little settlement of Quebec were aware of what was happening in the world beyond their immediate borders. Traders and fishermen undoubtedly carried news of events taking place in the New England colonies.

Father Lalemant was to remark with amazement that no lives were lost and there was little damage to the French settlements. "Near us we see great clefts that were formed, and a prodigious extent of country utterly wrecked, while we have not lost a child or even a hair of our heads. All around us we see evidences of overthrow and ruin, and yet we had only some chimneys demolished, while the surrounding Mountains were swallowed up."[4]

A majority of the settlers before 1663 were brought to the colony by the religious institutions. Their experiences in life were seen through the prism of their religious convictions. Disasters were often viewed as acts of God, as punishment for previous sin. Overnight, the irreligious became religious. The French in the New World embraced the Lenten season of 1663 with a newfound passion. Mother Marie noted "At the same time that God shook the rocks and the mountains of this wild country, he shook the souls of men."[5] As Father Lalemant put it:

> The days of the Carnival were turned into days of piety, mourning, contrition, and tears; private prayers were protracted till late at night; public supplications were Announced; pilgrimages were undertaken, and Fasts observed. Confessions were instituted, — and, among these, many which comprised the sins of a whole life, — and indeed they were generally made in that faith wherein each one wished to be Judged by God, and that these might prevent his eternal wrath and condemnation.[6]

The earthquake was not the only thing to rattle the colony that year. In the motherland across the Atlantic, events were happening that would directly affect the well-being and the future of the French colony. The affairs of New France would no longer be governed by the Company of One Hundred Associates. In 1661, the colony had come under the direct control of Louis XIV.[7] In 1663, three hundred persons from La Rochelle arrived in Quebec aboard two vessels.[8] Among the passengers were a number of girls who came to be known as the *filles du roi*,[9] or the King's daughters. The King had at last begun to take notice of the needs of the French settlement. Between 1663 and 1673, 770 young, single or widowed "marriageable" women would be sponsored by the King to come to the colony for the purpose of marrying and producing children.[10] Two of these *filles du roi* would become Hélène's daughters-in-law.

Men greatly outnumbered women in the colony. In 1663, there were six single men for every unmarried woman in the French colony. Two-thirds of the immigrants to New France between 1632 and 1659 had returned home. Among the reasons for returning to the mother country was the difficulty of finding a spouse and establishing a family in the New World.[11] In the 1600s, France was involved in a series of wars in Europe and reluctant to send large numbers of people to the colony. At the same time, the country did not want to miss out on the opportunities that the new territory offered. Louis XIV thought it would be easier to establish settlements in New France by encouraging the emigration of women and promoting births, rather than by sending massive numbers to the colony. In addition to skilled tradesmen and contract workers, whole families and single, marriageable women were encouraged to emigrate. Women would come with their husbands, their parents, another relative, or they came as *filles du roi*.[12]

Sending marriageable girls to New France required a significant investment on the part of the crown. Jean-Baptiste Colbert, the King's Minister of Finance, was responsible for the financing and recruitment of the young women in France. Recruiters were given ten *livres* for each girl. The French West India Company received one hundred *livres* for each woman brought to the colony. Thirty *livres* were allotted for the purchase of clothing and small household items. These personal articles included a bonnet, lace, a ribbon for the shoes, a taffeta handkerchief, a hairbrush, a pair of stockings, and a pair of gloves. The young women also received two knives (presumably for the kitchen), scissors, pins, needles, and thread. An additional sixty *livres* were provided for travel expenses. Upon marriage, the girls were supposed to receive a dowry from the King. Commoners might receive a monetary gift of fifty *livres*. Young ladies of higher birth might be given 100 *livres* or more. According to some studies, more than half received no dowry at all from the King.[13]

The origins and social status of the girls varied. The vast majority of women who received support from the King came from Paris and cities in Normandy. However, some came from other regions and several were not French by birth. Some sixty girls were of higher rank; they came from the lesser nobility and upper-middle-class families. In all likelihood, they were successfully recruited because their families lacked the money for the marriage dowry, essential for a good marriage in France. These girls were needed to provide suitable matches for officers and men of rank in the colony. The greatest number of women came from more humble backgrounds. They were the daughters of minor artisans, laborers, and servants. Most of these women could neither read nor write, as evidenced by the notation on their marriage records that they were "unable to sign." Some presented themselves at the port cities of Dieppe and La Rochelle on their own accord. Others were recruited by the Sulpicians and the Archbishop of Rouen. Opportunities in France for these young women were very limited. They were willing to face what was likely to be a dangerous trip across the Atlantic and the hardships of life in the untamed territory of the New World for a chance to marry, have a home, and rear children.[14]

Over one-third of the women came from the Hôpital Général de Paris.[15] Most, if not all, of these women were orphans. In the mid-seventeenth century, between ten and thirteen percent of the Paris population was homeless. In 1656, Louis XIV passed an edict requiring that the homeless in and around Paris be removed from the streets. The poor, the sickly, and the homeless thus found shelter in the city's Hôpital Général and the streets of Paris were rid of these unfortunates. Conditions were harsh in the charity hospitals.

The majority of girls lived in squalor, sleeping three to five girls to a lice-infested bed. Meals were meager. The work was hard.[16]

The *filles du roi* departed from the ports of Dieppe and La Rochelle and crossed the Atlantic in convoys. They were closely supervised on their journey and in the colony before they married. When they landed in Quebec, the young women were greeted and assisted with settlement by the Sovereign Council and, after 1665, by Intendant Talon. Some girls were housed with the Ursulines in Quebec, in a home built originally for Madame de La Peltrie; others found lodging with the Congregation of Notre-Dame in Montreal. In general, they spent about two weeks living with the nuns, who instructed them on life in the settlements, before marrying and beginning a family. Marguerite Bourgeoys, founder of the Congregation in Montreal, welcomed these women. She understood that they would be key to increasing French settlement in the New World.[17]

Anne Gasnier, widow of Jean Bourdon, made several trips to France to recruit suitable girls for the colony. She would look for young women from good peasant families or reputable institutions who expressed an interest in settling in the colony and came with the recommendation of the local priest. Upon their arrival and until they found a husband, she would also offer them accommodation in a home in the Lower Town left to her by her late husband.[18]

The *filles du roi* did not receive a warm welcome from everyone. Women traveling alone across the Atlantic were often considered to be women of ill repute. They were treated with contempt and subjected to all manner of bawdy jokes and sexual harassment.[19] Intendant Talon, Mother Marie de l'Incarnation, and Marguerite Bourgeoys all wrote of their concerns regarding their appropriateness for life in the New World. The colony needed women who were strong, had good housekeeping skills, and were willing to work hard in a harsh world. They needed girls who were accustomed to life on a farm. The unmarried girls who arrived at Quebec appeared unprepared for the rigors of pioneer life in the settlement. In France, the majority of these girls had been raised in an urban environment;

many were in questionable health. In 1668, Mere Marie de St. André, an Ursuline at Quebec, would write, "You wouldn't believe the damage these good creatures do, not counting the fact that they have already set the house on fire two or three times. . . . We are working as hard as we can to get rid of them."[20]

Marie de l'Incarnation expressed the sentiments of the day when she wrote to her son from Quebec in 1668: "From now on we would like to ask only for country girls who, like the men, are suitable for work, experience having revealed that those who have not been brought up for it are not suited for this country, being in a miserable state from which they cannot escape."[21] After Intendant Talon arrived in Quebec, he specified that the women sponsored by the King be of an age suitable for procreation and be in good health. Talon bluntly stated that "it would be wise to strongly recommend that the women destined for this country be entirely free of any natural blemish or of anything repulsive in their appearance, that they be healthy and strong for work in the fields, or at least that they have some skill for manual labors."[22]

All but thirty-two of the 770 *filles du roi* married. Most of the girls were between nineteen and twenty-five when they became brides. The majority married within six months of arriving in New France; some married within the month. Seventy percent of the girls would settle in Quebec, eighteen percent established a home in Montreal, and twelve percent in Trois-Rivières.[23]

In the coming years, two of the sons of Noël and Hélène would marry a *fille du roi*. On October 18, 1667, Jean-Baptiste signed a contract to marry Marie Anne Firman, a girl who had arrived from Dieppe, France, as a *fille du roi*. Marie Anne was from Paris. Her father was an advocate on the Grand Council in the Parliament of Paris.[24] Apparently one of the parties was unhappy with the arrangement; Marie-Ann returned to France on the ship Le Prophéte. A month later, Jean-Baptiste chose another young *fille du roi*. On November 22, 1667, Jean-Baptiste, now using the surname Morin dit Rochebelle, married Catherine de Belleau in a ceremony attended by the governor of the colony, Daniel de Rémy de Courcelle. Her father was François DeBelleau, esquire and Lord of Cantigny from the province of Picardy, in northwestern France.[25]

On February 10, 1670, Noël and Hélène's son Alphonse married Marie-Madeleine Normand, also one of the *filles du roi*. She was the daughter of Jean-Baptiste Normand and Catherine Pageau. Marie-Madeleine was born in Sens in the region of Bourgogne, some seventy-five miles southeast of Paris. Five years earlier, Marie-Madeleine's sister Catherine had come to Quebec as a *fille du roi* and married the pioneer Pierre Normand (no relation).[26]

The King's Minister of Finance went to extra lengths to promote these marriages. He wanted a strong colony, less dependent upon the mother country. In 1670, Colbert would publish an edict requiring the single men in the colony to marry. If men chose not to comply, they faced the loss of fishing and hunting rights, as well as other privileges. A number of hasty marriages resulted from this edict.[27]

No doubt the colonists were interested in learning from the recent arrivals what life was like in Paris. Many in the colony had ties to Paris. They were well-acquainted with the city and what went on there: they had been born there or had at least spent time within its boundaries. Both the elite and the poor of the city were represented in the colony. Samuel de Champlain, the colony's founder, and his wife, Hélène, had had a home in Paris. Louis Hébert, first farmer of New France, and his wife were Parisians. Many of the Jesuit missionaries had lived or studied there. In 1646, Hélène's seventeen-year-old nephew Louis Couillard, along with four other young lads, made the trip to France.[28] One cannot imagine that they would not have traveled to Paris. Others in the colony had traveled to the city on business. Jean Bourdon, Noël and Hélène's illustrious neighbor in the Upper Town, would make four trips to Paris: in 1641, 1650, 1660, and, lastly, in 1663.[29] Many of the *filles du roi* to emigrate in 1663 were from the city. Certainly, the political wisdom and policies, as well as the fashions and the customs that emanated from Paris, were of interest to the colonists and influenced life in Quebec.

Paris had been a center of trade since Roman times. With the creation of its university in the twelfth century, it had become a center of learning and higher education, drawing students from many places in Europe. It was the seat of the French kings and the attendant administration. By the mid-sixteenth century, it had a population between 280,000 and 300,000. Many people would die during the religious wars in the second half of that century. However, there would be a sharp increase in the population of the city in the early seventeenth century as a result of urban development and other policies initiated by Henry IV at the beginning of that century. By the 1630s, the population of Paris had more than doubled from some 200,000 in 1594 to 430,000. Paris in the seventeenth century was the largest city in France, and had been for some time.[30]

The face of the city changed dramatically over the course of the first half of the seventeenth century. Henry IV was assassinated by a Roman Catholic fanatic in 1610, but the work he had initiated to improve the city was continued by his widow, Marie de'Medici, and his successor, Louis XIII. The Pont Neuf, begun in the 1500s over the River Seine, was completed. The Louvre complex was expanded to connect with the palace of the Tuileries. The construction of two beautiful residential squares, the Place Dauphine and the Place Royale (later known as the Place des Vosges), as well as the building of the Luxembourg Palace and Gardens, were all made possible by the crown. The Place des Vosges, completed in 1612, was bordered on each side by a continuous line of stylish, gabled mansions constructed of brick and stone. The Île-St.-Louis became a desirable residential district for well-to-do commercial families, financiers, and royal officials. In 1624, Cardinal Richelieu commissioned his residence to be built near the Louvre-Tuileries complex, making the rue St. Honoré neighborhood another residential district of choice for high-ranking government officials. Noble families took up residence in town houses which had been recently built or newly remodeled.[31]

By 1643, Paris' city center had outgrown its medieval base and been transformed by a ring of new construction under royal sponsorship. In addition to the traditional aristocracy, Paris was home to a wealthy class of bankers, merchants and manufacturers. Trade in luxury goods flourished. For those with money, Paris became a city characterized by ostentation, grand boulevards, magnificent homes, beautiful gardens, and imposing monuments.[32]

During this building boom, thousands of jobs were created for laborers and skilled craftsmen. The households of the wealthy demanded the services provided by artisans; they also required servants of various ranks and skills. Emigrants from all over France, as well as other countries, moved to Paris to fill the newly created positions. Impoverished peasants moved from the countryside to the tenements on the outskirts of town, hoping to obtain work as servants or day laborers. If they failed to find work, they hoped to rely on assistance from the many charitable establishments active in seventeenth-century Paris.[33]

Meal preparation in the city was in sharp contrast to the labor-intensive work required of families in the countryside and in New France. The wealthy of Paris enjoyed their own version of fast or convenience food. There were a number of culinary guilds that supplied customers with all manner of ready-to-eat meals. Bakers sold bread; pastry chefs produced a variety of pies, both sweet and savory. Cooked poultry and joints of meat were obtained from *rôtisseurs*. From charcutiers came cured pork, ham, and sausage. Charcutiers also sold rillets (finely-chopped and heavily-seasoned meat, baked in a casserole or pot) and pâté (similar to rillets, but baked in a crust of pastry). There was also a sauce-maker's guild and another one offering lemonade and other liquid refreshment.[34]

Poorer Parisians also had access to ready-to-eat foods. There was a thriving market for what one person called "second-hand food." This was food left over from the dinners of the wealthy and sold by the servants of the household. Women from the lower classes often worked long hours and did not have the time to cook a meal. Many of these women lived with their families in a single room which would have only the most rudimentary of cooking facilities. Any food prepared in these lodgings was prepared over an open fireplace, which also served to heat and light the room. Wood was costly, so fires were a luxury. Soup and small pies were purchased to accompany bread, the dietary mainstay of the poor.[35]

Seventeenth-century French had developed a keen sense of propriety and etiquette, particularly when it came to meals. In the homes of the privileged, tables were set with linens that draped over the side and were long enough to serve as a common napkin. Bowls of scented water were placed in front of diners who were expected to wash their hands before eating. By mid-century, food was served on plates rather than over bread. Places were set with knives, forks, and spoons. A dinner might consist of several courses, including a variety of meats, vegetables, fruits, and salads. Wine was the beverage of choice. Good manners dictated that one should keep elbows off the table, not make noise when eating, and not talk with a full mouth. There were numerous books on etiquette, as well as cookbooks, published in the seventeenth century.[36]

This era was marked by a growing separation of the classes. The elegant residential neighborhoods of the wealthy contrasted sharply with the squalid tenements of the poor, where buildings often housed twenty or more families. Paris, as well as other older European cities, was ringed with elaborate fortifications so that it was not easy to expand outward. The city could not accommodate the larger population with enough clean water and waste management. The city became an unhealthy place to live due to the crowded conditions, especially for the lower classes.[37]

The letters of Mother Marie de l'Incarnation and the reports of the Jesuits in New France were filled with references to the filth of the natives. However, the Parisians were not paragons of cleanliness in the seventeenth century. If there was increased fastidiousness in food preparation and consumption, the streets of seventeenth-century Paris were a different story. Many of the streets were dark, narrow, deeply rutted, muddy, often unpaved, and littered with dung, sewage, garbage, flies, and foraging pigs and chickens. People on foot shared the passageways with horses and donkey-pulled carts.

Throughout the century, household waste was routinely tossed out the windows and doors onto the streets, often splashing anyone who happened to be passing by. At the sides of doorways were small mounds of household waste: human excrement from chamber pots and kitchen garbage, waiting to be carted away where the material would provide fertilizer for the gardens on the outskirts of the city. Before one could see Paris, one could smell the stench. Well-off Parisians wore perfumed gloves or held sweet-scented handkerchiefs to their noses when going about their business. The wealthier citizens were sometimes carried through the streets in sedan chairs. Parisians were complacent and resistant to regulations concerning hygiene. In 1666, a law was passed requiring homes to have some sort of privy or sanitary accommodation. It was not universally enforced. The River Seine was an open sewer, with all manner of waste tossed in. It was also a source of drinking water for Parisians, as well as where women washed their clothes. In the Louvre and other public places, people relieved themselves in the courtyards, on staircases, behind doors and from balconies.[38]

Bathing in a tub of water was a rare occurrence. A dip in the river in the summer months was more common. In Paris, there were open-air, well-patronized bathing places along the river for both men and women. French etiquette did call for daily hand washing and washing the face nearly as regularly. Gentlemen were advised to wash their feet occasionally. Parisians did not use soap and water; instead, they used a cloth soaked in alcohol or water diluted with wine and perfume. The latter would certainly have helped to mask the more unpleasant smells of the city.[39]

Paris in the mid-seventeenth century represented both the best and the worst that Europe had to offer. The Jesuits who had spent time in Paris and some of the wealthier settlers might have missed the luxuries and sophistication of Paris. It is doubtful that those at the bottom of the economic ladder regretted their decision to emigrate.

The French were a study in contrasts. They observed strict rules of hygiene and etiquette in the preparation and consumption of food; however, filth and disorder reigned in the streets. In matters of hygiene, the French of Quebec repeated the behavior of the French in the mother country. Prior to 1673, human waste was thrown from the windows and doorways of the cottages into the street. In the Lower Town, pigs were allowed to roam freely. In Quebec in 1673, legislation would require new home construction to include latrines or privies on the property. In older homes or neighborhoods where there was no room for a latrine, the owner of each home had to clean the street in front of his home each day.[40]

For many of the residents of Quebec, the year 1663 would be remembered as the year of the big earthquake. Noël and Hélène would certainly remember where they were the moment the earthquake struck. As with all of the settlers, stories of the quake and its aftermath would dominate conversation around the Morin family hearth for many months to come. Eventually life returned to normal. Most of the *filles du roi* who arrived in the summer married quickly and were adjusting to life in the New World. Other concerns dominated the thoughts of the French colonists.

CHAPTER SEVENTEEN

FALL OF 1666

———∞———

Louis XIV turns his attention to New France; Arrival of the Carignan-Salières regiment in 1665; Changes in the government of the colony; Census of 1666; The Morin household; Seigneuries and seigneurial rights and responsibilities; Noël's seigneury; Iroquois attacks on the colonists; Defeat of the Iroquois in 1666

It had been five years since Louis XIV personally began governing France. In 1665, the King of France, recognizing that the survival of the colony was in some jeopardy, had sent the Carignan-Salières Regiment to New France. They arrived at Quebec in the summer of that year under the command of Lieutenant-General Alexandre de Prouville, Marquis de Tracy. It was the first expedition of regular French troops and the only complete regiment to be sent to the New World during the French rule. There were twenty companies in the regiment and each company had about fifty soldiers, including three officers: a captain, a lieutenant and an ensign. Four other companies joined this regiment, making a total of about twelve hundred soldiers who arrived in the colony. The men were dressed in fashionable brown uniforms with a grey lining exposed in the upturned sleeves. On their heads they wore wide-brimmed black felt hats. Officers were provided with swords and pistols, while the enlisted men carried matchlock firearms and bayonets. Given that the population of New France at this time was about 3,200 inhabitants, the presence of the French troops had a significant impact on the ability of the colony to defend itself against the Iroquois warriors.[1] One can imagine the excitement in the settlement as the ships bringing the soldiers appeared in the harbor. Happy pandemonium greeted the men as they disembarked and unloaded their artillery and other cargo. Quebec was a beehive of activity that summer.

The colony was on the verge of economic collapse. The Company of One Hundred Associates and the Société Notre-Dame de Montreal, both disbanded in 1663, had been unsuccessful in establishing a strong French presence in the New World. Fortunately for the people of New France, the monarch believed in the opportunities offered by colonization of the New World. From this point on, the crown assumed direct responsibility for the development and colonization of New France. As far as the French colony was concerned, one of the first orders of business for the King was to create a dual government. A governor was appointed as the military chief and an intendant was appointed as the civil authority. In the fall of 1665, Governor Rémy de Courcelle and Intendant Jean Talon arrived in Quebec.[2]

France, as well as the other European nations, understood that to hold on to the territory in the New World a strong colony would have to be established. Recruitment of settlers was difficult. It took courage to undertake a two or three month voyage to settle in what was considered a wild and dangerous land. Beyond fish and fur, there wasn't much to lure would-be settlers to this land in the northern reaches of the new continent. The reasons for emigration varied. Clearly, some saw a chance for adventure. Others found life in France confining and options limited. Emigration offered a chance, however small, for success. Most came with the hope that life in the New World would be better than that in the old. While land ownership was more easily obtained in the New World, the hardships were very real. The heavily-wooded terrain and the long, bitterly cold winters were detriments to profitable farming. Colonists risked torture and death at the hands of unfriendly natives.[3]

When Jean Talon arrived in Quebec, he lost no time in ordering a census in New France. According to the census of 1666, the population of the province of Quebec was 3,200. Quebec City itself had only 555 inhabitants.[4] French men outnumbered the women two to one. While almost all of the women between the ages of fifteen and thirty were married, there was still a high number of single men.[5]

In this first census of Quebec, Noël and Hélène, along with their children, were listed as living in the region of "Sainct Jean, Sainct François and Sainct Michel", a district just west of the Upper Town. Noël's occupation was listed as *charron habitant*, that is, resident wheelwright.[6] There were nine people listed in the household of Noël Morin. Noël was listed as age fifty-seven. Hélène's age was given as forty-six. Five of their children were still living with them: Nicolas, age twenty-two; Jean-Baptiste, age twenty-one; Alphonse, age fifteen; Charles, age eleven; and Marie-Madeleine, age nine. Also living in the household was a daughter-in-law, Marie Charlotte Depoitiers, the widow of Hélène's son by her first marriage. Jean Ballie, a domestic "*engagé*", was living with the Morin family, as well.[7] A year later, in the census of 1667, just Alphonse, Charles and Marie-Madeleine would be living at home, along with Zacharie Jolly, a seventeen-year-old apprentice, and Jean Ballie, the domestic.[8] It would be noted in the census of 1667 that Noël's possessions included a dozen cows and forty *arpents* (thirty-four acres) of land.[9]

Jean Talon would serve as civil administrator from 1665 to 1668 and from 1670 to 1672. The colony would long feel the effects of his administration. He believed, as did Louis XIV, that the way to build the colony was from within, instead of having to depend on immigration. Toward that end, Intendant Talon introduced incentives to encourage early marriages and large families. Grooms, aged twenty and under, received a gift of twenty *livres* from the King on their wedding day. Parents who didn't marry their children off early faced hefty fines and other restrictions, such as the loss of hunting, fishing, and trading privileges.[10]

An annual allowance of three hundred *livres* was to be given to families with ten living, legitimate children. This allocation was increased to four hundred *livres* for families with twelve or more children. Children intended for the priesthood or convent were not counted in determining eligibility for these incentives. In addition to the allowances, civilian and military honors were bestowed on the heads of large families: The men might be made churchwardens or captains of the military.[11] No record remains identifying those who received the incentives. One wonders how many families actually qualified for them. It is doubtful that Noël and Hélène received the allowance. By 1665, two of their children had entered religious life, and several had died in childhood.

Talon's policies would remain in effect for a number of years and proved quite successful: The high birth rate of New France, rather than immigration, would be responsible for the population increase in the colony.[12] In 1664, Jean Poitras was married in Quebec. He would eventually sire twenty-seven children, seventeen with his first wife and ten with his second.[13]

Natives were not included in Talon's census. As mentioned in earlier chapters, the number of natives who lived in the territory north of the St. Lawrence River had diminished greatly. In August of 1664, Mother Marie de l'Incarnation wrote to Mother Angélique at the Ursuline Monastery in Tours, observing that "although there is still a large number, it is small in comparison with what it used to be, for out of twenty [Amerindians] there now remains only a single person."[14] The decline of the native population increased the need for French immigrants to maintain the fur trade. There had been little need for a large European settlement in the early days of the fur trade: the natives supplied the labor.

More farmers were also needed to sustain the colony and to decrease dependence on French imports. Land served as an inducement. Between 1631 and 1650, under the management of the Company of One Hundred Associates, six thousand *hectares* (15,000 acres) were granted to French colonists in the form of seigneuries and other smaller land grants. Between 1650 and 1655, an additional fifteen thousand *hectares* (37,500 acres) were granted. Within a span of five years, the distribution was more than double the amount distributed in the previous twenty years. In 1650, the population of the entire colony was 1,206. Ten years later, in 1660, the population would be 2,690. After 1650, more than half of the French immigrants remained in the colony.[15] Prior to that date, close to two-thirds of the immigrants had returned to France.[16]

The Company of One Hundred Associates relied primarily on the seigneurs to fulfill its contractual obligation to settle New France. The seigneurs were individuals who either bought or were given tracts of land. They were the most important members of society in the New World. Usually they had been members of the aristocracy or had had a military position of some importance prior to becoming a seigneur. The smaller seigneuries were granted to persons of less distinction. The Company granted seigneuries with the understanding that the seigneurs would bring colonists to develop the land.[17] Historians do not agree as to the number of seigneuries granted by the Company. The number ranges from seventy to more than one hundred.[18]

The early seigneuries were clustered around Quebec and, to a lesser extent, Trois-Rivières and Montreal. These seigneuries varied greatly in size. The largest were hundreds of square miles in size, while others, located in the towns, consisted of only a few *arpents* of land. (One arpent is .84 acre.) Some seigneuries overlapped with previous concessions. The Company did not have any idea how much land could reasonably be cleared and how much land would be needed to become a profitable enterprise and support the families settled on the land.[19]

The land grants were designed to take advantage of waterways, yet encourage development of interior land. Therefore, the seigneurie was generally a long, narrow strip of land with the short end bordering a body of water: the St. Lawrence River or another major river. In general, each lot had seven *arpents* (about six acres) of river frontage. This configuration provided easy access for transport of goods and communication with the outside world. Because people built their homes close to the river, it also promoted a tight-knit community and a measure of security for the settlers who could come to each other's aid when needed.[20]

The seigneurial system set up by the French along the St. Lawrence River was an adaptation of the French feudal system. The land grant came with specific rights and responsibilities. Under the conditions of the seigneurial system, the seigneur was responsible for clearing the land, building houses, and settling people on his land. The seigneur needed to grant enough land to each settler so that the farmer could support himself and his family. To this end, seigneuries were further divided, again into long and narrow parcels of land. The seigneur was required to build a communal flour mill and an oven for the use of all settlers on the seigneury. The mill would double as a fort when necessary. The building and maintenance of roads on the land was also the responsibility of the seigneur. Of course, there would be a manor house for the family of the seigneur, and there might also be a chapel on the property. In order to accomplish all of this, it fell upon the seigneur to recruit men to come to the New World.[21]

The religious institutions received huge land grants. By the end of the French regime, one fourth of the land in New France was owned by the church, and more than one third of the colonists of New France lived on the seigneuries of the church. The Jesuits had eight seigneuries and were the largest property owners in the colony. The seigneury of Sainte-Croix went to the Ursulines at Quebec. These seigneuries provided significant income for the church. As in France, the religious institutions in the colony were responsible for maintaining hospitals and educational institutions. Toward that end, the state was generous in supplying them with land, the development of which would meet their financial needs.[22]

With a few exceptions, notably the concessions to the Catholic Church, the seigneuries in New France were granted to individual men. Robert Giffard's land grant at Beauport in 1634 was the first of the seigneuries granted by the Company of One Hundred Associates. In 1653, the Beauport seigneury was enlarged to a depth of four leagues (twelve miles), and in the census of 1666 there were twenty-nine households living on the land. Over the course of the years, Giffard was granted two additional seigneuries: Saint-Gabriel, located northwest of Quebec and awarded in 1647, and Mille-Vaches, located near Tadoussac and granted in 1653.[23]

On November 15, 1653, Noël Morin was granted a small arriere-fief located within the Rivière-du-Sud seigneurie on the south shore of the St. Lawrence River, at a point known as the Pointe-de-la Caille at Montmagny, ten leagues (thirty miles) downstream from Quebec. Morin gave the name St-Luc to this land grant. From that time on, Noël Morin became known as the Sieur de St-Luc. In 1663, after the Company of One Hundred Associates was disbanded, Noël's land grant was re-conceded.[24] However, almost ten more years would elapse before Noël would develop this seigneurie. As noted in the various civil and church records, the Morin family continued to live on their property on the côteau Sainte-Geneviève.

As a seigneur, Noël and his wife, Hélène, were honored in a number of ways. The social life of the seigneury, as well as the colony itself, was centered on the church. For this reason, many of the honors paid to the seigneur were accorded him through the Church. The seigneur was granted a special pew, larger than the rest, and located in the most prominent place in the church, that is, the first row on the right. On May 17, 1655, Hélène and Noël were given a pew of their own at the parish church of Notre-Dame de Québec in the Upper Town. The pew was on the right-hand side, behind that of Sieur Charles Sevestre.[25] Noël was given the second pew, in all probability because the church had to accommodate two seigneurs. He and his family would have been mentioned by name in the prayers from the pulpit. In the various ceremonies, the seigneur was the first in line, after the church wardens, to receive Benediction, Communion, the ashes of Ash Wednesday, and palms on Palm Sunday. In processions, he marched behind the priest. When he died, the seigneur also had the right to be buried inside the church beneath the seigneurial pew.[26]

After 1663, Louis XIV assumed control of land development in New France. Many of the large seigneuries granted by the Company of One Hundred Associates were a problem. Much of this land had never been cleared or settled. The majority of seigneurs were unwilling or unable to bring settlers to establish homesteads on the land. In March of 1663, Louis XIV ordered all land grants made under the Company of One Hundred Associates to be cleared within six months or to be returned to the Royal Domain. Intendant Talon did not enforce the decree; however, in general, future land grants were considerably smaller.[27] Talon was particularly interested in organizing the colony to promote self-protection and to encourage trade and industry. To that end, he was instrumental in seeing that a number of seigneuries were given to officers of the military to encourage them to stay.[28]

There were two groups of people who worked the land: *engagés* and *habitants*. *Engagés* were indentured servants who came under signed contracts, generally of three years' duration, to work under the seigneur or for the religious institutions. Many of the French who came between 1632 and 1650 came as indentured servants of the Jesuits, Ursulines, or Hospitaller nuns. They provided labor and surplus foodstuffs for the seminary and convents. *Engagés* were also contracted to work for fur traders and merchants. At the end of the contract, some men were enticed to remain in the colony by being given parcels of land, in exchange for some form of dues, generally a small portion of their harvest. However, most did not stay at the end of their three-year contract: three-fourths returned to France.[29]

Habitants were farmers or laborers also brought to New France to live on and work the land. They were given a small piece of property from the seigneur, perhaps three *arpents* (two and a half acres) wide, bordering the body of water, and thirty *arpents* (twenty-five acres) deep. Thus the *habitant* would have access to water and good soil at the water's edge and to timber further back. In return for the use of the land, *habitants* paid rent and taxes to the seigneur. *Habitants* not fortunate enough to have sufficient land to meet their family needs turned to wage labor to supplement farm income.[30]

In the census of 1666, fifty percent of the Frenchmen listed a trade, even though they might also be living and working on a farm. One incentive to emigrate was to become a master tradesman. The charter of the Company of One Hundred Associates, established in 1627, encouraged tradesmen to emigrate. Those men who came and worked at this trade for six years in the New World would be considered masters upon their return to France. The position of master tradesman had become increasingly difficult to obtain in the mother country. In 1653, some one hundred tradesmen immigrated in a group. They held varying degrees of experience in their trade, but came with high hopes of returning to their homeland and opening up a shop of their own. In return for passage plus room and board, paid by the man who recruited them, tradesmen signed a contract to work for three years. They became known as the "treinte-six mois."[31] Unfortunately, those who returned to France did nothing to contribute to the growth of the colony.

There was one man who came under a three-year contract who stayed and contributed greatly to the cultural and educational development of Quebec. That man was Martin Boutet, originally from Sceaux near Paris. He had been a neighbor of the Morin family for years, having purchased a parcel of land adjoining their property in the Upper Town in 1649.[32] Boutet had come to the colony in 1643 as an *engagé* from La Rochelle, along with his wife and a young daughter. He was a man of many talents. Boutet initially served as a soldier, probably stationed at Fort Saint-Louis on Cap Diamant, just down the road from the Morin family. After his wife's death in 1664, Martin went to work for the Jesuits. He served them first as a business agent and later as a teacher at the Jesuit College, instructing the students in mathematics, surveying, hydrography, and piloting. For his efforts, Louis XIV awarded him an engineer's certificate in 1678. Boutet also had a significant role in bringing music to the colony.

In 1645, he played the violin at Christmas Mass at the Church of Notre-Dame in Quebec. One can imagine that Noël and Hélène, along with their children, were in the church listening to him. In 1651, Boutet was appointed music director of the church. He sang at the services, directed the children's choir, and provided money for the purchase of music books for the church. Louis Jolliet, another friend of the Morin family, would also benefit from the instruction of Martin Boutet. While Jolliet would become famous for his explorations in New France, he also became one of the first organists in the country. It is believed that Jolliet initiated his organ studies under Boutet.[33]

The business of a tradesman was generally a family affair; however, it appears that none of Noël's sons was interested in becoming a *charron* and following in his father's footsteps. In the census of 1667, as noted earlier, Noël had a seventeen-year-old apprentice named Zacharie Jolly working with him. This would have been the norm: the artisan worked alone or perhaps with one apprentice, a son or another boy, who would became a part of the tradesman's family. Generally, the apprenticeship lasted from three to seven years; at the end of the service, the apprentice received a small payment. Young men or boys who served as apprentices learned a trade and provided cheap labor for the craftsman in the process. As has been noted as well, many artisans were also farmers. They needed the foodstuffs and extra income produced by the farm to adequately provide for their families.[34]

The French settlers were hampered in their efforts to establish farms by the continuing attacks from the Iroquois. Initially it fell to the trading companies to employ a small number of soldiers to protect the colonists and keep order in the settlements. In 1620, Samuel de Champlain constructed Fort Saint-Louis at Quebec on the precipice overlooking the St. Lawrence River to take advantage of the area's natural defenses. Later the compound was fortified with batteries at weak points and cannons facing east. In the first fifty years of its existence, the west side was never enclosed. The fort was never destroyed, in spite of various sieges and assaults. As attacks from

natives increased, the colonists formed militias to protect themselves. In 1651, Pierre Boucher formed a militia of able-bodied men
in Trois-Rivières. In 1663, Maisonneuve did the same in Montreal.[35]

Between the founding of Quebec in 1608 and the arrival of the
Carignan-Salières regiment in 1665, approximately two hundred
French settlers had been killed by the Iroquois. Native attacks against
the French had been sporadic and warfare was guerilla-style. The Iroquois did not attack the French in the vicinity of Quebec until after
1650. Most of the deaths in that area occurred in 1661. Montreal had
endured twenty years of attacks, beginning in 1643.[36]

Hélène's daughter Marie Morin, who had entered the convent of
the Hôtel-Dieu of Montreal in 1662, provided a vivid account of
the Iroquois attacks experienced in that community in her *Annales de
L'Hôtel-Dieu de Montreal*. At the first sign of an Iroquois attack, one
of the nuns would race to ring the alarm bell, calling all able-bodied
men to battle. She observed that some of the women also grabbed
weapons and joined the battle, fighting just as valiantly as did the
men. The priests in the settlement moved among the fallen, offering
what comfort they could. The braver nuns at the hospital continued
about their business of caring for the sick and wounded, while the
less brave made their way to the chapel to prepare for death. During
these years, the French settlers learned to live with the constant threat
of an attack, at least during the warmer months. Sister Morin noted
that frequently there were Iroquois warriors hiding in the brush near
the Hôtel Dieu and other buildings, just waiting for some foolish
person to venture outside after dark.[37]

There were instances where women were captured, tortured, and
killed. In one incident, however, there was a happier ending. In 1652,
in an attack that took place near the fort in Montreal, three Iroquois warriors, hatchets in hand, threw themselves upon a woman
named Martine Messier. This woman had only her hands and feet for
weapons, but she fought back ferociously. After a couple of blows,
the natives believed that they had killed her. One bent down, in an
attempt to scalp her.

But as our amazon felt herself so seized, she at once recovered her senses, raised herself and, more fierce than ever, caught hold of this monster so forcibly by a place which modesty forbids us to mention that he could not free himself. He beat her with his hatchet over the head, but she maintained her hold steadily until once again she fell unconscious to the earth, and so allowed this Iroquois to flee as fast as he could, that being all he thought of for the moment.[38]

Over the years in their pursuit of the Hurons, the Iroquois massacred several French families. Others were taken prisoner. French captives were often, but not always, tortured before being killed. Over half of the French taken prisoner by the Iroquois were freed, escaped, or remained willingly with their captors.[39] One prisoner of the Iroquois was a French girl named Jeanne Baillargeon. The child was captured when she was four years old and kept prisoner for nine years. During that time, she had come to live and think like her captors. So much so that, when she was released, she was afraid of returning to the French. She came out of the woods only upon the insistence of one of the nuns. The Marquis de Tracy, Commander of the Carignan-Salières regiment, was responsible for obtaining her release and he gave her money for a dowry upon her marriage. However, first she needed to re-learn French ways, a task willingly undertaken by the Ursulines.[40]

Marie de l'Incarnation commented that generally the Amerindians left French women alone. She would declare that she was more in fear of dying from lack of provisions than from the natives: "To speak with you, frankly, the difficulty of getting the necessities of life and of clothing will be the reason for leaving, if we leave – rather than the Iroquois."[41] Even so, the threat of an Iroquois attack weighed heavily upon the settlers. Not all were as courageous as Mother Marie and Martine Messier.

To the newly arrived Governor Rémy de Courcelle and the Marquis de Tracy fell the task of eliminating the Iroquois threat. Upon arrival in the colony in the summer of 1665, the soldiers of the

Carignan-Salières regiment were put to work in the construction of three forts on the Richelieu River. Two more would be constructed the following year. These fortifications were to serve as defensive outposts, as the Richelieu River was the principal route taken by Iroquois raiding parties. In the summer of 1666, the French met with representatives of all five of the Iroquois nations; however, efforts to negotiate a peace failed. At the end of September in 1666, Courcelle and Tracy organized an expedition of thirteen hundred men and marched south of the St. Lawrence River into Mohawk country. Upon seeing the strength of the French army, most of these Iroquois panicked and abandoned their villages. Although no battles were fought, the native settlements were destroyed. The expedition took seven weeks and covered nine hundred miles. When the soldiers returned to Quebec, they were given a hero's welcome by the jubilant French citizens. The Iroquois, who for twenty-five years had menaced French settlers, traders, and missionaries, as well as the Huron and Algonquin tribes, were sufficiently chastised in their own country. Following the defeat of the Iroquois in 1666, the French colonists would enjoy some eighteen years of relative peace.[42]

Although native assaults on the colonists lasted half a century, some would argue that they were less terrible than the constant warfare in France during the same time. The French settlers were generally not the main target of native warfare. The Iroquois were fighting to control the fur trade. Their most savage and cruel attacks were directed at the natives who supplied the French with furs rather than directly at the colonists.[43]

The Carignan-Salières military expedition had a two-fold mission. In addition to providing protection for the colonists, it was hoped that the men would stay, marry, and establish families. Many did just that, taking advantage of financial incentives offered by the King. Some four hundred officers and soldiers, about one third of the Carignan-Salières Regiment, remained and settled in the colony, generally becoming traders or farmers. Many of these married the *filles du roi* who had been sent to New France for the explicit purpose of marrying and increasing the population. The Carignan-Salières regiment was in the New World just a short time, returning to France in 1667 and 1668. In 1669, Louis XIV would order the Governor of New France to organize a militia for the protection of all the country.[44]

CHAPTER EIGHTEEN
JUNE OF 1675

———❧❧❧———

Hélène and Noël put their affairs in order and help their children to become established; A summary of Quebec and the colony in 1675; Accomplishments of the religious institutions; Civil government and Intendant Talon's legacy; Power struggles; Neighbors in the Upper Town; Only a few Amerindians to be found in the French settlements; Explorations; Deaths of Hélène and Noël; Hélène's legacy

It is likely that the victories of the Carignan-Salières soldiers, followed by the establishment of a militia for all of New France in 1669, helped to convince Noël Morin that it was now safe to establish homesteads on his seigneury on the south shore of the St. Lawrence.[1] Owners of arrière-fiefs or sub-seigneuries were required to pay *foi et hommage* to the owner of the larger seigneury. Accordingly, on November 12 of 1671, Noël rendered faith and homage to Louis Couillard de Lespinay, owner of the seigneurie de la Rivière-du-sud, of which Noël's fief St-Luc was a part.[2] On June 4, 1672, Louis XIV issued another ordinance requiring all uncleared seigneurial land to be returned to the royal domain.[3] Certainly this measure provided more incentive for Morin and other landowners to develop their property. On August 22, 1672, Noël granted a parcel of land within the fief to his son Alphonse. At the same time, he gave another parcel to his son-in-law Guillaume Fournier. In 1673 and 1674, he would grant land at St-Luc to Jean Prou, Jean Ballie, and Michel Isabel.[4] On February 25, 1668, he sold a parcel of land located on the outskirts of Quebec to his son Jean-Baptiste.[5] Notarial records from the civil archives of Quebec indicate that Noël also included his daughters in the distribution of his assets.[6]

Noël was advancing in age and wanted to make sure that each of his children was provided with land or equivalent monetary compensation. In the French colony, just as in the mother country, much attention was paid to the transfer of property from one generation to the next. Families in New France were large and parents wrestled with the challenge of dividing their land among the many children. Having property of a sufficient size was key to establishing a viable farm. French law stipulated that all legitimate children should inherit a portion of the property. Under the Coutume de Paris, the eldest son would inherit the manor house and half the land. The rest of the property was divided equally among the remaining children. Parents needed to expend considerable effort to ensure that the farm was not divided into parcels too small to support a family. After a couple of generations and without sufficient foresight, the family land might indeed be minutely divided. The Intendants and the Sovereign Council of early Quebec handled hundreds of disagreements involving boundary lines and other property issues. Those who could afford to do so worked to acquire large holdings of land to ensure that each child was given a farm of sufficient size to support a new family. If resources were limited, a son might be apprenticed to a craftsman to learn a trade or be forced to find employment as a day laborer.[7]

Parents also used the transfer of land to guarantee their care and security in their old age when they were no longer able to work. In what was known as the *pension alimentaire*, elderly parents would give the farm to one of their children, often a younger child, in return for their material support until their deaths. Sometimes, to ensure equality among the children, this youngest child was required to pay a sum of money to each of his or her siblings upon receipt of the family farm.[8] Now that Hélène and Noël were getting older, they wanted to make sure that there was someone to care for them in their old age. On January 4, 1671, the couple signed an agreement giving their household possessions and farm animals to their sons Alphonse and Charles on the condition that they care for their parents until their death.[9] Alphonse was twenty-one at the time and Charles, just sixteen. However, life doesn't always go as planned: Charles died on October 4 of that year.

Three of Hélène and Noël's children, Agnés, Jean-Baptiste, and Marie-Madeleine, along with their spouses, established homes and raised their families in Quebec City.[10] Alphonse would establish his home at Montmagny. So did Françoise, Hélène's daughter by her first marriage. Louise Morin would move to Château-Richer with her husband. Sister Marie Morin remained with the Hospitallers of Montreal for the rest of her life. Germain Morin, ordained a priest in 1665, would serve in a number of communities along the St. Lawrence River, but eventually returned to Quebec.[11]

Evidently Noël and Hélène chose to stay in Quebec. Noël continued to practice his trade as cartwright, at least through 1673. On June 15 of that year, he agreed to make twenty-four wheeled cannon mountings for the artillery of Quebec at the request of Charles Legardeur and François Prévost. These men were representing Governor Frontenac who had arrived in New France in 1672. Noël would be paid forty *livres* for each mounting.[12] Between 1671 and 1674, Hélène's name continued to appear as godmother or midwife in the baptism records of Notre-Dame de Quebec.[13]

One can just imagine the changes in Quebec witnessed by Hélène over the years. By 1675, Quebec was an infant city. Beyond it, toward the east and the west, were a series of communities firmly established on both sides of the St. Lawrence River.[14] This was in stark contrast to Quebec's inauspicious beginnings. In 1608, the year of Quebec's founding, there were twenty-eight men who spent the winter with Samuel de Champlain. When Hélène was born twelve years later, in 1620, there were only sixty French. In 1627, there were one hundred colonists in all of New France. In a letter written in 1669, Mother Marie de l'Incarnation would recall that when she first came to Quebec thirty years earlier there were only a few homes. The little colony was surrounded by an immense forest and a great many natives.[15]

In the seventeenth century, between 10,000 and 14,000 French would emigrate to the New World. Most of these immigrants did not originate from the poorest sections of France and many came from the cities. In the seventeenth century, the western and central provinces of France, those situated to the north of the Loire River, provided the majority of French colonists. One third of the settlers came from Normandy and the Paris area. However, two-thirds of the immigrants would return home. Less than four thousand remained to form the core of the French population in New France. There was little financial incentive to emigrate or to stay in the colony. France didn't need to import agricultural products. While there was a market for furs, a large French force was not needed to prepare the pelts for shipment to France. This resulted in little demand for French laborers in the fur trade.[16]

The royal policies to increase population had been, in large measure, successful. In 1666, the population of New France was 3,215. Seven years later, in 1673, the population of New France had doubled to 7,600.[17] The census of 1681 would identify a population of close to ten thousand in the colony.[18] Three-fourths of the French who would immigrate to New France came before 1680. From that date on, the population increased through natural growth, rather than from any significant immigration. The last group of *filles du roi* had arrived in 1673. The number of female immigrants to Canada dwindled greatly after 1679. However, in contrast to many male immigrants, the majority of women who made the journey to the New World remained. They crossed the Atlantic with the intention of marrying and settling in the new colony. Women who had married and produced children were less disposed to leave the country.[19]

By 1675, there were few Amerindians to be found in Quebec. In the first seventy years of the colony, the missionaries had been minimally successful in their attempts at evangelization of the native population and at conversion of the aborigines to the French way of doing things. In truth, each absorbed little from the other culture. The French borrowed from the natives birch bark canoes, snow-shoes, toboggans, moccasins, corn, and tobacco. Native people borrowed from the French copper kettles, metal tools, firearms, clothing, and blankets, as well as a love of bread and alcohol. They did not see themselves as inferior to European immigrants. They valued their personal freedom and independence. They were proud of their fortitude in adversity and their survival skills in a harsh environment.[20]

The Récollet missionary Le Clercq would report in 1691 that natives appeared at the French settlements each year with their furs in their canoes, eager to trade. However, they showed little interest in the Christian faith, attending services only to show some respect for the French leaders. At the time of his writing, LeClerq observed that none of the indigenous people were living among the French Canadians, but only in neighboring villages. They were following their native ways. The only signs of the Christian religion were the chanting of prayers, hymns, and observance of some of the religious ceremonies of the French. Over the course of the years, there had been many baptisms of dying infants and sick adults, but few conversions of healthy adults. Christianity required that the natives reject many of their own traditions. The missionaries were unable to claim large numbers of converts to Christianity.[21]

Another observer of colonization in the Americas provided an apt description of the Native American attitude towards Christianity:

> Those who entered a mission generally did so because it seemed to be the best way to obtain a specific goal: food in times of drought or in the face of a landscape so changed that it could not produce the traditional resources; the promise of health when unknown diseases were ravaging traditional communities; the hope of security that might come from alignment with the obviously well-armed soldiers; or the help of a powerful deity in times of distress and confusion. Once at the missions, the [Amerindians] often grafted a Christian surface onto their ancient ways and created their own forms of syncretistic Christianity.[22]

By 1675, agriculture and commerce in the colony were well-launched. In addition, a defense system, a legal structure, religious institutions, and administration by the French monarchy were in place. The Upper Town, built on the cliff above the St. Lawrence River, had become the seat of the religious and administrative establishments. Situated here were the Cathedral of Notre-Dame, the Bishop's Seminary, the Jesuit College,[23] Fort Saint-Louis, and the Château Saint-Louis, the last being the Governor's residence. Also in the Upper Town were the Hôtel Dieu run by the Augustinian Sisters, as well as the Ursuline Convent and School for Girls.[24]

Although the framework for governing the colony was in place, this doesn't mean that religious and civic affairs went smoothly. Controversy and conflict accompanied many of the decisions made by the community's leaders. Powerful positions brought big egos; petty rivalries often interfered with the business at hand. At the very least, there were strong opinions and disagreements on almost everything. Quebec was still a small community. If residents weren't actually participating in the political arena, they had front-row seats. Conversations around the hearth might have been just as heated as the contents of the pot hung above the fire.

The Lower Town and its port remained the market place for the colony. Ships brought manufactured goods from Europe and carried away furs and some lumber. Here, the settlers bartered or bought what they needed to sustain them through the year: goods that were beyond what they themselves could produce. One of the proprietors in the Lower Town was Charles Aubert de la Chesnaye, a fur trader and leading merchant in seventeenth-century New France. His store was stocked with goods worth 50,000 *livres*.[25] One can imagine that all sorts of prized items could be found in the barrels and crates that filled his shop. There would be fine imports from France, as well as local products. As the years went by, agriculture was to assume an ever greater role in the economy of New France. Produce from the farms was consumed by the family or traded for needed goods in the neighborhood. Surpluses were also consumed by the colony's tradesmen, the elite, and the religious communities.[26]

The judicial system of Quebec at this time consisted of the Sovereign Council which had been created in 1663 and the royal courts at Quebec, Montreal, and Trois-Rivières. The Sovereign Council served mainly as an appeals court for civil decisions and criminal punishment issued by the royal court. Its membership consisted of the governor, the intendant, the bishop, and five councilors. Royal courts judged both civil disputes and criminal cases. Debt recovery and disputes over property and seigneurial dues made up about ninety-eight percent of the activity in Quebec. For the most part, those who used the system were the merchants, artisans, and landed members of the colony.[27]

In 1674, Monsignor François de Montmorency Laval was made the first bishop of New France.[28] Msgr. Laval had arrived in 1658, some fifteen years earlier. Prior to his becoming bishop, he had served as Apostolic Vicar in the New World. The Church of Notre-Dame de Quebec, built in the Upper Town of Quebec in 1647, became the first parish church in New France in 1664. When Laval became bishop, the Church of Notre-Dame de Quebec, as the residence of the bishop, became the first Cathedral in New France.[29]

From the beginning, Laval's appointment to New France was controversial. He would soon be involved in many of the colony's social as well as religious issues.[30] The most serious issue that Bishop Laval faced upon his arrival in New France was the controversy over the sale of alcohol to the natives. There was also conflict between the French monarchy and the religious authorities in France on one hand, and the Pope and Papal authority in Rome on the other, over who had the ultimate authority over the missionaries and religious institutions in New France. The nuns were not anxious to submit to the authority of Laval. They had arrived twenty years earlier and wanted to manage their own affairs. The religious who had come to New France were men and women of uncommon vitality and character who held strong convictions. Those halfhearted in the practice of their religion and more interested in worldly comforts had stayed behind in France. An equally determined and strong-willed man, Monsignor Laval set out to control all religious matters in the colony, including those of the Jesuits and the nuns. His goal was to consolidate religious power in New France under his person.[31]

Prior to Laval's arrival, the Jesuit missionaries had ministered to the spiritual needs of the French. Laval wanted a community of secular priests who would serve the French settlements as parish priests and who would be supervised by the Bishop of Quebec. Toward this end, he founded the Seminary of Quebec on March 26, 1663, under an ordinance published in Paris and confirmed by the King. Laval's Seminary was built on the grounds of Louis Hébert's homestead.[32] It was established to provide training for parish priests in ministering to the spiritual needs of the growing colony. The revenue needed to support the seminary and parish churches would come from tithing. Laval was to clash with the civil authorities and colonists over the amount of the tithe to be paid to the church by the *habitants*. In 1663, as a result of complaints from the colonists, tithing was set at one-twentieth of the harvest; Laval had wanted it to be one-thirteenth.[33]

Under Laval's leadership, the number of parishes grew from five in 1659 to thirty-five in 1688. Prior to that time, the missionary chapels served the colonists as well as the natives. In the colony, the number of priests had increased from 24 to 102, including 13 priests born in the New World. In 1659, there were 32 nuns; by 1688, there were just under 100 nuns, 50 of them native to New France.[34] In Quebec, there was no lack of individuals devoted to the spiritual needs of the colony. The census taken in 1681 revealed that in the city of Quebec itself twelve percent of the population were priests, nuns, or people employed by the religious institutions.[35] In large measure, it was the work of the Ursulines and Jesuits that preserved French culture and the amenities of a civilized society in New France.

The Confraternity of the Holy Family was founded in 1663 to increase religious piety and devotion in the French-Canadian households. Men received spiritual guidance from the priests. The Ladies of Piety ministered to the women. This devotion, inaugurated by Madame d'Ailleboust and officially recognized by Bishop Laval, would also play a role in promoting strong religious conviction and practice among the French Canadians.[36]

Since their arrival in 1639, the Ursulines had worked indefatigably in Quebec, doing what they could to educate and evangelize the often restless native children as well as the children of the French settlers. They learned the native languages and shared their food and lodging with the poor and the sick. By 1669, the Ursuline Monastery had twenty-two religious living in the Cloister and regularly twenty to thirty boarders at the School. The French brought their daughters from as far away as sixty leagues (some 180 miles). There were also day pupils from the Upper and Lower Town.[37] The French families gave the nuns 120 *livres* for board or the equivalent "in-kind" contributions. In 1646, Mother Marie would note that, for the board of one of her young students, she received three and one half cords of firewood in January and another four cords in March, along with a pot of butter weighing twelve *livres*. In November, the family delivered a fat pig, one barrel of peas, and one barrel of salted eel.[38] The native girls enjoyed free board, living and studying with the French girls. Marie observed that the indigenous, who dearly loved their children, believed that they were doing the nuns a favor in handing over their little ones to be educated in the French way. Marie wrote in 1668 that they did not always have the resources to accommodate everyone who came to their doors. She noted that she had needed to refuse seven Algonquin boarders because of the lack of food and supplies. Some French girls also had to be returned to their families. In 1672, Mother Marie de l'Incarnation died after a bout of hepatitis, having spent the last thirty-three years of her life in Quebec. Mother Marie is considered to be the founder of the first school for girls in North America.[39]

From the beginning, Marie de l'Incarnation had included needlework in the instruction of the girls. In addition to learning their catechism, reading, writing, and arithmetic, the girls were taught "*les ouvrages de goût*": fine sewing, embroidery, lace-making, and possibly painting. Marie Lemaire arrived in New France to join the Ursulines on September 19, 1671. She had been born in 1641, the daughter of a bourgeois merchant family living in the Saint Germain-l'Auxerrois district of Paris. This district was known in the seventeenth century for the number of its residents who excelled in the art of embroidery. In her childhood, Marie spent a lot of time in the workshops of the embroiderers and developed some skill in the art. At the boarding school in the Ursuline Convent of the Faubourg Saint-Jacques, she refined her techniques in embroidery.[40] Under the tutelage of Mother Marie Lemaire, nuns and students at Quebec produced beautiful work. In mastering the art of embroidery, the girls needed to develop skills in composition and dexterity, as well as a knowledge of drawing, engraving, painting, and sculpture. Many of the nuns found great satisfaction in making beautiful altar cloths. Some also learned to make lovely beaded collars. The nuns produced a collection of richly decorated embroidered pieces which graced the Monastery chapel, as well as the altars of the other chapels and churches of New France. Tapestries were woven in threads of gold and silver, as well as reds, blues, and other rich colors. The Ursuline nuns were to note that the skills and talents exhibited by the girls after they left the Ursuline School were evidence of the quality of the education they received at this institution.[41]

By the last quarter of the seventeenth century, the hospitals run by religious orders in Montreal and Quebec City were well established. These institutions had a better reputation than those in France. People who were sick when they disembarked from the ships were immediately taken to the hospital. Efforts were made to contain diseases and limit their spread in the colony.[42]

The early settlers of New France who had survived the challenges of life along the St. Lawrence River were reaching the autumn of their lives. They were beginning to die of the infirmities of old age. In January of 1668, Jean Bourdon died at his home in Quebec at the age of sixty-seven; he had suffered from gout for a number of years.[43] Guillaume Couillard, Hélène's brother-in-law, had died five years earlier in 1663. He was survived by his wife, Guillemette Hébert, daughter of Quebec's first farmer. Guillemette would spend the last years of her life as a boarder at the Hôtel-Dieu. Over the years, she and her husband had donated a sizeable amount of their property to the various religious institutions of Quebec. In 1666, she sold property which contained the original Hébert homestead in the Upper Town to Bishop Laval for his "petite seminary"; this was done over the objections of her offspring.[44] Guillemette would die in October of 1684, at the age of seventy-six. She was the mother of ten children, seven of whom married. At the time of her death, Guillemette already had 143 descendants.[45] Her body was buried under the chapel of the Hôtel-Dieu, next to that of her husband. Abraham Martin, Hélène's uncle, died in September of 1664. Five months later, in February of 1665, his widow, Marguerite Langlois, would marry René Branch. Marguerite died in December of 1665, some ten months after her second marriage. Although their dates of birth are unknown, Marguerite would have been at least sixty; Abraham's age is estimated to be about seventy-five.[46]

Robert Giffard, a long-time friend of Hélène and Noël, died at his seigneury at Beauport on April 14, 1668, at the age of eighty-one. He had spent his last thirty-four years in New France. This man, so esteemed in the community, was the first surgeon of the Hôtel-Dieu, established in Quebec in 1639. Giffard was a devout Catholic. He held the position of church warden at the parish of Quebec in 1645. Bishop Laval, along with other clerics, attended his funeral. Giffard and his wife, Marie Renouard, were the parents of six children. In addition to the daughter who became a nun, there were three other daughters who grew to adulthood, married, and provided descendants. However, Giffard's name died out in the colony, as his son Joseph left no issue and his other son returned to France.[47]

In 1675, Quebec's economy was still based on the export of furs. Early merchants had relied on natives for the labor involved in collecting and transporting pelts to the storehouses in Quebec and other trading posts. Since 1650, the greatly diminished Huron population no longer served as intermediaries in the transport of furs to the markets. In the *Jesuit Relations* of 1644, it was noted that whereas in the past three to four hundred native canoes showed up for the trading fair, now a mere twenty or thirty canoes appeared.[48] The situation had not improved over the years. Frenchmen, who came to be known as *coureurs de bois*, assumed this role of purchasing and transporting the furs.[49]

Many men in the colony found the life of a *coureur de bois* more appealing than a life spent cultivating the land. It offered adventure, independence, the possibility of wealth, and freedom from the responsibilities of marriage and family. One can see that it might be a more attractive option, especially for the soldiers with the Carignan-Salières regiment who were already an independent group of men. Intendant Talon had offered incentives to the soldiers to stay and marry. Those who remained single faced forfeiture of hunting and fishing privileges. In 1672, Talon forbade anyone from entering the woods without a license from the Governor or the Intendant. Apparently, his efforts were largely a failure. Talon would soon bemoan the fact that so many men were stealing away to the forests and living like the natives. They behaved like bandits: plying the natives with alcohol and stealing their furs when they got drunk.[50] Marie de l'Incarnation would comment that it was easier for a Frenchman to follow the native ways than for the Amerindians to become French.[51]

The Comte de Frontenac had arrived as governor of the colony in the summer of 1672.[52] He was another controversial figure in the small colony. Frontenac had been born to a noble family and, when he was not serving his country as a soldier, he and his wife resided among the royalty of Paris. The man had a reputation in France for extravagance and vanity. He was not used to sharing power. In Quebec, he had to contend with the Sovereign Council, the Intendant, and the Bishop. Frontenac clashed with Bishop Laval over the sale of liquor to the aborigines. He sided with the merchants in their belief that liquor was needed to do business in the fur trade; otherwise, the natives would take their pelts to the English and Dutch. He was an ambitious man and supported previous efforts to expand the French fur trade to the west. To that end, he had a number of forts built in the region of the Great Lakes. Frontenac turned to the settlers to supply the labor; taxes from the seigneurs and *habitants* provided the funds. These actions did not endear him either to the farmers or the merchants, who felt that the governor might become too involved in the fur trade.[53]

As the native population decreased, French settlements spread west. The *coureurs de bois,* the first to travel inland, were soon followed by farmers. France's population in the New World was concentrated along the St. Lawrence River. However its holdings extended from the Gulf of St. Lawrence to the Gulf of Mexico. French fur traders were active as far west as the Ohio Valley.[54] The French were competing with the English: both wanted to expand their possessions in the New World. In addition to profiting from the fur trade, the French also held onto the dream of finding a route to China. Quebec, under the leadership of Intendant Talon, would continue to be a starting point for further exploration of the New World.[55]

One of the colony's most esteemed explorers was a good friend of Hélène and Noël. Louis Jolliet, born in Quebec in September of 1645, was the talented son of Jean Jolliet, a wheelwright who was employed by the Company of One Hundred Associates. His mother, Marie d'Abancourt, was the godmother of Germain Morin, Hélène and Noël's oldest son.[56] The fact that Noël Morin and Jean Jolliet were both wheelwrights might have drawn the two families together. Louis and Germain were classmates at the Jesuit College at Quebec. Louis had entered the college at the age of eleven. There, he studied philosophy, defending a thesis in that discipline in the summer of 1666. The young man was also quite musical and became the first organist at Notre-Dame de Quebec, where he played the organ for many years. Jolliet was initially interested in becoming a priest and took the minor orders on August 19, 1662. Apparently, Louis decided the priesthood was not for him, as he left the seminary five years later. By 1668, Jolliet was embarking on a career as a fur trader, business man, and explorer. This was at a time when the French were very interested in extending their holdings in the New World in order to further develop commercial interests. The French had heard from the natives of a beautiful river to the west, one that was long, wide, and deep, but they didn't know where it ended. They wondered if this mighty Mississippi, as it came to be known, was the fabled route to China.[57]

Louis Jolliet was chosen by Intendant Talon to embark on a voyage to find the mouth of the river. In May of 1673, Jolliet, accompanied by the Jesuit priest Jacques Marquette, set out to explore the Mississippi River. The expedition, composed of seven men in two canoes, left the mission of Saint-Ignace on Lake Michigan. The canoes carrying the Frenchmen traveled many miles beyond known territory to enter the Mississippi River on June 15. From there they advanced along the river some 450 miles until they reached the village of the Quapaw natives. Increasing hostility from the aborigines and the possibility that they might be captured by the Spanish forced them to stop there. Before returning home, they ascertained that the river emptied into the Gulf of Mexico. By the fall of 1675, Louis Jolliet had returned to Quebec. He married Claire-Françoise Byssot and resumed his business in the fur trade. However, he continued to explore and map other territory. He died in the summer of 1700, internationally acclaimed for his exploration of the Mississippi River.[58]

The French who came to the New World and established a home there lived longer than the general population of France. This was due to a number of factors. The men and women sent to the colony by the crown or the trading companies were carefully selected. Those who were allowed to emigrate were generally individuals in good shape, mentally and physically. Those found to be sick, crippled or otherwise unfit were not allowed to emigrate. The hazards of a trip across the Atlantic also eliminated weaker individuals. It is estimated that nearly ten percent of the passengers died during the ocean crossing and never reached the New World. Life was not easy in the wilderness along the St. Lawrence River. Those who did not adapt well to the harsh climate, the isolation, and the other hardships of New France usually returned to France once their service contracts had ended. Only the sturdiest and most courageous of individuals stayed to populate the land.[59]

On June 24, 1675, Hélène died in the land of her birth; she was fifty-five years old. Hélène's death and burial were not recorded in the parish church records of the province of Quebec. Instead, the date of Hélène's death is known by an annotation in the Register of the Confraternity of the Holy Family, established in Quebec some ten years earlier.[60] She last appears in the church archives of Quebec on February 18, 1674. In this record, Hélène is listed as present for the baptism and burial of the newborn child of Jean Soulard and Catherine Boutet.[61] She was in all probability there in the capacity of midwife as well as a friend. Catherine was the daughter of Martin Boutet, their neighbor on the outskirts of the Upper Town.

In spite of an earlier arrangement made in 1671 with his sons Alphonse and Charles regarding his care in his old age, Noël decided to retire to the home of his son Jean-Baptiste after his wife's death. On October 30, 1675, Noël entered into an agreement whereby this son would provide food and lodging for his father. The initial recompense was rather complicated. In a document executed on December 4 of that year, it was decided that Noël would pay a pension of 200 *livres* a year for six years for a total of 1200 *livres*. There are notarial records indicating that Noël paid the pension through 1678. On November 1, 1675, four months after Hélène's death, Noël Morin, with the agreement of all of his children, sold his holdings on the côteau Sainte-Geneviève on the outskirts of the Upper Town to Charles Bazire, one of the city's chief merchants. The house, barn, stable, and garden, along with fifty-eight *arpents* (fifty acres) of land, were sold for three thousand *livres*.[62] At some point, Noël either moved to or was visiting in the home of his son Alphonse at St-Thomas de la Riviere-du-Sud in Montmagny. Parish records note that Noël Morin, *ancien habitant de ce pays*, died there on February 10, 1680 and was buried in Quebec five days later, in the presence of his son Jean-Baptiste and his son-in-law Gilles Ragout. His age at death was listed as seventy-four.[63]

There is no doubt that Hélène was among the leading citizens of the colony in the seventeenth century. Although of more humble backgrounds than many, the Morins mingled with the most prominent figures in Quebec. Hélène was a respected *sage-femme* and an esteemed member of the church community. She and her husband raised their children to be responsible citizens. Hélène was undoubtedly strong in body and in spirit. Born in Champlain's Habitation in 1620, she survived nine years in the tiny settlement that was little more than a trading post.[64] Following the capture of Quebec by the English in 1629, Hélène lived five years in France and endured two dangerous ocean crossings. She returned to Quebec and spent the last forty years of her life in the Upper Town or on its outskirts, where she survived bitterly cold winters, insufficient food, fires, a big earthquake, epidemics of disease, and periodic threats from the Iroquois. There were many times when the continued existence of the little colony was in jeopardy.

The early settlers were encouraged by both religious and civil authorities to have large families; their descendants, in turn, would also have large families. Women growing up in the colony were often married in their early teens; they were healthy and fertile. The average number of children and grand-children for each couple was thirty-six.[65] Hélène, first French child to be born and survive in New France, produced fifteen children from her two marriages and had seventy grandchildren.[66] Serving as *sage-femme* and godmother, she had welcomed into the New World many other French infants. Hélène had certainly done her part in peopling the French settlements of the St. Lawrence River valley. She had given one daughter to the convent and a son to the priesthood. Hélène embodied the qualities that Champlain and the King sought in the women of the New World. As much as anyone, she earned her place on the plaque located in Montmorency Park in Quebec City which lists the pioneer settlers of the city.

In 1759, the course of Canadian history was changed with a twenty-minute battle fought on the Plains of Abraham, an area just outside the walls of Vieux Quebec in the Upper Town. As a result of this battle, New France came under British rule. However, down through the centuries to the present day, the French-Canadians have held fast to their language, their culture, their traditions and, to a lesser extent, their religion. With so many progeny, Hélène's impact on the future of her beloved settlement at Quebec is undeniable.

CHAPTER NINETEEN

THE NEXT GENERATION

———— ❧ ————

Hélène's first marriage was to Guillaume Hébert, son of Louis Hébert and Marie Rollet. Guillaume was born in Paris, Île-de-France, and immigrated to New France as a young child, along with his parents in 1617. He died on September 23, 1639, leaving nineteen-year-old Hélène a widow with three young children. Two would marry and produce fifteen children.

The children of Hélène Desportes and Guillaume Hébert[1]

1. **Joseph Hébert** was baptized on November 3, 1636. Charles de Montmagny, the governor of the small colony at the time, was his godfather. His grandmother, Marie Rollet, was his godmother. On October 12, 1660, Joseph married Marie Charlotte Depoitiers, the daughter of Pierre Charles Depoitiers Buisson and Hélène de Belleau. A year later, Joseph was captured, tortured, and murdered by Iroquois. The actual date of his death in the fall of 1661 is unknown. Joseph, the only child of Joseph and Marie Charlotte, was born on October 15, 1661. It is quite possible that Joseph might never have met his son. Presumably, this child died young, as there is only a baptism record for him. After her husband's death, Marie Charlotte remained in the household of Hélène and Noël for several years. She, but not her son, is listed with the other members of the household in the census record of 1666. Marie Charlotte married Simon Lefebvre Angers

on January 11, 1667. Father Germain Morin, her brother-in-law by her first marriage, performed the ceremony. Marie Charlotte would remain close to the Hébert/Morin family. In 1697, Marie Charlotte's son Louis, the oldest of her eight children, would marry Anne Félicité Bonhomme, the daughter of Agnés Morin, her former sister-in-law.

2. **Françoise Hébert** was baptized on January 23, 1638. Her godparents were Guillaume Hubou and Guillemette Hébert. She was thirteen when she married Guillaume Fournier on November 20, 1651. When she was fifteen, her first child was born. In the census of 1667, the family was listed as living in the nearby village of Charlesbourg.[2] The couple had fourteen children, all but the last one born in Quebec. By 1679, the family had moved to the settlement of Montmagny. Eleven of the children grew to adulthood and married. Two died as infants. The fate of the last child, born in Montmagny in 1679, is unknown. It seems that, in her later years, Françoise followed in her mother's footsteps as midwife, at least as far as providing emergency baptisms for infants in danger of dying shortly after birth. Although she is never listed as "*sage-femme*," she is listed as having baptized a couple of infants on their baptism records in the parish records of Montmagny. Françoise died on March 16, 1716, at the age of 78 and was buried at Montmagny.[3] On her burial record is the notation that her husband Guillaume was the founder of the church at Montmagny. There are a number of records in the civil archives of Quebec where Guillaume is listed as a litigant. Apparently there were more than a few disagreements between neighbors. Françoise lived in Montmagny for the last 37 years of her life. Many of her living children also settled in Montmagny.

3. **Angélique Hébert** was baptized on August 2, 1639. Her godparents were Olivier Le Tardif and Marguerite Langlois, the child's great-aunt. Angélique was just six weeks old when her father died. On October 29, 1639, she was named in a document signed by Governor Montmagny appointing a guardian for the minor chil-

dren of Guillaume Hébert. Presumably she died before she was five, as there is another document in the Quebec civil archives, dated October 7, 1644, concerning the sale of land on behalf of Joseph and Françoise Hébert, minor children of Guillaume Hébert. Angélique is not mentioned.

In late December of 1639, three months after the death of her first husband, Hélène contracted to marry Noël Morin, a cartwright. The marriage took place on January 9, 1640. Hélène had twelve children over a period of just fifteen years with Noël: six boys and six girls. Five of these children married and produced a total of fifty-five children. Hélène and Noël's oldest son Germain became a priest. Their daughter Marie would join the Hospitallers of Montreal. Three of Hélène and Noël's children died before adulthood and one died as a young, unmarried adult. There is a baptism record for another child, but no further record. Presumably she also died as a child.

The Children of Hélène Desportes and Noël Morin[4]

1. **Agnés Morin** was born and baptized on January 21, 1641. Her godparents were Marie Giffard and Louis Houel. Agnés married Nicolas Gaudry dit Bourbonnière on November 17, 1653 at the age of twelve. Their first child was born when she was fifteen. She and Nicolas had eight children together. Nicolas died in June of 1669, leaving Agnés a widow at the age of twenty-eight. A year and a half later, on January 12, 1671, Agnés married Ignace Bonhomme Beaupré. With this man, she had nine more children. In the civil archives of Quebec is a communication dated December 5, 1678 from the Deputy Attorney General to the Attorney General of the Provost of Quebec regarding the case of "Agnés Morin, wife of Ignace Bonhomme, accused of uttering insulting words against the Governor." Agnés had delivered her thirteenth child six weeks earlier and one can imagine that she might have felt harassed and ill-disposed. Agnés had two husbands and seventeen children before she died on August 30, 1687, at the age of forty-six. Agnés' signature appears on some baptism records,

indicating that she had a basic education, one can assume at the hands of the Ursulines of Quebec.

2. **Germain Morin** was the first native-born French-Canadian priest. Baptized on January 15, 1642, he was the second child and oldest son of Hélène and Noël. His godmother was Marie d'Abancourt Lacaille, the mother of Louis Jolliet, the man who would become a famous French explorer. Germain's godfather was Germain Legardeur. Germain was living in the Jesuit College as early as November of 1659 and was ordained a priest on September 19, 1665, at the age of twenty-three. Father Germain Morin baptized Françoise Laberge on January 28, 1666 in Château-Richer. This is the first instance in the church records where he is listed as the officiating priest. In the census of 1667, Germain was living with the other Jesuit fathers in Quebec. Also listed as residing in the seminary were Louis Jolliet, whose occupation is given as "clerk," and Charles Amador Martin, Germain's cousin once-removed. Charles became the second native-born French-Canadian priest. It must have been with special joy that Father Germain officiated at family events. In April of 1666, he baptized his sister Agnés' baby in Quebec City. In 1667, Germain officiated at the wedding in Quebec of Marie Charlotte Depoitiers, the widow of Germain's half-brother Joseph Hébert. Germain Morin served for a time as Secretary for Monsignor Laval in Quebec. In his capacity as diocesan clerk, he was responsible for maintaining the official church registers. He later served as missionary priest for the parishes of Pointe-aux-Trembles, Château-Richer, Sainte-Anne de Beaupré, Champlain, Repentigny, and others. On September 20, 1697, he was appointed Canon of the Quebec chapter. Germain died at the Hôtel Dieu in Quebec on August 20, 1702, and was buried inside the choir of the Cathedral of Quebec. His age is listed as sixty years, seven months and six days.[5]

3. **Louise Morin** was baptized on April 27, 1643. Marguerite Couillard and Antoine Taboureau were her godparents. At the age of sixteen, she married Charles Cloutier in a ceremony in Quebec on April 20, 1659. Three years later, the young family moved to

Château-Richer, where they established their home and spent the remainder of their lives. Louise and Charles had twelve children: eight girls and four boys. Significantly, none of these children died in infancy or childhood. All of them grew to adulthood and nine of them married. Louise followed in her mother's footsteps as a midwife. She is listed as a *sage-femme* on the death record of the infant of Jean Gagnon, born in Château-Richer in 1691. Louise died in 1713 at the age of seventy and was buried in Château-Richer.

4. **Nicolas Morin** was baptized on April 26, 1644. His godparents were Nicolas Maquart and Marie Le Barbier. He was confirmed in Quebec with two of his brothers in 1659. There is a record in the archives of Quebec that, on February 24, 1663, Jérôme Lalemant, the Jesuit Superior, granted Nicolas Morin a parcel of land situated on the côteau Sainte-Geneviève along the route Saint-Michel within the seigneurie of Sillery.[6] He is listed as twenty-two years old in the census records of 1666 and living in the household of his parents in the Comté de Quebec. There is no mention of him in the census of 1667. On February 26, 1668, Noël sold the land of his "late son Nicolas" for 250 *livres*.[7] Although there is no death or burial record, the above records indicate that he died sometime between 1666 and early 1667, at the age of twenty-two.

5. **Jean-Baptiste Morin Rochebelle** was baptized on May 25, 1645. His godparents were Jean Bourdon and Marie Langlois, the spouse of Jean Juchereau. On October 18, 1667, twenty-two-year-old Jean-Baptiste signed a contract to marry Marie-Ann Firman, a girl who had arrived from Dieppe, France, as one of the *filles du roi*. The couple did not marry though and Marie-Ann returned to France. A month later, on November 22, 1667, Jean-Baptiste, now using the surname Morin dit Rochebelle, married Catherine de Belleau, another of the *filles du roi*, in a ceremony attended by the governor of the colony, Daniel de Rémy de Courcelle. Catherine de Belleau was the daughter of François de Belleau and Anne de Breda of Evéché d'Amiens in Picardie, France and a cousin

of Marie Charlotte Depoitiers, who had married Jean-Baptiste's half-brother Joseph Hébert in 1660. Jean-Baptiste is listed as *habitant* of the Comté de Quebec on the census of 1667. Again, he uses the name Morin De Belle Roche or Rochebelle. He probably chose this name to distinguish himself from another colonist also named Jean-Baptiste Morin. In 1668, he purchased a parcel of land on the route of St. Michel on the outskirts of Quebec from his father for 250 *livres*.[8] On various records, including the baptism record of Marie Madeline Boucher in 1692, Jean-Baptiste is listed as a bourgeois.[9] Jean-Baptiste and Catherine had only two children. The first, a daughter named Marie, was born on January 1, 1672. Marie's god-parents were Marie Charlotte Depoitiers and Governor Daniel de Rémy de Courcelle. This child died and was buried on January 26, before she was one month old. Jean-Baptiste and Catherine had a second child Marie-Anne born on July 31, 1675. She grew up and married Jacques Pinguet Beaucour, with whom she had ten children. Jean-Baptiste died in Quebec on December 12, 1694, at the age of forty-nine. He is listed in the records of the Hôtel Dieu the previous month, so it is possible that he had been sick for some period of time.

6. **Marguerite Morin** was baptized on September 29, 1646. Her godparents were Abraham Martin and Marguerite Martin Racine. The infant died three weeks later and was buried on October 17, 1646.

7. **Hélène Morin** was baptized on September 30, 1647. Noël Pinguet and Hélène Martin, the wife of Médard Chouart, the Sieur de Groseillers, were her godparents. She died on May 10, 1661, at the age of thirteen.

8. **Marie Morin** was born and baptized on March 19, 1649. Her godparents were Governor Louis D'Ailleboust and Marie-Madeleine Legardeur, the spouse of Jean-Paul Godefroy. In 1659, as a ten-year-old boarding student with the Ursulines of Quebec, she made the acquaintance of Jeanne Mance and Marguerite Bourgeoys who were returning from France and stopped briefly

on their way to Montreal. They must have spoken highly of the Hôtel-Dieu in their city. Three years later, Marie left her native Quebec to join the Hospitallers in Montreal as a novice nun. On March 20, 1665, she took her first vows. Her solemn permanent vows were professed on October 27, 1671. Sister Marie Morin became the first Canadian-born girl to become a Hospitaller of Montreal. Marie served her community as Mother Superior of the Convent on two different occasions: from September 3, 1693 to September 3, 1696, and from July 9, 1708 to July 9, 1711. She was also the author of the *Annales de l'Hôtel Dieu*. She died in Montreal on April 8, 1730 at the age of eighty-one, after a long illness.[10]

9. **Alphonse Morin Valcourt** was born on December 12, 1650 and baptized the following day. His godparents were Guillaume Odoart de St-Germain and Marguerite Besnard. On February 10, 1670, Alphonse, age twenty, married Marie-Madeleine Normand, the daughter of Jean-Baptiste Normand and Catherine Pageau. Marie-Madeleine had come to Quebec as one of the *filles du roi*. They married in Quebec and their oldest children were born there. By 1675, the family had settled in Montmagny, on the south side of the St. Lawrence River. At the baptism of their son Joseph in 1675, Alphonse and Marie-Madeleine were listed as living in Riviere-de-la-Caille, Montmagny and Alphonse was using the surname Morin Valcour (Valcourt). A total of eleven children would be born to the couple. However, Alphonse would suffer the loss of four family members within six months in 1690. His wife Marie-Madeleine died on April 27, 1690 in Montmagny. On May 2, five days after her death, their newborn son Charles died. In June, their three-year-old son Louis died, followed by eight-year-old Marie-Madeleine in September. Two years later, on November 24, 1692, Alphonse married Angélique Destroismaisons at Cap St-Ignace. This couple had four children, all born in Montmagny, but the oldest and the youngest died before they were a month old. Alphonse himself died on August 29, 1711, two weeks before his last child, a little girl named Hélène, was born. With his two wives, Alphonse fathered fifteen children.

10. **Noël Morin** was baptized on October 12, 1652. His godmother was Françoise Pinguet, spouse of Pierre de Launay. A godfather is not listed. No other record of this child of Hélène and Noël exists. It is presumed that he died sometime in childhood, as he is not listed in the census record of 1666.

11. **Charles Morin** was born on August 29, 1654, and baptized the following day. His godparents were Charles D'Ailleboust De Mousseaux and Marie Bourdon, the wife of Jean Gloria. Charles died on October 4, 1671, at the age of seventeen. No details of his death have survived.

12. **Marie-Madeleine Morin**, the last of Hélène's children, was born on December 28, 1656. She was baptized the following day. Her godparents were Jean Madry, a surgeon, and Jacquette Vivier, the spouse of Jean Normand. On May 29, 1673, at the age of sixteen, she married Gilles Rageot (Rajotte). Gilles, born in Orne, France, had come to Quebec ten years earlier and initially worked as clerk of the registry of the Sovereign Council. In 1666, in addition to being court clerk, he was given the position of Royal Notary by Intendant Talon. This commission was confirmed in a document signed by Louis XIV on May 17, 1675. Thus, Gilles Rageot became the first Royal Notary in New France. The couple settled in Quebec and had nine children, eight boys and one girl, between 1674 and 1692. Gilles Rageot died on January 3, 1692, at the age of fifty. His youngest child, his only daughter, was born a month later. Marie-Madeleine, at the age of thirty-six, was left a widow with seven children to raise. Two of their sons had died in childhood. Three sons, Charles, Nicolas, and François, followed in their father's footsteps and became court clerks and notaries. Two sons, Philippe and Jean-Baptiste, became priests. The youngest son became a successful businessman. Only four of the children married: their daughter and three sons.[11] Marie-Madeleine never remarried and died in Quebec on July 21, 1720, at the age of sixty-four, twenty-eight years after the death of her husband.

ENDNOTES

Chapter One

1   Hélène's baptism record does not appear in the church records of Quebec.
    If it ever existed, it might well have been lost in the fire that destroyed
    Notre-Dame-de-la-Recouvrance on June 4, 1640 (Tanguay, *À Travers
    les Registres*, 25). Her date and place of birth are based on other records.
    Champlain and his wife, Hélène Boullé, arrived in Quebec in late July of
    1620. Champlain's wife was chosen godmother of the newborn infant so
    presumably Hélène Desportes was born in Quebec after that date. In the
    census record of 1666 for the Comté of Quebec, Hélène's age is listed as
    46. This would support a birth year of 1620. However, the following year,
    on the census record of 1667 for Comté of Quebec, Hélène's age is given
    as 48. At her Confirmation on August 10, 1659, her age was recorded as
    38. Based on these surviving records, it appears that the date of "1620, in
    the second half of the year" comes as close to the truth as any. Tanguay
    came to much the same conclusion, listing her date of birth as "1620" in
    his *Dictionnaire Genealogique des Familles Canadiennes*, 302. Hélène's place of
    birth has been determined to be Quebec because on the marriage contract
    between Hélène and her second husband Noël Morin, dated December 27,
    1639, she is listed as a native of the parish of Notre-Dame-De-La-Recou-
    vrance in Quebec. Noël is listed as a native of the parish of St. Etienne in
    Brie-Comte-Robert, France. This last document is found in the *Parchemin –
    Banque de données notariales (1626-1789), Bibliothèque et Archives nationales du
    Québec* (BAnQ).

2   Quebec was not the only seventeenth-century European settlement in North
    America. In 1607, the English founded a colony at Jamestown, Virginia.
    This was to become the first permanent English settlement in America. In
    1620, Plymouth Colony, Massachusetts became the second permanent Eng-
    lish settlement in America. Farther to the south were the Spanish colonies.
    Christopher Columbus, an Italian sailor sponsored by King Ferdinand and
    Queen Isabella of Spain, landed in the Bahamas on October 12, of 1492.
    The following year, in 1493, Columbus established the first European colony
    in America with the Spanish settlement of Isabela on the northern coast

of the island of Hispaniola. (This part of the island is now known as the Dominican Republic.) In 1521, Hernán Cortés, another Spaniard, conquered Mexico. In 1565, the Spaniards established St. Augustine, Florida, the oldest city in what is now the United States. The Spanish were firmly planted on the soil of South America by the end of the sixteenth century.

3   Trudel, *Introduction to New France*, 8-9. Historians maintain that the Venetian John Cabot sailed for America under the English flag in 1497. The Portuguese Corte-Real brothers were in the North Atlantic in 1501 and 1502.

4   Dickinson and Young, *A Short History of Quebec, 14;* Trudel, *Introduction to New France*, 9, 21.

5   Slafter, "Memoir of Samuel de Champlain," 105-6.

6   Trudel, *Introduction to New France*, 14.

7   Dickinson and Young, *A Short History of Quebec*, 14-18, 71.

8   Dickinson and Young, *A Short History of Quebec*, 14-18.

9   Trudel, *Introduction to New France*, 3-22.

10 Champlain, *Voyages of Samuel de Champlain*, ed. Slafter, II:183-84; Trudel, *Introduction to New France*, 14-19. Cartier made three trips to the St. Lawrence River Valley: in 1534, 1535, and 1541.

11 Slafter, "Memoir of Samuel de Champlain," 30-31.

12 *Jesuit Relations*, ed. Thwaites, IV: 256-58. These trading companies are described in the Notes section of this volume.

13 *Jesuit Relations*, ed. Thwaites, IV: 256. (Notes section)

14 Slafter, "Memoir of Samuel de Champlain," 28-78.

15 Champlain, *Voyages of Samuel de Champlain*, ed. Slafter, II: 163-64.

16 Champlain, *Voyages of Samuel de Champlain*, ed. Slafter, II: 174-76.

17 Charbonneau et al., *The First French Canadians: Pioneers in the St. Lawrence Valley*, 18.

18 Champlain, *Voyages of Samuel de Champlain*, ed. Slafter, II:182-83.

[19] Champlain, *Voyages of Samuel de Champlain*, ed. Slafter, II:197-99.

[20] Slafter, "Memoir of Samuel de Champlain," 147; Champlain and Sagard, as quoted in Tanguay, *À Travers les Registres, 9.* Tanguay states that 6 people arrived that year.

[21] Slafter, "Memoir of Samuel de Champlain," 147. Fischer, *Champlain's Dream*, 369-371. Both authors state that Champlain and his party left Tadoussac for Quebec on July 11; neither give an exact date for Champlain's arrival in Quebec. Apparently that date is not known. Tanguay lists only the year of their arrival (Tanguay, *À Travers les Registres*, 9).

[22] Germe, "Champlain (De), Samuel." *Fichier Origine Database.*

[23] Slafter, "Memoir of Samuel de Champlain," 104-5; Trudel, "Champlain, Samuel De"; Fischer, *Champlain's Dream*, 287-88. The Church of Saint-Germaine dates back to the 12th century and is still standing at the beginning of the 21st century. It is located near the Louvre in the center of Paris. When the Louvre was the Royal Palace, this was the parish church of the king. Church services were attended by royalty, as well as courtesans and local artisans. (Sacred Destinations, Web 29 Sept 2011)

[24] Fischer, *Champlain's Dream*, 287-88; Slafter, "Memoir of Samuel de Champlain," 105.

[25] Slafter, "Memoir of Samuel de Champlain," 105.

[26] Fischer, *Champlain's Dream*, 352-53. Little is known of their personal affairs. Champlain did not discuss his private life in his writings.

[27] Trudel, "Champlain, Samuel De," *Dictionary of Canadian Biography Online.*

[28] Slafter, "Memoir of Samuel de Champlain," 147. This was not Eustache's first trip to Quebec; he had originally come to the colony in 1618 (Tanguay, *À Travers les Registres*, 8).

[29] Macouin, "Hébert, Louis," *Fichier Origine Database.*

[30] Bennett, "Hébert, Louis," *Dictionary of Canadian Biography Online.*

[31] Champlain, *Voyages of Samuel de Champlain*, ed. Slafter, II: 174.

[32] Bennett, "Hébert, Louis," *Dictionary of Canadian Biography Online.*

33   Tanguay, *À Travers les Registres*, 8; Champlain, *Voyages of Samuel de Champlain*, ed. Slafter, III: 203.

34   "Even the most prosperous streets in the central part of the city were no more than muddy tracks and only the wealthiest Parisians were able to cross the city, on horseback or in one of the few working carriages, without being covered in muck and excrement. . . . For the visitor new to the city, the most striking aspect of this dereliction was the stench from stagnant or flooded sewage systems. . . . Houses and streets were alive with rats and almost as many Parisians died from plague or other diseases as from violent conflict during the three decades of civil war" (Hussey, *Paris: The Secret History*, 137).

35   Pinkard, *A Revolution in Taste: The Rise of French Cuisine, 1650–1800*, 51-52; Hussey, *Paris: The Secret History*, 137.

36   Tanguay, *À Travers les Registres*, 9; Moreau-Desharnais, "Langlois, François" and "Martin/L'Ecossais, Abraham." *Fichier Origine Database*.

37   Hayes, *Historical Atlas of Canada*, 24, 26. Concerning sixteenth and seventeenth-century exploration of lands across the Atlantic, Hayes notes "Kings may grant permission for such voyages, but it was the merchants of places such as Dieppe and Bristol who paid for them!"(26)

38   Tanguay, *À Travers les Registres*, 19.

39   Tanguay, *À Travers les Registres*, 8-9.

40   Hélène Desportes is identified as the godchild of Champlain's wife in Champlain's will, completed in 1635.

41   Tanguay, *À Travers les Registres*, 9.

42   Récollets, also spelled Recollects, were of the order of Reformed Franciscans (Le Clercq, *First Establishment of the Faith in New France*, I:6).

43   Champlain, *Voyages of Samuel de Champlain*, ed. Slafter, III:104-6.

44   Champlain, *The Works of Samuel de Champlain*, ed. Biggar, IV: 352-56; Tanguay, *À Travers les Registres*, 9-11; Fischer, *Champlain's Dream*, 369.

45   Slafter, "Memoir of Samuel de Champlain," 147-48.

[46]   Champlain, *The Works of Samuel de Champlain*, ed. Biggar, IV: 352-56.

[47]   Champlain, *The Works of Samuel de Champlain*, ed. Biggar, IV: 352-56.

Chapter Two

[1]   *Programme de recherche en démographie historique (PRDH) Genealogical Database*, Marriage Record # 66317. The marriage was witnessed by Samuel de Champlain and Eustache Boullé; Tanguay, *À Travers Les Registres*,10.

[2]   There is a baptism record in the church records of Quebec for Eustache Martin, dated October 24, 1621. He is listed as the son of Abraham Martin and Marguerite Langlois. Eustache Boullé, was his godfather. (Source: *Programme de recherche en démographie historique Genealogical Database*, Baptism record 57096) No further record of Eustache Martin exists, so that it is assumed that he died. The birth and death of the newborn infant of Abraham Martin is also listed in Tanguay, *À Travers les Registres*, 10.

[3]   *Jesuit Relations*, ed. Thwaites, IV: 267-68 (Notes section).

[4]   *Jesuit Relations*, ed. Thwaites, VI: 49.

[5]   The chapel, Notre-Dame-des-Anges established by the Récollets on the banks of the St. Charles River in 1620, was taken over by the Jesuits when the Récollets were not allowed to return to Quebec in 1632 (Le Clercq, *First Establishment of the Faith in New France*, 327-28; Sulte, Fryer, and David, *A History of Quebec*, 37).

[6]   Labine, *Histoire des Premiers Travaux des Péres Récollets en la Nouvelle France, 1615-1629*. 61-63. Sagard, quoted in Labine, was the colony's first religious historian, publishing his *L'Histoire du Canada* in 1636.

[7]   Champlain, *Voyages of Samuel de Champlain*, ed. Slafter, III: 1-8, 105-06.

[8]   Champlain, *Voyages of Samuel de Champlain*, ed. Slafter, II: 193, 198; Champlain, *The Works of Samuel de Champlain*, ed. Biggar, IV: 62.

[9]   Bennett, "Hébert, Louis," *Dictionary of Canadian Biography Online*.

[10]   Champlain, *The Works of Samuel de Champlain*, ed. Biggar, IV: 352-56.

[11]   *Jesuit Relations*, ed. Thwaites, V: 35,37.

12   Forty thousand years ago, tribes crossed the Bering Strait from Asia to North America. At the end of an Ice Age 10,000 years ago, the natives spread south and east, across North and South America, following herds of caribou, moose, deer, and other game. Three thousand years ago, tribes settled in the region around Quebec. (Dickinson and Young, *A Short History of Quebec*, 4)

13   Champlain, *Voyages of Samuel de Champlain*, ed. Slafter, II: 175, 186-88; Trudel, *Introduction to New France*, 15-16.

14   Trudel, *Introduction to New France*, 25-26; Dickinson and Young, *A Short History of Quebec*, 6-7.

15   Champlain, *Voyages of Samuel de Champlain*, ed. Slafter, III:168.

16   *Jesuit Relations*, ed. Thwaites, V:105.

17   Goubert, Pierre. *The French Peasantry in the Seventeenth Century*, 52-53.

18   *Jesuit Relations*, ed. Thwaites, V:211.

19   Dickinson and Young, *A Short History of Quebec*, 7.

20   Trudel, *Introduction to New France*, 27, 29.

21   Trudel, *Introduction to New France*, 27, 29; *Jesuit Relations*, ed. Thwaites, XV:153.

22   Champlain, *Voyages of Samuel de Champlain*, ed. Slafter, III: 160-61. A fathom measures six feet in length. Years later, Father LeJeune would have occasion to visit two Huron villages where the missionaries had established a post. In one of the villages he noted that there were eighty cabins; in the other, forty. He described their cabins as being made of large sheets of tree bark and constructed in the shape of an arbor, long, high, and wide. LeJeune gives much smaller dimensions for the Huron cabins than Champlain. According to him, the cabins were as much as seventy feet long. There were five fireplaces in each cabin. One cabin could house as many as ten families, two at each fire pit. (*Jesuit Relations*, ed. Thwaites, XV:151,153)

23   Champlain, *The Works of Samuel de Champlain*, ed. Biggar, VI: 244.

24   *Jesuit Relations*, ed. Thwaites, XV:151.

[25] Trudel, *Introduction to New France*, 29; Simpson, *Marguerite Bourgeoys and Montréal, 1640-1665*, 84.

[26] The horse made its first appearance in New France in June of 1647 as a gift to Governor Charles Huault Montmagny. (Gagnon, *Le Fort et Le Château Saint-Louis*, 233) This is more than 100 years after the Spanish first brought horses to the New World. In 1519, the Spanish conquistador Hernán Cortés landed in what is now Mexico with thirteen horses. These animals astonished and frightened the natives who had never before seen such beasts.

[27] The canoes and the native mode of travel are described in a number of places in the writings of Champlain and the Jesuits, including the following: Champlain, *Voyages of Samuel de Champlain*, ed. Slafter, II:167; *Jesuit Relations*, ed. Thwaites, IV:205; XV:149. (Note that a pace is equal to one natural step, about 30 inches long.)

[28] Champlain, *Voyages of Samuel de Champlain*, ed. Slafter, III:143 (footnote).

[29] Champlain, *Voyages of Samuel de Champlain*, ed. Slafter, II:191.

[30] *Jesuit Relations*, ed. Thwaites, XV: 149; Dickinson and Young. *A Short History of Quebec*, 17-20.

[31] Tooker, *An Ethnography of the Huron Indians, 1615-1649*, 26-27.

[32] *Jesuit Relations*, ed. Thwaites, V: 239.

[33] *Jesuit Relations*, ed. Thwaites, V:183-85.

[34] Dickinson and Young, *A Short History of Quebec*, 17.

[35] Dickinson and Young, *A Short History of Quebec*, 17-18; Trudel, *Introduction to New France*, 194.

[36] Dickinson and Young, *A Short History of Quebec*, 12.

[37] *Jesuit Relations*, ed. Thwaites, IV: 207; Dickinson and Young, *A Short History of Quebec*, 17-18; Trudel, *Introduction to New France*, 194-95. In the *Jesuit Relations*, the number of pelts collected each year was reported to be between 12,000 and 15,000.

[38] *Jesuit Relations*, ed. Thwaites, IV: 256-8, 267-68 (Notes section).

39 Le Clercq, *First Establishment of the Faith in New France*, I:164-167. Pierre Desportes signed the document as "Des Portes." The fact that his signature is on the document indicates that he was literate enough to sign his name and that he had some standing in the community.

Chapter Three

1 Tanguay, *À Travers les Registres*, 11-12.

2 *Programme de recherche en démographie historique (PRDH) Genealogical Database*, Baptism record # 57097. Godparents were Thierry Desdames and Marguerite Lesage. The Récollet Father Paul baptized the infant. Abraham Martin and Marguerite Langlois also gave birth to a son in 1621, whom they named Eustache, but the child died later that year (*Programme de recherche en démographie historique (PRDH) Genealogical Database*, Baptism record # 57096; Tanguay, *À Travers les Registres*, 10).

3 *Programme de recherche en démographie historique (PRDH) Genealogical Database*, Baptism record # 57098. Godparents were Émery De Caën and Marie Roolet (Rollet), the child's grandmother. Father Joseph LeCaron, Récollet, baptized the infant.

4 Children's clothes are described in Goubert, *The French Peasantry in the Seventeenth Century*, 53. The fashion of the era is also revealed in seventeenth-century paintings as found in Lewis, *The Splendid Century: Life in the France of Louis XIV*.

5 Tanguay, *À Travers les Registres*, 12. From Tadoussac, Champlain's party traveled to Gaspé where they formed a convoy of four ships and sailed for France. They arrived at Dieppe on the first of October and from there traveled on to Paris. (Fischer, *Champlain's Dream*, 583)

6 Hélène Boullé remained in Paris until after her husband's death (Shafter, "Memoir of Samuel de Champlain," 194).

7 Paul, "The Servants of God in Canada," *The Pilgrim of Our Lady of Martyrs*, 186-88.

8 Le Clercq, *First Establishment of the Faith in New France*, I:229-41; *Jesuit Relations*, ed. Thwaites, IV:258, 260.

9 *Jesuit Relations*, ed. Thwaites, IV:169,171; LeClercq, *First Establishment of the Faith in New France*, I:239, 282.

[10]   The Jesuit College of La Flèche was established in 1604 and was considered by some to be one of the most prestigious schools of higher learning in seventeenth-century Europe. One of its most illustrious students was the French philosopher René Descartes who attended the school from 1604 to 1612. Descartes was later to remark, "I was in one of the most famous schools in Europe" (Quoted in Haudrère, "Royal College de Flèche, Wellspring of Missionary Zeal"). The number of French missionaries to New France who attended the school included Charles Lalemant, Enemond Massé and Paul le Jeune, as well as François Montmorency de Laval, New France's first bishop. Laval was a resident of the college between 1631 and 1641. The school was notable in the numbers of its students and teachers who later served in the Americas. The Jesuit order sent 254 missionaries to New France between 1610 and 1760. Of that number, one fourth, or more than sixty men, were from the college. This is remarkable, given that La Fléche was one of forty-six Jesuit educational institutions in France in 1616. Education at the college was considered to be of the highest quality. It complied with orthodox Roman Catholic teaching and competed successfully with the Calvinist Academy located sixty kilometers away in Samur. (Haudrère, "Royal College de Flèche, Wellspring of Missionary Zeal")

[11]   Pouliot, Léon. "Lalemant, Charles," *Dictionary of Canadian Biography Online.*

[12]   Champlain, *Voyages of Samuel de Champlain*, ed. Slafter, III:166-67.

[13]   *Jesuit Relations*, ed. Thwaites, IV:205; V:23, 25; XV:153.

[14]   Champlain, *Voyages of Samuel de Champlain*, ed. Slafter, III:166-67; *Jesuit Relations*, ed. Thwaites, XV: 153.

[15]   Champlain, *Voyages of Samuel de Champlain*, ed. Slafter, III:166-67.

[16]   *Jesuit Relations*, ed. Thwaites, V:23; Trudel, *Introduction to New France*, 30, 195. Trudel notes that the Amerindians favored the woolen blankets made by the English in red, white or blue cloth, with an edging of black striping. This obliged the French traders to purchase at least some of their trading supplies from the English.

[17]   Champlain, *Voyages of Samuel de Champlain*, ed. Slafter, III:166-67; *Jesuit Relations*, ed. Thwaites, IV:23, 205.

[18]   *Jesuit Relations*, ed. Thwaites, V:23.

[19]   *Jesuit Relations*, ed. Thwaites, V:105.

20 *Jesuit Relations*, ed. Thwaites, V:105.

21 *Jesuit Relations*, ed. Thwaites, XV:153.

22 Champlain, *Voyages of Samuel de Champlain*, ed. Slafter, III: 167.

23 The only domesticated animal known to the natives of North America was the dog. The turkey had been domesticated in Mesoamerica. In the Andes Mountains of South America, the alpaca, the llama, the Muscovy duck, and the guinea pig had been domesticated. (Mann, *1491: New Revelations of the Americas Before Columbus*, 109)

24 *Jesuit Relations*, ed. Thwaites, VII:41-45.

25 *Jesuit Relations*, ed. Thwaites, IV:205.

26 Champlain, *Voyages of Samuel de Champlain*, ed. Slafter, III:167-68.

27 Champlain, *Voyages of Samuel de Champlain*, ed. Slafter, III:168.

28 *Jesuit Relations*, ed. Thwaites, V:133.

29 Dickinson and Young. *A Short History of Quebec*, 11-14.

30 *Jesuit Relations*, ed. Thwaites, V:105.

31 Champlain, *Voyages of Samuel de Champlain*, ed. Slafter, II:190.

32 Champlain, *Voyages of Samuel de Champlain*, ed. Slafter, III:38.

33 Champlain, *Voyages of Samuel de Champlain*, ed. Slafter, II:190.

34 Champlain, *Voyages of Samuel de Champlain*, ed. Slafter, II:191-92; *Jesuit Relations*, ed. Thwaites, IV:201.

35 Dickinson and Young. *A Short History of Quebec*, 12. The Jesuit Lalemant noted that the natives along the St. Lawrence River called the sun Jesus. Prior to the arrival of the French, the natives had been in contact with the Basques who probably acquainted them with some basic Christian beliefs and words. (*Jesuit Relations*, ed. Thwaites, IV:201)

36 "Because their spirituality commanded genuine respect for the welfare of other life forms, the native people can be seen as the first environmentalists" (Dickinson and Young. *A Short History of Quebec*,12).

[37]   *Jesuit Relations*, ed. Thwaites, XV:175-77.

[38]   Champlain, *Voyages of Samuel de Champlain*, ed. Slafter, II:192.

[39]   *Jesuit Relations*, ed. Thwaites, IV:203.

[40]   *Jesuit Relations*, ed. Thwaites, IV:221-23.

[41]   As quoted in Simpson, *Marguerite Bourgeoys and Montréal, 1640-1665*, 120.

Chapter Four

[1]   Fischer, *Champlain's Dream*, 398-400. According to Fischer, later excavations by Canadian archeologists have confirmed that this was the manner of construction; they found no evidence of stone fireplaces so they assume that the fireplaces were made of clay, common in peasant cottages of seventeenth-century Normandy.

[2]   Sulte, Fryer and David, *A History of Quebec*, 23.

[3]   At the beginning of the twenty-first century, the land in the Upper Town where Hébert established his homestead is the site occupied by the Basilica of Notre-Dame de Quebec and the seminary, as well as Hébert and Couillard streets (Bennett, "Hébert, Louis" *Dictionary of Canadian Biography Online*).

[4]   Bennett, "Hébert, Louis," *Dictionary of Canadian Biography Online*. The first fief entered on the Canadian Feudal Register was the fief of Saint Joseph. This land, which bordered the St. Charles River, was conceded by the Duke of Ventador to Louis Hébert, Sieur de l'Espinay, in 1626. (Garneau, *History of Canada*, 183)

[5]   An *arpent* of land is approximately 5/6 of an acre.

[6]   Labine, *Histoire des Premiers Travaux des Péres Récollets en la Nouvelle France, 1615-1629*, 45-63.

[7]   *Jesuit Relations*, ed. Thwaites, IV:217, XLVII:259; Le Clercq, *First Establishment of the Faith in New France*, I:282.

[8]   Goubert, *The French Peasantry in the Seventeenth Century*, 83-84.

[9]   Goubert, *The French Peasantry in the Seventeenth Century*, 86-87.

[10]   Dickinson and Young. *A Short History of Quebec*, 91.

11   *Jesuit Relations*, ed. Thwaites, IX:155.

12   A report prepared in 1637 reveals the type of food and the quantity eaten by Parisians in seventeenth-century France. It noted that "each week the city consumed an average of 86,400 bushels of wheat (almost 4,500,000 bushels a year), 900 head of cattle (at least 40,000 a year, allowing for Lent) and 8,000 head of sheep (358,000 a year). Other foodstuffs mentioned in the report included 4,200 veal calves a year (mostly consumed between Easter and Pentecost), 25,000 pigs, 1,456,000 dry or salted codfish, 18,200 salted mackerel, 23,600 white herrings, 360,000 red herrings, 108,350 salmon, and 240,000 muids of wine (about 72,000,000 gallons.) These figures probably did not include foodstuffs grown on land owned by Parisians outside the walls and brought into town for their own use nor the produce of the many kitchen gardens, cow pastures, hen houses, and vineyards that lay within the confines of the city itself." (Pinkard, *A Revolution in Taste: The Rise of French Cuisine*, 54)

13   Archeological findings at Champlain's Second Habitation, as presented in the little museum beneath Notre-Dame- des-Victoires at Place Royale in Quebec in 2012.

14   In his book, *1491: New Revelations of the Americas Before Columbus*, Mann noted that "Mesoamerica would deserve its place in the human pantheon if its inhabitants had only created maize, in terms of harvest weight the world's most important crop. But the inhabitants of Mexico and northern Central America also developed tomatoes, now basic to Italian cuisine; peppers, essential to Thai and Indian food; all the world's squashes (except for a few domesticated in the United States); and many of the beans on dinner plates around the world." (196-97)

15   Pinkard, *A Revolution in Taste: The Rise of French Cuisine*, 30-31.

16   As quoted in *Jesuit Relations*, ed. Thwaites, V:213.

17   Pinkard, *A Revolution in Taste: The Rise of French Cuisine*, 15-16. Nicolas de Bonnefons, the seventeenth-century author of the cookbook *Les Délices de la campagne*, dedicated his chapter on vegetables to the Capuchin monks, who consumed only plant foods and cultivated many of those selected for inclusion in his book.

18   Pinkard, *A Revolution in Taste: The Rise of French Cuisine, 1650 – 1800*, 36-37.

19   Pinkard, *A Revolution in Taste: The Rise of French Cuisine, 1650 – 1800*, 60-61, 77.

[20] Champlain, *Voyages of Samuel de Champlain*, ed. Slafter, III:204.

[21] Champlain, *The Works of Samuel de Champlain*, ed. Biggar, IV:49-51.

[22] *Jesuit Relations*, ed. Thwaites, VII:69-207.

[23] *Jesuit Relations*, ed. Thwaites, V:89.

[24] Modern maize developed in the southern part of Mexico more than six thousand years ago. Its cultivation spread throughout the Americas, halted only where the land was too dry or the climate too cold. By the seventeenth century, there were fields of maize, along with beans and squash, all along the coast of New England and in many places inland. (Mann, *1491: New Revelations of the Americas Before Columbus*, 218, 223-24)

[25] *Jesuit Relations*, ed. Thwaites, XV:155.

[26] Champlain, *Voyages of Samuel de Champlain*, ed. Slafter, III:162-64.

[27] *Jesuit Relations*, ed. Thwaites, XV:159, 161.

[28] *Jesuit Relations*, ed. Thwaites, XV:161.

[29] Champlain, *Voyages of Samuel de Champlain*, ed. Slafter, III:164.

[30] *Jesuit Relations*, ed. Thwaites, XV:157.

[31] *Jesuit Relations*, ed. Thwaites, IV:201.

[32] Champlain, *Voyages of Samuel de Champlain*, ed. Slafter, II:195.

[33] Champlain, *Voyages of Samuel de Champlain*, ed. Slafter, II:190, 194-95.

[34] *Jesuit Relations*, ed. Thwaites, XV:155.

Chapter Five

[1] Le Clercq, *First Establishment of the Faith in New France*, I:282-84; Laverdiere, *Samuel de Champlain*, 141-45.

[2] *Jesuit Relations*, ed. Thwaites, XV:153.

[3] Champlain, *Voyages of Samuel de Champlain*, ed. Slafter, I:285; *Jesuit Relations*, ed. Thwaites, IV:217.

[4] The practice of giving away or kidnapping young girls as recompense for crimes committed by an adult family member continues to exist in the twenty-first century. It appears to be deeply rooted and still flourishing in some of the more isolated tribal societies. In the Islamic world the practice is known as "baad," and although illegal, it is still used as a form of tribal justice in rural Afghanistan. In an article appearing in February of 2012 in *The New York Times*, the author reports on the kidnapping of an eight-year-old Afghan girl from a remote village in retaliation for the wrong-doing of an uncle. "The idea is that the giving of a girl to the aggrieved family as a de facto slave and having her marry a member of that family ties the two warring families together, so they are less likely to continue a blood feud. The practice also helps to compensate the family for the labor of a lost relative. And when the girl gives birth to children, the offspring are at least a symbolic replacement for the relative who has been lost." (Ruben, "In Punishment for Elder's Misdeeds, Afghan girl pays the price")

[5] Sagard, *Histoire du Canada*, 829; Le Clercq, *First Establishment of the Faith in New France*, I:283-84.

[6] *Parchemin Notarial Records (1626-1789)*, Bibliothèque et Archives nationales du Québec (BAnQ). Document of M. Piraube, Notary of Quebec, dated December 27, 1639. Guillemette Hébert witnessed the signing of the marriage contract between Hélène Desportes and Noël Morin. Her signature appears on this document.

[7] Mann, *1491: New Revelations of the Americas Before Columbus*, 46-7. Montagnais celebrations prior to engaging the Iroquois in war are described in Champlain, *Voyages of Samuel de Champlain*, ed. Slafter, I: 285.

[8] Champlain, *Voyages of Samuel de Champlain*, ed. Slafter, II:245.

[9] Champlain, *Voyages of Samuel de Champlain*, ed. Slafter, II:245.

[10] *Jesuit Relations*, ed. Thwaites, V: 27, 29, 31, 53.

[11] *Jesuit Relations*, ed. Thwaites, XXXVI:164.

[12] Dickinson and Young. *A Short History of Quebec*, 39.

[13] Miethe and Lu. *Punishment: A Comparative Historical Perspective*, 43-44.

[14] Champlain, *Voyages of Samuel de Champlain*, ed. Slafter, II:176-82.

15   Lewis, *The Splendid Century: Life in the France of Louis XIV*, 104-108.

16   Bosher, "View of France from La Rochelle," 3,8, 9.

17   *Jesuit Relations*, ed. Thwaites, IV: 256 (Notes section); Trudel, "Caën, Émery De" and "Caën, Guillaume De," *Dictionary of Canadian Biography Online*.

18   Trudel, "Caën, Guillaume De," *Dictionary of Canadian Biography Online*.

19   *Jesuit Relations*, ed. Thwaites, IV:267-68 (Notes section).

20   *Jesuit Relations*, ed. Thwaites, IV:259 (Notes section).

21   Trudel, "Caën, Guillaume De," *Dictionary of Canadian Biography Online*.

22   *Jesuit Relations*, ed. Thwaites, IV:227.

23   Slafter, "Memoir of Samuel de Champlain," 154-56; *Jesuit Relations*, ed. Thwaites, IV:257-58 (Notes section); Trudel, "Caën, Guillaume De," *Dictionary of Canadian Biography Online*.

24   Bosher, "View of France from La Rochelle," 15.

25   Fischer, *Champlain's Dream*, 404.

26   Slafter, "Memoir of Samuel de Champlain," 154-56; Fischer, *Champlain's Dream, 314*, 402-404.

27   *Jesuit Relations*, ed. Thwaites, IV:257-58 (Notes section); Slafter, "Memoir of Samuel de Champlain," 154-56. The ships that sailed in 1628 under the command of Claude de Roquemont, a member of the Company of One Hundred Associates, were intercepted by the English and never reached Quebec.

28   Tanguay, *À Travers les Registres*, 7-10, 13. On May 16, 1629, another French settler Guillaume Hubou married Marie Rollet, the widow of Louis Hébert. Champlain, a long-time close friend of Marie and her first husband, stood up for the couple. (*Programme de recherche en démographie historique (PRDH) Genealogical Database, Marriage Record # 66318*)

29   *Quebec Registers*, as noted by Tanguay, *À Travers les Registres*, 13. This daughter was named Hélène.

30   Tanguay, *À Travers les Registres*, 13.

[31] At the same time that all of New France numbered 100 colonists, Plymouth alone had a population of 200; Salem had a population of 100. Virginia at that point was the most successful of the colonies in North America. This colony had a population of 2,000 and was producing 500,000 pounds of tobacco a year. The English colonists found a ready market for their products in Europe. (Trudel, *Introduction to New France,* 42)

Chapter Six

[1] Tanguay, *À Travers les Registres,* 15.

[2] Champlain, *The Works of Samuel de Champlain,* ed. Biggar, VI:40-52.

[3] Champlain, *The Works of Samuel de Champlain,* ed. Biggar, VI:40-52.

[4] Tanguay, *À Travers les Registres,* 8. Tanguay records the arrival of the Hébert family in Quebec in 1617. The family was described as Louis, his wife, two daughters and *"un petite garçon."* Guillaume Hébert's exact age is unknown. His baptism record has not been found.

[5] Tanguay, *À Travers les Registres,* 3-16. According to Tanguay's records, in the twenty years since the founding of the colony in 1608, there had never been more than 85 French at the settlement of Quebec (Tanguay, À Travers les Registres, 19). Note: Every author's numbers vary a bit; Tanguay based his population figures on the information gained from the books and reports of Champlain, Sagard, Leclercq, *Jesuit Relations,* and the Church registers.

[6] Tanguay, *À Travers les Registres,* 15; Slafter, "Memoir of Samuel de Champlain," 160-65; Champlain, *The Works of Samuel de Champlain,* ed. Biggar, VI:27-29; Le Clercq, *First Establishment of the Faith in New France,* I:285-87.

[7] Le Clercq, *First Establishment of the Faith in New France,* I:290-91; Tanguay, *À Travers les Registres,* 15; Slafter, "Memoir of Samuel de Champlain," 160-65; Moir, "Kirke, Sir David," *Dictionary of Canadian Biography Online.*

[8] A shallop is a two-masted sailing vessel.

[9] Champlain, *The Works of Samuel de Champlain,* ed. Biggar, VI:26-27. Salt was valuable because it was used to preserve meat and fish.

[10] Champlain, *The Works of Samuel de Champlain,* ed. Biggar, VI:25.

11   Tanguay, *À Travers les Registres*,16; Champlain, *The Works of Samuel de Champlain*, ed. Biggar, VI:81-82.

12   Champlain, *The Works of Samuel de Champlain*, ed. Biggar, VI:52-55. On July 24, 1629, the French merchant Émery de Caën arrived in New France to get his furs. Champlain learned that the French had delayed in leaving France. Champlain bemoaned the fact that, if the French had left port earlier, they might have successfully avoided the English, and brought with them the supplies the French sorely needed to withstand the assault from the English. (Champlain, *The Works of Samuel de Champlain*, ed. Biggar, VI:74-97)

13   Champlain, *The Works of Samuel de Champlain*, ed. Biggar, VI:63-64.

14   Slafter, "Memoir of Samuel de Champlain," 161; Moir, "Kirke, Sir David," *Dictionary of Canadian Biography Online*.

15   Champlain, *The Works of Samuel de Champlain*, ed. Biggar, VI:52-82.

16   Champlain, *The Works of Samuel de Champlain*, ed. Biggar, VI:70-74.

17   Champlain, *The Works of Samuel de Champlain*, ed. Biggar, VI:74.

18   A number of earlier historians, including Tanguay (*À Travers les Registres*, 16-17) and Sulte, Fryer, and David (*A History of Quebec*, 30), believed that the families of Abraham Martin and Pierre Desportes remained in Quebec. It has only been in recent years that documents have been discovered placing both families in Dieppe, France during the years between 1629 and 1632.

19   Foi, the third Amerindian girl given to Champlain in 1627, had returned to her parents, according to the Récollet historian Sagard (Champlain, *The Works of Samuel de Champlain*, ed. Biggar, VI:51, footnote).

20   Champlain, *The Works of Samuel de Champlain*, ed. Biggar, VI:121.

21   Champlain, *The Works of Samuel de Champlain*, ed. Biggar, VI:122-23.

22   Le Clercq, *First Establishment of the Faith in New France*, I:306; Champlain, *The Works of Samuel de Champlain*, ed. Biggar, VI:142-44.

23   *Jesuit Relations*, ed. Thwaites, V:11-15; Simpson, Marguerite Bourgeoys and Montréal, 1640-1665,149-50; Brault, The French-Canadian Heritage in New England, 115.

24 Charbonneau et al., *The First French Canadians: Pioneers in the St. Lawrence Valley*, 171.

25 *Jesuit Relations*, ed. Thwaites, IV:264 (Notes section).

26 *Jesuit Relations*, ed. Thwaites, VIII:175.

27 *Jesuit Relations*, ed. Thwaites, IV:265 (Notes section).

28 Fischer, *Champlain's Dream*, 90.

29 Fischer, *Champlain's Dream*, 90; Durand-Gasselin, "Huguenot Pirates in the Seventeenth Century," *Musée Virtual Du Protestantisme Francais*.

30 Jesuit Relations, ed. Thwaites, IV:235-45.

31 Jesuit Relations, ed. Thwaites, IV:235-41.

32 Jesuit Relations, ed. Thwaites, IV:241.

33 Jesuit Relations, ed. Thwaites, IV:245.

34 Champlain, *The Works of Samuel de Champlain*, ed. Biggar, VI:144-45. In Le Clercq's accounting, the fleet of ships sailed for England on September 14, 1629 and arrived at Plymouth on the 18th of October. The French were taken from London to Calais on October 29. (*First Establishment of the Faith in New France*, I: 306) In his "Memoir of Samuel de Champlain," Slafter states that the fleet sailed for England about the middle of September and arrived in Plymouth on November 20 (171).

35 According to Tanguay, four families remained in Quebec after the surrender to the British in the summer of 1629: (1) Guillaume Hubou and Marie Rollet with Guillaume Hébert, son of Louis Hébert (deceased); (2) Guillaume Couillard and Guillemette Hébert with their children Louise, Marguerite, and Louis; (3) *Abraham Martin and Marguerite Langlois with their children Marguerite and Hélène. (They also had a girl named Ann, age 25, living with them.); (4) Pivert and his wife, Marguerite Lesage, a niece, and a young man. Others who remained were Adrien Duchesne (surgeon), Le Bailly, Etienne Brule, Nicolas Marsolet, Pierre Boyer (cartwright), LeBocq (carpenter), and Gros-Jean. Hélène Desportes and her parents are not mentioned. (Tanguay, *Through the Registers*, 16-17.) *Tanguay's work is incorrect. According to Bernadette Foisset and Gail Moreau-Desharnais in their research for the *Fichier Origine Database*, Abraham Martin and his family returned to France in 1629,

after the capture of Quebec by the Kirke brothers. Abraham's son Pierre was baptized in Dieppe in January 1630.

36   Moreau-Desharnais, "Exiles from Québec Found in the Parish of St-Jacques de Dieppe During the Kirke Occupation (1629-1632).''; Moreau-Desharnais, "Langlois, Françoise," and Foisset & Moreau-Desharnais, "Martin/ L'Ecossais, Abraham," *Fichier Origine Database*.

37   Hayes, *Canada: An Illustrated History,* 26; Hayes, *Historical Atlas,* x; Rider, *Short Breaks in Northern France,* 154-55.

38   The Dieppe citizen Jean Ango, a wealthy ship owner, funded many expeditions for trade and exploration in the sixteenth century. He became the city's richest man and is buried in the Church of Saint-Jacques in Dieppe. In the twenty-first century, he is a local hero and is commemorated in various ways about town. (Rider, *Short Breaks in Northern France,* 154)

39   Hayes, *Canada: An Illustrated History,* 26; Hayes, *Historical Atlas,* x; Rider, *Short Breaks in Northern France,* 154-55.

40   Hayes, *Canada: An Illustrated History,* 26; Hayes, *Historical Atlas,* x; Rider, *Short Breaks in Northern France,* 154-55; Trudel, *Introduction to New France,* 9.

41   The first horse to come to the colony was the one given to Governor Montmagny in 1647. In 1665, a dozen more horses arrived with the Carignan-Salières regiment. (Trudel, *Introduction to New France,* 207)

42   El Camino de Santiago, or the Way of Saint James, is a pilgrimage that has existed since the eleventh century, and perhaps earlier. By the twelfth century, it was an important part of the culture of Europe. In the Middle Ages, there were three important Christian pilgrimages: pilgrims traveled to Jerusalem, to Rome, or to Santiago de Compostela in northwestern Spain. A massive infrastructure was created to support pilgrims on their journey to Santiago. Roads were improved and bridges were built. Churches and hostels were established along the famous route. The popularity of the pilgrimage diminished in the centuries following its peak, but beginning in the late twentieth century, there has been a resurgence of interest in this pilgrimage.

43   Rider, *Short Breaks in Northern France,*150, 154-55. The population of Dieppe at the beginning of the 21st century is 35,000. Although its former grandeur has faded, the old harbor remains and fishermen still ply their trade. The massive stone gateway, the Porte des Tourelles, is all that is left of the walls that were built around the city in the fourteenth century. The thirteenth-cen-

tury Church of Saint-Rémy, the fifteenth-century Church of Saint-Jacques, and the castle complex built above the town in the fifteenth century (now the Château Musée) remain as historical landmarks. Although the weather is often cold and grey, Dieppe has the closest beach to Paris. In the nineteenth and twentieth centuries, this seaport town became a fashionable destination for Parisians. Many artists, including the likes of Monet, Pissarro, and Miró, were also drawn to Dieppe, drawing inspiration from its landscape, sea, and sky. Today, it has one of the better Saturday markets in all of Normandy. (Rider, *Short Breaks in Northern France,*150, 154-55)

Chapter Seven

1   It is not known for certain whether Hélène was among the French who returned with Champlain in 1633, or whether she came the following year with a group headed by Robert Giffard. Since her parents had died in France, it is assumed that Hélène returned with her uncle Abraham Martin and her aunt Marguerite Langlois. In the *Fichier Origine* record for Abraham Martin, it states that he returned to New France in 1633 with his wife and son Charles; however, no civil or church record has survived indicating exactly which year this couple returned. There is good reason to believe that Hélène returned in the summer of 1634. One indication may be found in the 1634 marriage record of Hélène and Guillaume. The witnesses to the marriage were Robert Giffard and Henri Pinguet. Since both Giffard and Pinguet arrived from France in 1634, it might well have been that Hélène had made their acquaintance on the ocean crossing. If she had arrived the previous year, she might well have chosen as witnesses other settlers with whom she was better acquainted. Also, as Léon Roy notes in his article, "Pierre Desportes et sa descendance," there were many more men than women in the small colony. A lot of pressure was placed on families to marry their girls at a young age. It was not unusual for girls in early Quebec to be married at the age of twelve or thirteen. This would suggest that if, in fact, Hélène had returned in the summer of 1633, she would have been married to Guillaume that fall, when she was thirteen years old.

2   *Programme de recherche en démographie historique (PRDH) Genealogical Database,* Marriage Record #66320; "Quebec, Catholic Parish Registers, 1621-1979" FamilySearch online, Notre-Dame de Quebec, 1621-1679, Image 128.

3   Champlain, *The Works of Samuel de Champlain,* ed. Biggar, VI:144-50.

4   Champlain, *The Works of Samuel de Champlain,* ed. Biggar, VI:72.

[5]   Moreau-Desharnais, "Exiles from Québec Found in the Parish of St-Jacques de Dieppe During the Kirke Occupation (1629-1632)."

[6]   Moreau-Desharnais, "Langlois, Françoise," *Fichier Origine Database*. Lisieux is 155 km. south of Dieppe, France.

[7]   Slafter, "Memoir of Samuel de Champlain," 176.

[8]   *Jesuit Relations*, ed. Thwaites, V:11.

[9]   *Jesuit Relations*, ed. Thwaites, V:11-21,39.

[10] *Jesuit Relations*, ed. Thwaites, V:39-43; Slafter, "Memoir of Samuel de Champlain," 178.

[11] *Jesuit Relations*, ed. Thwaites, V:39-45.

[12] Father Le Jeune was to remark in his *Relations* of 1632 that this was the only French family that had stayed in Quebec (*Jesuit Relations*, ed. Thwaites, V:41,43).

[13] Tanguay, *À Travers les Registres*, 18.

[14] *Jesuit Relations*, ed. Thwaites, V:41-43.

[15] Olivier served as a domestic in the household of Couillard until his death on May 10, 1654 at about the age of thirty. There is no record of other black slaves in New France until the end of the seventeenth century. However, enslaved Native Americans were reported in Montreal in 1670. Some Native American captives were held as slaves by other Native Americans or by their European conquerors (Winks, *The Blacks in Canada: A History*, 1-2). "Slavery was given its legal foundation in New France between 1689 and 1709 . . . Economic rather than social ends had shaped the conventional wisdom of the time. The fur trade required no skilled labor; it required no gang labor either. A full-blown slave system had not been needed, and although the Indians enslaved many of their captives, on occasion selling a pani (Indian) to work as a field hand or as a domestic servant for the French, there had been no economic base upon which slavery could profitably be built" (Winks, *The Blacks in Canada: A History*, 3).

[16] *Jesuit Relations*, ed. Thwaites, V: 63, 197, 199.

[17] The Récollet missionaries felt keenly their removal from the missions that they had founded in the New World. Récollet Father Christian Le Clercq,

writing in 1691, speaks bitterly about this matter. Their exclusion was presumed to be due to the fact that Cardinal Richelieu was known to favor the Jesuit order and oppose the Récollets. As Prime Minister and highest ranking member of the Company of One Hundred Associates, his word ruled. (Le Clercq, *First Establishment of the Faith in New France*, I:7)

[18] Le Clercq, *First Establishment of the Faith in New France*, I:327-28.

[19] *Jesuit Relations*, ed. Thwaites, V: 2 (Preface), 187, 189.

[20] No passenger lists of the voyages of 1633 have been found. It is not known for sure whether the returning colonists came back that year, accompanying Champlain, or in 1634.

[21] *Jesuit Relations*, ed. Thwaites, V:199-203.

[22] Champlain was present for the birth of Françoise Giffard, daughter of Robert Giffard and Marie Renouard on June 12, 1634. (*Programme de recherche en démographie historique (PRDH) Genealogical Database*, Baptism Record for Françoise Giffard)

[23] Provost, "Giffard de Moncel, Robert," *Dictionary of Canadian Biography Online*; Montagne, *Tourouvre et les Juchereau: Un chapitre de l'émigration percheronne au Canada*, 107; Sulte, Fryer, and David, *A History of Quebec*, 32.

[24] *Jesuit Relations*, ed. Thwaites, IV:261 (Notes section).

[25] The narrative detailing Le Jeune's winter with the Montagnais natives appears in the *Jesuit Relations* of 1634, published in Paris in 1635 (*Jesuit Relations*, ed. Thwaites, VII:69-207).

Chapter Eight

[1] *Jesuit Relations*, ed. Thwaites, IX:205.

[2] *Jesuit Relations*, ed. Thwaites, IX:205, 207.

[3] According to Trudel, this chapel was lost in the fire that destroyed Notre-Dame-de-la-Recouvrance as well as the Jesuit Residence in 1640. The chapel was rebuilt almost immediately. However, it is not mentioned in any records after 1664. The assumption is that any bodies buried beneath the chapel were moved and placed under the new church of Notre-Dame de Quebec. Work was done on the basement of this church in 1877, and apparently there is

now no possibility of confirming whether or not the remains of Champlain lie beneath the church. (Trudel, "Champlain, Samuel," *Dictionary of Canadian Biography Online*) In 1908, Sulte, David, and Fryer had also observed, "It is a lamentable fact that the resting place of the founder of Quebec and the first governor of Canada is not known with any degree of exactness. Assuming that he was placed in a vault within the church which he himself built to commemorate the recovery of the city (Notre-Dame-de-la-Recouvrance), and that the vault was not destroyed by the fire of 1640, it is conceivable that the foundation walls of the parish church which absorbed the old structure of Notre-Dame-de-la-Recouvrance, and out of which developed successively the cathedral, and the present basilica, may yet contain the remains of the immortal founder of the city." (Sulte, Fryer, and David, *History of Quebec*, 31)

4   The historian Trudel reports that there were only about 150 French settlers in the colony at the time of Champlain's death (Trudel, "Champlain, Samuel," *Dictionary of Canadian Biography Online*).

5   Champlain's godchildren and his wife's godchild are mentioned by name in Champlain's Last Will and Testament.

6   In his article on the birthplace of Champlain, the historian Marcel Fournier notes that Champlain identified himself as from Brouage in his writings in 1632. Champlain's father owned property in both Brouage and La Rochelle. There was no Protestant church in Brouage, so his parents would naturally have taken him to the one in La Rochelle if they had wanted him baptized in the Protestant faith. (Fournier. "Samuel de Champlain de Brouage ou de La Rochelle? – Les deux!") The historian Tanguay also notes that Champlain was born in Brouage, in Xaintonge, the child of Antoine de Champlain, a ship's captain, and Marguerite LeRoy. (Registers of Quebec, as quoted in Tanguay through the Registers, 25)

7   Until very recently Champlain's date of birth was unknown. In the spring of 2012, the French genealogist Jean-Marie Germe discovered Samuel de Champlain's baptism record in the register of the temple of Saint-Yon in La Rochelle. It gives the date of his baptism as August 13, 1574. It is presumed that he was born earlier in the year. On the document, the surname of Samuel's father is given as Chapeleau; it was not uncommon in that era for there to be variations in the spelling of surnames. (Fournier, "Samuel de Champlain de Brouage ou de La Rochelle?- Les deux!") Prior to the discovery of his baptism record, various authorities estimated Champlain's year of birth as between 1567 and 1580. They based their estimate on what was known of his life on the sea and his records of military service. It was assumed that

he undertook these activities after reaching maturity. (Slafter, "Memoirs of Champlain," 1-2; Fischer, *Champlain's Dream*, 21)

8   Slafter, "Memoirs of Champlain," 2-3.

9   Slafter, "Memoirs of Champlain," 3-13.

10   Slafter, "Memoirs of Champlain," 19-26.

11   Slafter, "Memoirs of Champlain," 26-28.

12   Quoted in Slafter, "Memoirs of Champlain," 10.

13   Champlain, *The Works of Samuel de Champlain*, ed. Biggar, VI:255.

14   Fischer, *Champlain's Dream*, 586. Trudel records twenty-one trips across the Atlantic, from 1603 onwards (Trudel, "Champlain, Samuel," *Dictionary of Canadian Biography Online*).

15   Slafter, "Memoirs of Champlain," 1-2.

16   Champlain, *The Works of Samuel de Champlain*, ed. Biggar, VI:268.

17   Champlain, *The Works of Samuel de Champlain*, ed. Biggar, VI:260.

18   Champlain represented the thinking of others of that era. Antonio De Ascención, a Carmelite priest who came to New Spain in 1597, wrote that "a ship captain should know how to command with love and authority and will treat each person as an individual. And be certain that this is a God-fearing man, one who keeps his own counsel, and someone who is not only zealous in his service to His Majesty, but also in matters relating to the conversion of souls." (Beebe, *Lands of Promise*, 49)

19   Champlain, *The Works of Samuel de Champlain*, ed. Biggar, VI:258.

20   Champlain received a copy of the document later that year, but it was after the English had seized the colony and Champlain had returned to France. (Champlain, *The Works of Samuel de Champlain*, ed. Biggar, VI:151-2.) Unfortunately, Champlain failed to receive any other official recognition from Cardinal Richelieu or Louis XIII for his life's work and accomplishments. He was never given a patent of nobility or a land grant, although others who settled in the New World would receive such honors. (Fischer, *Champlain's Dream*, 520-21)

21   Lake Champlain is in the United States, in upper Vermont and New York
      states.

22   Fischer, *Champlain's Dream*, 254-80; Trudel, "Champlain, Samuel," *Dictionary
      of Canadian Biography Online;* Sulte, Fryer, and David, *History of Quebec*, 15-16;
      Simpson, *Marguerite Bourgeoys and Montréal, 1640-1665,* 84.

23   Fiske, John. *New France and New England,* 57-58.

24   Slafter, "Memoirs of Champlain," 72-74 (Quoted material on 73).

25   According to historians Robert LeBlant and David Hackett Fisher, the
      will was discovered in August of 1959 by a conservator with the National
      Archives in Paris. However, historians were noting the existence of the will
      and its specifics at a much earlier date. Louise Paul refers to the will, the
      beneficiaries, the controversy surrounding the document, and the court deci-
      sion to nullify the will in her article on Hélène Boullé, which appeared in the
      monthly magazine *The Pilgrim of Our Lady of Martyrs* in 1905. (Paul, "The Ser-
      vants of God in Canada") N. E. Dionne, in *The Makers of Canada: Champlain,*
      published in 1905, also refers to details in Champlain's will.

26   Le Blant, Robert. "Le testament de Samuel Champlain, 17 novembre 1635."

27   Hélène Boullé entered the novitiate of the Ursulines in the Faubourg St-
      Jacques in Paris on November 7, 1645, ten years after Champlain's death.
      There she took the name of Sister Hélène of St. Augustin. In 1648, she
      established a convent of the same order in Meaux, France, bringing with her
      a dowry of 20,000 *livres*, assistants, and some furnishings. As the foundress
      of the convent, she was allowed certain privileges, including a higher quality
      of food and exemption from attending some of the longer prayer services.
      Hélène lived for 6 years at the Convent in Meaux, dying on December 20,
      1654, at the age of 56.(Shafter, "Memoir of Samuel de Champlain,"194; Le
      Blant, "Le triste veuvage d'Hélène Boullé.")

28   Marie Cameret was the daughter of Captain George Camaret, deceased,
      and the wife of sieur d'Arsaut, who lived in La Rochelle. At the end of his
      will, Champlain directed that any remaining assets were to go to this cousin.
      Champlain also made other bequests to various charities. (Trudel, "Cham-
      plain, Samuel," *Dictionary of Canadian Biography Online;* Le Blant, Robert. "Le
      testament de Samuel Champlain, 17 novembre 1635).

29   Champlain, *The Works of Samuel de Champlain,* ed. Biggar, VI:123.

30   Charles Lalemant's ties to the French court were the fact that he was the son of a criminal court lieutenant in Paris. With respect to pleading the case of the colonists in Quebec, Father Lalemant had come to understand that the de Caën merchants were interested solely in the fur trade and not in establishing a French colony in the New World, much less in supporting any missionary effort. (Pouliot, "Lalemant, Charles," *Dictionary of Canadian Biography Online*)

31   Father Lalemant continued his support of the French settlers of Quebec in various posts held in France, including the position of procurator of the mission. It was in this role that he was instrumental in the selection of Paul de Chomedey de Maisonneuve and Jeanne Mance to lead the founding of Montreal in 1642. While a number of his fellow Jesuit missionaries suffered death in the New World, Lalemant lived to be 84, dying in Paris in November of 1674. (Pouliot, "Lalemant, Charles," *Dictionary of Canadian Biography Online*)

32   *Jesuit Relations*, ed. Thwaites, V:275 (Notes section).

Chapter Nine

1   Hamelin, "Huault de Montmagny, Charles," *Dictionary of Canadian Biography Online*.

2   *Parchemin – Banque de données notariales (1626-1789)*, Bibliothèque et Archives nationales du Québec (BAnQ). Document of M. Piraube, Notary of Quebec, dated 4 September, 1640. The home and the grant of land by Champlain were confirmed in this document signed by Governor Montmagny on September 4, 1640.

3   *Pistard Database*, Bibliothèque et Archives nationales du Québec (BAnQ), Quebec, Canada. Civil document concerning Guillaume Hébert, dated October 10, 1636.

4   *Programme de recherche en démographie historique (PRDH) Genealogical Database*, Family Record # 223: Family of Guillaume Hébert and Hélène Desportes.

5   *Programme de recherche en démographie historique (PRDH) Genealogical Database*, Family Record # 85: Family of Guillaume Couillard and Guillemette Hébert.

6   *Programme de recherche en démographie historique (PRDH) Genealogical Database*, Family Record # 86: Family of Abraham Martin and Marguerite Langlois.

[7] Fraser, *Love and Louis XIV: The Women in the Life of the Sun King, 3,187*. Marriages made at such a young age were often not consummated until what was considered a more appropriate age. In the case of Louise-Françoise, it was a year later, just before her thirteenth birthday. (187)

[8] Fischer, *Champlain's Dream*, 314-15.

[9] Eccles, W.J. "Buade De Frontenac et De Palluau, Louis De," *Dictionary of Canadian Biography Online*.

[10] Charbonneau et al., *The First French Canadians: Pioneers in the St. Lawrence Valley*, 88-99.

[11] Champlain, *Voyages of Samuel de Champlain*, ed. Slafter, II:191; III:168-69.

[12] Trudel, *Introduction to New France*, 32.

[13] Tanguay, *À Travers les Registres*,15; Champlain, *The Works of Samuel de Champlain*, ed. Biggar, VI:41-45. (Tanguay records twenty-one men in his register; however, Champlain reports twenty men in his account of events in 1629.)

[14] Warrick, Gary A. "European Infectious Disease and Depopulation of the Wendat-Tionontate (Huron-Petun)," 272.

[15] Mann, *1491: New Revelations of the Americas Before Columbus*, 97.

[16] Mann, *1491: New Revelations of the Americas Before Columbus*, 103.

[17] It is believed that the smallpox virus evolved from a cattle virus that causes cowpox. Similar viruses caused horsepox and camelpox. Europeans had frequent contact with these domesticated animals. Those who developed the disease in one of its forms and survived developed an immunity to the virus. The Americas, at the time of the initial European immigration, did not have these animals. (Mann, *1491: New Revelations of the Americas Before Columbus*, 97)

[18] Though largely eradicated, smallpox was still found in certain parts of the world late in the twentieth century. In the early 1960s, there were seven thousand unvaccinated smallpox cases in the south of India. Of that number, 43 percent of the infected died. (Mann, *1491: New Revelations of the Americas Before Columbus*, 97)

[19] Fraser, *Love and Louis XIV: The Women in the Life of the Sun King*, 295.

[20] Mann, *1491: New Revelations of the Americas Before Columbus,* 109.

[21] Mahoney, *Marie of the Incarnation: Selected Writings,* 257-58; Simpson, *Marguerite Bourgeoys and Montréal, 1640-1665,*149-52; Charbonneau et al., *The First French Canadians: Pioneers in the St. Lawrence Valley,* 74.

[22] English colonists were very familiar with smallpox. Many bore the scars of the disease. In none of the contemporary accounts of the epidemic of 1616 was smallpox mentioned. There are accounts of a smallpox epidemic in the New England settlements in 1633 and 1634. (Morton, *The New English Canaan,* footnote on 133)

[23] Mann, *1491: New Revelations of the Americas Before Columbus,* 59-61; Morton, *The New English Canaan,* footnote on 133.

[24] Morton, Thomas. *The New English Canaan,* 132-33. (Spelling in original version altered to read correctly in modern English.)

[25] Mann, *1491: New Revelations of the Americas Before Columbus,* 61.

[26] *Jesuit Relations,* ed. Thwaites, XV:21.

[27] *Jesuit Relations,* ed. Thwaites, XV:17.

[28] *Jesuit Relations,* ed. Thwaites, XV:19-55.

[29] *Jesuit Relations,* ed. Thwaites, XV:29.

[30] Dickinson and Young, *A Short History of Quebec,*13.

[31] The Jesuits, along with the rest of Europeans, did not have a clear understanding of the infectious nature of these diseases; however, they did understand the concept of quarantine. This practice of separating sick individuals from the healthy has been around for a long time. Lepers were isolated from the well in the Old Testament. In the years to come, sick immigrants arriving in Quebec would be taken off the ships and sent to the hospital to avoid infecting others. Or, they would be required to remain on board the ship. What seventeenth-century Europeans did not understand was that healthy individuals could carry disease to others.

[32] Champlain, *Voyages of Samuel de Champlain,* ed. Slafter, II:193.

[33] Champlain, *The Works of Samuel de Champlain,* ed. Biggar, VI:145.

34 *Jesuit Relations*, ed. Thwaites, XV:165.

35 Sulte, Fryer, and David, *A History of Quebec*, 7.

36 Champlain, *Voyages of Samuel de Champlain*, ed. Slafter, II:197-99.

37 Lewis, *The Splendid Century: Life in the France of Louis XIV*, 177-87.

38 Lewis, *The Splendid Century: Life in the France of Louis XIV*, 177-87.

39 Lewis, *The Splendid Century: Life in the France of Louis XIV*, 180-81.

40 Pinkard, *A Revolution in Taste: The Rise of French Cuisine, 1650 – 1800*, 69.

41 In the century following his death, scientists and physicians who were followers of Phillip von Hohenheim, also known as Paracelsus, devoted themselves to developing a chemical theory of health and sickness. Their efforts resulted in the establishment of chemistry as part of medical science. While Paracelsus and his followers believed in the healing properties of metals (including mercury) and minerals, they also studied the medicinal value of chemical substances found in common herbs and other plants. There were several believers of Paracelsus' theories among seventeenth-century physicians in the Royal Court. One of them persuaded Louis XIII to establish the Jardin Royal des Plantes Médicinales in 1635 as an institution for the conduct of chemical research and preparation of herbal remedies. Paracelsian supporters won the support of the powerful Cardinal Richelieu who gave his approval for research into the therapeutic qualities of plant substances. (Pinkard, *A Revolution in Taste: The Rise of French Cuisine, 1650 – 1800*, 69-70)

42 Lewis, *The Splendid Century: Life in the France of Louis XIV*, 187-89.

43 Lewis, *The Splendid Century: Life in the France of Louis XIV*, 185.

44 Champlain, *The Works of Samuel de Champlain*, ed. Biggar, VI:264- 66.

45 Lewis, *The Splendid Century: Life in the France of Louis XIV*, 182.

46 Harris, *Practice of Medicine and Surgery by the Canadian Tribes in Champlain's Time*, 11.

47 Harris, *Practice of Medicine and Surgery by the Canadian Tribes in Champlain's Time*, 16-19.

48 *Jesuit Relations*, ed. Thwaites, V:105.

[49] Harris, *Practice of Medicine and Surgery by the Canadian Tribes in Champlain's Time*, 11-12, 22.

[50] Harris, *Practice of Medicine and Surgery by the Canadian Tribes in Champlain's Time*, 19.

[51] *Jesuit Relations*, ed. Thwaites, XV:177.

[52] Champlain, *Voyages of Samuel de Champlain*, ed. Slafter, III;174-77. Champlain provides a detailed description of the native treatment of the sick in this volume.

Chapter Ten

[1] Mother Marie speaks of their arrival in Quebec in her *"Relation of 1654"* (Mahoney, *Marie of the Incarnation: Selected Writings*, 136-40).

[2] Mahoney, *Marie of the Incarnation: Selected Writings*, 23, 117.

[3] The Religious Order of Ursulines was founded in 1535 at Brescia, Italy by a woman named Angela de Merici. To the Augustinian vows of poverty, chastity and obedience, Angela added a fourth: the instruction of girls. The order was established in Tours, France by the end of the sixteenth century. (Mahoney, *Marie of the Incarnation: Selected Writings*, 15, 25-26)

[4] Mahoney, *Marie of the Incarnation: Selected Writings*, 22-24, 117, 125-27, 132; Sulte, Fryer, and David, *A History of Quebec*, 36-37; *Glimpses of the Monastery: Scenes from the History of the Ursulines of Quebec during the Two Hundred Years 1639-1839*, 8-12.

[5] Chabot, "Chauvigny De La Peltrie, Marie-Madeleine De," *Dictionary of Canadian Biography Online*; *Glimpses of the Monastery: Scenes from the History of the Ursulines of Quebec during the Two Hundred Years 1639-1839*, 8-9.

[6] Chabot, "Guyart, Marie dite Marie de l'Incarnation," *Dictionary of Canadian Biography Online*; Mahoney, *Marie of the Incarnation: Selected Writings*, 2, 10, 43.

[7] The other Ursulines who came with Marie were Mother Cécile de Ste. Croix and Mother St. Joseph. Charlotte Barré was a young woman who came as the maid of Madame de La Peltrie, but then entered the Ursuline convent at Quebec in 1646. (Mahoney, *Marie of the Incarnation: Selected Writings*, 22-23, 132; Chabot, "Chauvigny De La Peltrie, Marie-Madeleine De," *Dictionary of Canadian Biography Online*)

[8]   The Hospitallers were Marie Guenet de Saint Ignace, Marie Forestier de Saint Bonaventure, and Anne Le Cointre de Saint Bernard (Chabot, "Guyart, Marie dite Marie de l'Incarnation," *Dictionary of Canadian Biography Online*).

[9]   Mahoney, *Marie of the Incarnation: Selected Writings*, 132-35, 220-21.

[10] Mahoney, *Marie of the Incarnation: Selected Writings*, 24-25,136, 273; Repplier, *Mère Marie of the Ursulines*, 77.

[11] Mahoney, *Marie of the Incarnation: Selected Writings*, 25, 136.

[12] "History: Dieppe". Monastère Communauté Augustines Malestroit.

[13] *Jesuit Relations*, ed. Thwaites, XV:215, 217.

[14] The Assumption of Mary into Heaven is one of the oldest and most important feasts in the Roman Catholic Church. This was originally a celebration in the Eastern Churches and was known as the Dormition. It was celebrated in Palestine before the year 500.

[15] *Jesuit Relations*, ed. Thwaites, XV:221-31.

[16] For everyday wear, women wore aprons over their dresses. Capots or cloaks kept them warm in winter.

[17] Seventeenth-century paintings and etchings serve as sources for the clothing worn by the French colonists.

[18] *Jesuit Relations*, ed. Thwaites, XV:221-31.

[19] *Jesuit Relations*, ed. Thwaites, XV:219.

[20] *Jesuit Relations*, ed. Thwaites, XXIII:301-20; Mahoney, *Marie of the Incarnation: Selected Writings*, 25.

[21] Mahoney, *Marie of the Incarnation: Selected Writings*, 25.

[22] It later became evident that the mixed-race children, the metis, were not fully accepted in either culture (Mahoney, *Marie of the Incarnation: Selected Writings*, 253).

[23] Warrick, "European Infectious Disease and Depopulation of the Wendat-Tionontate (Huron-Petun)," 273.

24   Over the years, the simple hospital would go through many changes. The original building was replaced in 1646 and again in 1658. In 1672, an addition to the hospital was constructed . (Sulte, Fryer, and David, *A History of Quebec*, 35-36)

25   *Jesuit Relations*, ed. Thwaites, XIX:7.

26   Mahoney, *Marie of the Incarnation: Selected Writings*, 138-139.

27   *Les Expositions* (incl. "Marie Lemaire des Anges et son atelier: Le Grand Art de la broderie"), Musée des Ursulines de Quebec.

28   Mahoney, *Marie of the Incarnation: Selected Writings*, 137.

29   *Jesuit Relations*, ed. Thwaites, XIX:125.

30   Fischer, *Champlain's Dream*, 325.

31   There is no burial record for Guillaume in the Church archives. The date of death is given on a document of the Notary Piraube, dated October 21, 1639, providing an inventory of Guillaume's possessions (Pistard Archives, Bibliothèque et Archives nationales du Québec *(BAnQ)*.

32   In the records of Quebec, the cause of death is listed when the death was the result of an accident or when the individual was killed by the natives. Apparently, when death was a result of illness this was not recorded, perhaps because there was no physician to identify the exact cause of death. According to the Church's burial records, accidents were the most common cause of death in the young colony; people died by drowning, fires and falls. More often than not, the victim was a young male. (Charbonneau et al., *The First French Canadians: Pioneers in the St. Lawrence Valley*, 172)

33   Rousseau, "Sarrazin, Michel," *Dictionary of Canadian Biography Online*.

34   *Pistard Archives*, Bibliothèque et Archives nationales du Québec *(BAnQ)*. Document of October 21, 1639. There is also an ordinance of Governor Montmagny, concerning guardianship of the children of Hélène, dated October 29, 1639.

35   Hélène's signature appears on two other documents in the National Archives of Quebec: those dated December 27, 1639 and February 25, 1668.

36   Harris, *The Seigneurial System: A Geographical Study*. 3, 46.

37 *Parchemin Notarial Records (1626-1789)*, Bibliothèque et Archives nationales du Québec (BAnQ). Document of M. Piraube, Notary of Quebec, dated October 21, 1639.

38 *Parchemin Notarial Records (1626-1789)*, Bibliothèque et Archives nationales du Québec (BAnQ). Document of M. Piraube, Notary of Quebec, dated November 11, 1639.

39 *Parchemin Notarial Records (1626-1789)*, Bibliothèque et Archives nationales du Québec (BAnQ). Document of M. Piraube, Notary of Quebec, dated November 12, 1639.

40 The church of Notre-Dame-de-la-Recouvrance was constructed in 1633 upon Champlain's return to Quebec, some thirteen years after Hélène's birth. Presumably the notary Piraube was implying that Hélène was a native of Quebec.

41 *Parchemin Notarial Records (1626-1789)*, Bibliothèque et Archives nationales du Québec (BAnQ). Document of M. Piraube, Notary of Quebec, dated December 27, 1639.

42 There is no mention of the twenty-two arpents of land ceded to Guillaume by Governor Montmagny on October 10, 1636. Perhaps it was considered that this land belonged to the children of the deceased.

43 Some translations of the document state that the sign featured a blue horse. The original document is very difficult to read; the handwritten French words blanc and bleu are very similar.

44 *Parchemin Notarial Records (1626-1789)*, Bibliothèque et Archives nationales du Québec (BAnQ). Marriage contract signed before M. Piraube, Notary of Quebec, dated December 27, 1639.

45 *Parchemin Notarial Records (1626-1789)*, Bibliothèque et Archives nationales du Québec (BAnQ). Document of M. Piraube, Notary of Quebec, dated December 27, 1639.

Chapter Eleven

1 *Programme de recherche en démographie historique (PRDH) Genealogical Database, Marriage Record # 66340*. On June 14, 1640, there was a fire at Notre-Dame-de-Recouvrance. The register of marriages, baptisms, and burials was destroyed.

Fortunately, Father LeJeune had a copy of this record. (Tanguay, *À Travers les Registres*, 25)

2   Charbonneau et al., *The First French Canadians: Pioneers in the St. Lawrence Valley*, 99-111.

3   Goubert, *The French Peasantry in the Seventeenth Century*, 37-39.

4   Trudel, *Introduction to New France*, 207; Goubert, *The French Peasantry in the Seventeenth Century*, 37-39.

5   Dickinson and Young. *A Short History of Quebec*, 89-91.

6   Simpson, *Marguerite Bourgeoys and Montréal, 1640-1665*, 173-74.

7   Dickinson and Young. *A Short History of Quebec*, 89-91; Brault, *The French-Canadian Heritage in New England*, 10-11. A Swedish traveler who visited the St. Lawrence River valley in 1749 described the housing thus, "The farm-houses are generally built of stone, but sometimes of timber, and have three or four rooms. The windows are seldom of glass, but most frequently of paper. They have iron stoves in one of the rooms, and chimneys in the rest. The roofs are covered with boards. The crevices and chinks are filled up with clay. The other buildings are covered with straw." (Sulte, Fryer, and David, *A History of Quebec*, 55)

8   Burke-Gaffney, "Canada's First Engineer Jean Bourdon (1601-1668)," 89-91; Hamelin, "Bourdon, Jean," *Dictionary of Canadian Biography Online*.

9   The côteau Sainte-Geneviève is also known as the côte Sainte-Geneviève; however, the former is more accurate, as côteau is the French word for hill.

10   Pinkard, Susan. *A Revolution in Taste: The Rise of French Cuisine, 1650 – 1800*, 108-10.

11   Trudel, *Introduction to New France*, 207; Dickinson and Young. *A Short History of Quebec*, 90.

12   *Jesuit Relations*, ed. Thwaites, V:147.

13   Dickinson and Young. *A Short History of Quebec*, 89-91; Brault, *The French-Canadian Heritage in New England*, 14.

14   In the *Jesuit Relations* of 1634, Father LeJeune estimated that it took a year for one man to clear one and a half arpents of land (a little over an acre), if he

was not working on anything else. Twenty men, working for a year, would be needed to clear thirty arpents of land (twenty-five acres). (*Jesuit Relations*, ed. Thwaites, IX:153)

15   Dickinson and Young. *A Short History of Quebec*, 84-85, 89-91; Brault, *The French-Canadian Heritage in New England*, 14-15.

16   Dickinson and Young. *A Short History of Quebec*, 84; Trudel, *Introduction to New France*, 204-07.

17   Dickinson and Young. *A Short History of Quebec*, 85; Trudel, *Introduction to New France*, 207.

18   *Jesuit Relations*, ed. Thwaites, XXXII:97, Quote on 105.

19   They were generally tradesmen or military recruits. In the census of 1666, carpenters, masons, weavers, tailors, sailors and other tradesmen would be listed. (Trudel, *Introduction to New France*, 203-04)

20   Trudel, *Introduction to New France*, 204-07; Harris, *The Seigneurial System in Early Canada: A Geographical Study*, 17.

21   Goubert, *The French Peasantry in the Seventeenth Century*, 86-90.

22   Lewis, *The Splendid Century: Life in the France of Louis XIV*, 209.

23   Pinkard, *A Revolution in Taste: The Rise of French Cuisine, 1650 – 1800*, 84-87.

Chapter Twelve

1   *Glimpses of the Monastery: Scenes from the History of the Ursulines of Quebec during the Two Hundred Years 1639-1839*, 24 (footnote).

2   *Jesuit Relations*, ed. Thwaites, XXIII:269.

3   Louise's son is not mentioned further in the records; presumably he died as an infant. Louise appears to have been in demand as a godmother. She is listed in this role on the baptism records of a dozen infants in Quebec, between 1636 and 1641. (*Programme de recherche en démographie historique (PRDH) Genealogical Database*)

4   Letardif held this commoner's land grant jointly with Jean Nicollet. In 1653, Letardif relinquished this property and obtained land at Château-Richer. He died there in January of 1665. (Trudel, "Letardif, Olivier," *Dictionary of*

Canadian Biography Online) He was another pioneer moving beyond Quebec to expand colonization of New France.

5   Simpson, *Marguerite Bourgeoys and Montréal, 1640-1665*, 83.

6   Daveluy, "Chomeday de Maisonnueve, Paul de." *Dictionary of Canadian Biography Online;* Simpson, *Marguerite Bourgeoys and Montréal, 1640-1665,*73-74, 78.

7   He was the first-born son of Louis de Chomeday, the seigneur of Chavanne, Germenoy-en-Brie. De Maisonneuve had entered the army at the age of 13 and was posted to Holland during the Thirty Years War. There are no surviving records of his early education. However, it is known that his grandfather was a scholar and a writer. It has also been noted that the elegance of expression and the clarity of thought found in surviving documents written by Maisonneuve suggest that he had more than a minimal education. (Simpson, *Marguerite Bourgeoys and Montréal, 1640-1665,*74-75)

8   Jeanne Mance is considered the co-founder of Montréal. As the first lay nurse in North America, she established the Hôtel-Dieu of Montréal and served as its administrator until her death in 1673. (Daveluy, "Mance, Jeanne," *Dictionary of Canadian Biography Online*)

9   Simpson, *Marguerite Bourgeoys and Montréal, 1640-1665,* 76-77.

10 Daveluy, "Chomeday de Maisonnueve, Paul de." *Dictionary of Canadian Biography Online*; Simpson, *Marguerite Bourgeoys and Montréal, 1640-1665,* 83,86.

11 Simpson, *Marguerite Bourgeoys and Montréal, 1640-1665,* 83-84.

12 Burke-Gaffney, "Canada's First Engineer Jean Bourdon (1601-1668)," *Canadian Catholic Historical Association (CCHA),* 93; Daveluy, "Chomeday de Maisonnueve, Paul de," *Dictionary of Canadian Biography Online.*

13 Simpson, *Marguerite Bourgeoys and Montréal, 1640-1665,* 86-87.

14 Daveluy, "Chomeday de Maisonnueve, Paul de," *Dictionary of Canadian Biography Online.* The success of the colony at Montreal was due in large measure to the skillful leadership of Maisonneuve and the courage of a handful of men and women. Maisonneuve had established Montreal in opposition to the settlers in Quebec City who called it a foolhardy undertaking. A religious zeal governed much of the activity in Montreal. Jeanne Mance founded Hôtel-Dieu in 1644. The Hospitalières of La Flèche in Anjou took over the hospital in 1659. Marguerite Bourgeoys began her first school in Montreal in

1653. She also founded a religious order of women in Montreal, dedicated to teaching. The Roman Catholic Church canonized her in 1982, in recognition of her holiness and saintly work. (Simpson, *Marguerite Bourgeoys and Montréal, 1640-1665,3-8*)

[15] Simpson, *Marguerite Bourgeoys and Montréal, 1640-1665*, 87-88; Mahoney, *Marie of the Incarnation: Selected Writings*, 225-226; Chabot, "Chauvigny De La Peltrie, Marie-Madeleine De," *Dictionary of Canadian Biography Online*. Although Madame de La Peltrie never took the veil, she lived with the Ursulines of Quebec until her death in 1671.

[16] Mahoney, *Marie of the Incarnation: Selected Writings*, 138-40; Chabot, "Guyart, Marie dite Marie de l "Incarnation," *Dictionary of Canadian Biography Online; Glimpses of the Monastery: Scenes from the History of the Ursulines of Quebec during the Two Hundred Years 1639-1839*, 38.

[17] *Glimpses of the Monastery: Scenes from the History of the Ursulines of Quebec during the Two Hundred Years 1639-1839*, 41; Mahoney, *Marie of the Incarnation: Selected Writings*, 140 (footnote).

[18] Marie Morin (daughter of Hélène Desportes), as quoted in Bernier, "Morin, Marie," *Dictionary of Canadian Biography Online*.

[19] *Glimpses of the Monastery: Scenes from the History of the Ursulines of Quebec during the Two Hundred Years 1639-1839*, 39.

[20] It is presumed that Angélique, the third child born to Hélène and Guillaume Hébert, died in infancy. According to church records, she was born in August of 1639. She is mentioned as a child of the widow Hélène in the Quebec civil archives in October of that year, on the document concerning guardianship of Guillaume's minor children. There is no further record of Angélique. In the notary archives dated July 10, 1644, regarding the sale of property on behalf of the minor children of Guillaume Hébert, only Joseph and Françoise are mentioned. (*Parchemin Notary Records (1626-1789)*, Bibliothèque et Archives nationales du Québec (BAnQ). Documents of the notary Piraube)

[21] *Jesuit Relations*, ed. Thwaites, XII:87, 89; Dickinson and Young, *A Short History of Quebec*, 42-43; Pinkard, *A Revolution in Taste: The Rise of French Cuisine, 1650 – 1800*, 83; Lewis, *The Splendid Century: Life in the France of Louis XIV*, 169.

[22] Fraser, *Love and Louis XIV: The Women in the Life of the Sun King*, 43.

23 "L' Exposition L'Académie des demoiselles." Musée des Ursulines de Quebec; Simpson, *Marguerite Bourgeoys and Montréal, 1640-1665*, 158.

24 Mahoney, *Marie of the Incarnation: Selected Writings*, 136-38, 223.

25 The resources of the Ursulines were severely taxed. They depended on wealthy benefactors in France to support their missionary efforts in New France. In addition to Madame de La Peltrie who had come to Quebec with Marie de l'Incarnation, Mademoiselle de Luynes also provided alms for the religious community. (Mahoney, *Marie of the Incarnation: Selected Writings*, 225)

26 *Glimpses of the Monastery: Scenes from the History of the Ursulines of Quebec during the Two Hundred Years 1639-1839*, 23.

27 *Jesuit Relations*, ed. Thwaites, XXIII:301-05.

28 *Jesuit Relations*, ed. Thwaites, XXIII:307, 309.

29 Burke-Gaffney, "Canada's First Engineer Jean Bourdon (1601-1668)," *Canadian Catholic Historical Association (CCHA), Report*, 94.

30 Simpson, *Marguerite Bourgeoys and Montréal, 1640-1665*, 95.

Chapter Thirteen

1 *Programme de recherche en démographie historique (PRDH) Genealogical Database*, Family Records # 223 (Guillaume Hébert and Hélène Desportes) and #344 (Noël Morin and Hélène Desportes).

2 Trudel, *Le Terrier Du Saint-Laurent en 1663*, 176, 224. According to Trudel, the hôpital du Saint-Sacrement in Quebec currently occupies a portion of the land originally known as the côte Sainte-Geneviève. The original grant to Morin also included property south and west of the hospital.

3 Trudel, *Le Terrier Du Saint-Laurent en 1663*, 176.

4 *Parchemin Notary Records (1626-1789)*, Bibliothèque et Archives nationales du Québec (BAnQ). Document of Audouart dit Saint-Germain, Notary of Quebec, dated February 6, 1650.

5 Langlois, Michel. *Dictionnaire Biographique Des Ancêtres Québécois (1608-1700)*, III:484. The property was described in its sale to Charles Bazire in 1675.

6 According to another translation, the "handsome pastries" were pigeon-pies. (*Glimpses of the Monastery: Scenes from the History of the Ursulines of Quebec during the Two Hundred Years 1639-1839*, 54.)

7 *Jesuit Relations*, ed. Thwaites, XXVIII:141,143. It is assumed that the *Jesuit Relations* written between 1645 and 1650 were written by Father Jérôme Lalemant. He served as superior of the Jesuits in Canada during that time period and resided at Quebec. (Pouliot. "Lalemant, Jérôme")

8 *Jesuit Relations*, ed. Thwaites, XXXVI:167. Mère Marie writes in her *Relation of 1654*: "fire occurred at the end of 1650" (Mahoney, *Marie of the Incarnation: Selected Writings*, 163-64).

9 Mahoney, *Marie of the Incarnation: Selected Writings*, 163.

10 Mahoney, *Marie of the Incarnation: Selected Writings*, 163-64.

11 Mahoney, *Marie of the Incarnation: Selected Writings*, 164.

12 *Jesuit Relations*, ed. Thwaites, XXXVI:171.

13 This would not be the only time that fire would destroy the Ursuline Convent in the seventeenth century. On a Sunday morning in October of 1686, a second fire broke out while the nuns and their pupils were attending Mass. The convent, school, and chapel were consumed in the fire. Only Madame de La Peltrie's house was spared. Again, the Ursulines would rebuild. When the convent re-opened, fifty years after the first Ursulines landed in Quebec, there were thirty-four members devoted to teaching. (Douglas, "Education in Quebec in the 17th century")

14 Repplier, *Mére Marie of the Ursulines*, 133.

15 *Jesuit Relations*, ed. Thwaites, XXXVI:171.

16 Repplier, *Mére Marie of the Ursulines*, 132-35. Quote on 132.

17 Quotation from the permanent exhibit, "L'Académie des demoiselles", *Ursuline Museum, Quebec City*, on display in August of 2011.

18 Repplier, *Mére Marie of the Ursulines*,149.

19 Pious individuals in France were stirred by the letters received over the years from Mother Marie and the other sisters. The Jesuits, in their annual reports,

also mentioned the good work of the Ursulines and the poverty the convent experienced. Monsieur de Bernières of Caën had become a devoted friend of Madame de La Peltrie and Mother Marie and continued his support of the Ursulines for many years. Other wealthy benefactors included the Queen of France (Anne of Austria), as well as the Duchesses d'Aiguillon and de Brienne. The Ursuline Convents in Paris and in Tours also provided financial assistance and gifts: "clothing for their seminarists, tools for their workmen, a chalice for their altar." (*Glimpses of the Monastery: Scenes from the History of the Ursulines of Quebec during the Two Hundred Years 1639-1839,*12, 23)

20 Mahoney, *Marie of the Incarnation: Selected Writings*, 241-48.

21 Simpson, *Marguerite Bourgeoys and Montréal, 1640-1665*, 104.

22 Sulte, Fryer, and David, *A History of Quebec*, 42.

23 *Jesuit Relations*, ed. Thwaites, XIX: 63-65. The conflagration of 1640 in the Upper Town was described thus, "Our house at Kebec took fire and was reduced to ashes, as was also the Chapel of Monsieur the Governor, and the public Church [Notre-Dame-de-la-Recouvrance], — all was consumed. It took place so suddenly, that in less than two or three hours nothing was to be seen of all these buildings and the greater part of all our furniture, but a few cinders, and some large pieces of the walls which remained, to proclaim this desolation. . . . A rather violent wind, the extreme [drought], the oily wood of the fir, of which these buildings were constructed, kindled a fire so quick and violent that hardly anything could be saved."

24 *Jesuit Relations*, ed. Thwaites, XXXVI: 165,167.

25 *Programme de recherche en démographie historique (PRDH) Genealogical Database,* Confirmation Records # 403661 and 403664.

26 Trudel, *Introduction to New France*, 252-57; Goubert, *The French Peasantry in the Seventeenth Century*, 220-21; Johnston, A. J. B. *Life and Religion at Louisbourg 1713-1758*, 16-19; Lewis, *The Splendid Century: Life in the France of Louis XIV*, 80-81.

27 Trudel, *Introduction to New France*, 252-57.

28 Lewis, *The Splendid Century: Life in the France of Louis XIV*, 170.

29 Johnston, A. J. B. *Life and Religion at Louisbourg 1713-1758*, 16-19; Lewis, *The Splendid Century: Life in the France of Louis XIV*, 80-81.

30   Accounts of processions and pageantry celebrating the various Holy Days
      are found in a number of places in the *Jesuit Relations*.

31   Goubert, *The French Peasantry in the Seventeenth Century*, 220-21.

32   *Jesuit Relations*, ed. Thwaites, XLVIII:191.

33   Fraser, *Love and Louis XIV: The Women in the Life of the Sun King*, 21, 26, 79,
      161.

34   This is the first such marriage to take place in Quebec for which there is
      a church record (The New Peoples: Being and Becoming Métis in North
      America, 27).

35   Quebec registers, as quoted in Tanguay, *À Travers les Registres*, 27; *Programme
      de recherche en démographie historique (PRDH) Genealogical Database*, Individual
      Record # 83388. Marie's surname is also listed as Ouchistaouichkoue, the
      name used by her mother.

36   Provost, "Prévost (Provost), Martin," *Dictionary of Canadian Biography Online*;
      Trudel, "Letardif, Olivier," *Dictionary of Canadian Biography Online*.

37   Mahoney, *Marie of the Incarnation: Selected Writings*, 230, 238-39.

38   Gabriel Lalemant was the nephew of Charles and Jérôme Lalemant; all three
      served as Jesuit missionaries in New France.

39   Mahoney, *Marie of the Incarnation: Selected Writings*, 162.

40   Mahoney, *Marie of the Incarnation: Selected Writings*, 162, 239, 270.

41   *Jesuit Relations*. ed. Thwaites, XXXVI:163.

42   Mahoney, *Marie of the Incarnation: Selected Writings*, 230, 238-39.

43   Dickinson and Young, *A Short History of Quebec*, 20.

Chapter Fourteen

1   Goubert, *The French Peasantry in the Seventeenth Century*, 47.

2   *Programme de recherche en démographie historique (PRDH) Genealogical Database*,
      Baptism and Burial Records.

3   In France, physicians were beginning to attend some births in the seventeenth century. However, there were no physicians in the colony during Hélène's lifetime. In general, childbirth belonged entirely to the realm of women: No men were allowed to be present for the birth, not the father of the baby, not a priest. (Goubert, *The French Peasantry in the Seventeenth Century*, 47) In the case of royalty, childbirth might be attended by men and others in the Royal Court to ensure that there were no substitutions for the royal child (Fraser, *Love and Louis XIV: The Women in the Life of the Sun King*, 12).

4   Stock-Morton, "Control and Limitation of Midwives in Modern France: The Example of Marseille."

5   Goubert, *The French Peasantry in the Seventeenth Century*, 47.

6   Stock-Morton, "Control and Limitation of Midwives in Modern France: The Example of Marseille." Louyse Bourgeois was the first to publish a book on the practice of midwifery.

7   Lewis, *The Splendid Century: Life in the France of Louis XIV*, 193.

8   *Programme de recherche en démographie historique (PRDH) Genealogical Database*.

9   Performing a baptism in an emergency does not automatically indicate the status of midwife. Apparently others, including men, could perform an emergency baptism in the absence of a priest. In the parish records of Château-Richer, on the baptism record of Charles LeTardiff, dated July 9, 1652, François Bellenger is listed as having baptized the infant. He is listed as performing the baptism on other records as well. (*Programme de recherche en démographie historique (PRDH) Genealogical Database*) One wonders if François might have been involved in some organization such as the Third Order of Carmelites, organized for devout men and women who did not enter the priesthood, brotherhood or a women's religious community, but did commit themselves to prayer and the practice of good works.

10   Laforce, Hélène. *Histoire de la sage-femme dans la région de Québec*, 149.

11   *Programme de recherche en démographie historique (PRDH) Genealogical Database*, Baptism and Burial Records.

12   Lessard, Renald. "De France à Nouvelle-France: la practique médicale canadienne aux XVIIe et XVIIIe siècles," 424.

13 LaForce, Hélène. "L'Univers de la sage-femme aux XVIIe aux XVIIIe siècle,"3-6.

14 One particularly notorious case was that of the midwife Catherine Monvoisin. She was arrested in Paris in 1679 on suspicion of witchcraft: casting spells, providing aphrodisiacs, reading ladies' horoscopes, and participating in black magic. Known as La Voisin, she had supplied the ladies of the court of Louis XIV with a variety of potions and powders designed to assist in keeping a lover or losing a husband. La Voisin implicated a great many others in her craft, including a number of other midwives. A tribunal, known as the Burning Chamber, was set up to investigate and judge. Three hundred people were arrested. La Voisin was executed a year later, along with thirty other individuals. An additional thirty were sent to the galleys or into exile. Their crimes varied from poisonings to the use of horoscopes. (Fraser, *Love and Louis XIV: The Women in the Life of the Sun King,* 179-80)

15 Stock-Morton, "Control and Limitation of Midwives in Modern France: The Example of Marseille."

16 Tanguay, *À Travers les Registres,* 13.

17 *Jesuit Relations,* ed. Thwaites, V:277; *Programme de recherche en démographie historique (PRDH) Genealogical Database.*

18 Thompson, *Mystery and Art of the Apothecary,* 103-4.

19 Lewis, *The Splendid Century: Life in the France of Louis XIV,* 193.

20 Goubert, *The French Peasantry in the Seventeenth Century,* 46.

21 *Jesuit Relations,* ed. Thwaites, XV:179, 181.

22 Provost, "Cloutier, Zacharie," *Dictionary of Canadian Biography Online.*

23 *Programme de recherche en démographie historique (PRDH) Genealogical Database.* Family record #86; Kallmann, "Martin, Charles-Amador," *Dictionary of Canadian Biography Online.*

24 Lewis, *The Splendid Century: Life in the France of Louis XIV,* 116, 150. According to one source, seventeenth-century records in New France show that a dowry requested by the convents might be several times more than that which was expected for marriage. However, the full amount of this religious dowry was not always paid. (Mahoney, *Marie de l'Incarnation: Selected Writings,*

254; Simpson, *Marguerite Bourgeoys and Montréal, 1640-1665*,196, Notes section)

25   Lewis, *The Splendid Century: Life in the France of Louis XIV*, 116-24.

26   Fraser, *Love and Louis XIV: The Women in the Life of the Sun King*, 71-73, 81,146-48.

27   Provost, "Giffard de Moncel, Robert," *Dictionary of Canadian Biography Online.*

28   *Programme de recherche en démographie historique (PRDH) Genealogical Database*, Burial record # 94065.

29   Mahoney, *Marie of the Incarnation: Selected Writings*, 248 (footnote); *Jesuit Relations*, ed. Thwaites, XXXIV: 119.

30   Hamelin, "Bourdon, Jean," *Dictionary of Canadian Biography Online.*

31   In 1659, new hospital sisters arrived aboard the Saint André on their way to the hospital at Montreal. These nuns stayed with the Ursulines during their time in Quebec. Evidently, they made a great impression on ten-year-old Marie Morin who was a day student with the Ursulines in 1659. (Simpson, Patricia. *Marguerite Bourgeoys and Montréal, 1640-1665*, 161-62)

32   Simpson, Patricia. *Marguerite Bourgeoys and Montréal, 1640-1665*, 160-62; Bernier, "Morin, Marie." *Dictionary of Canadian Biography Online.* Sister Morin would write her *Annales* between 1697 and 1725.

33   The book *Constitutions et Règlements des premières Ursulines de Québec, 1647*, was showcased at "L' Exposition L'Académie des demoiselles." Musée des Ursulines de Quebec, August, 2011.

34   "L' Exposition L'Académie des demoiselles." Musée des Ursulines de Quebec.

35   "L' Exposition L'Académie des demoiselles." Musée des Ursulines de Quebec.

36   Mahoney, *Marie of the Incarnation: Selected Writings*, 271-72.

37   Mahoney, *Marie of the Incarnation: Selected Writings*, 33, 247.

38   Mahoney, *Marie of the Incarnation: Selected Writings*, 247 (footnote).

39   Mahoney, *Marie of the Incarnation: Selected Writings*, 264.

Chapter Fifteen

1   *Jesuit Relations*, ed. Thwaites, XXVIII:237.

2   Bennett, "Couillard De Lespinay, Louis," *Dictionary of Canadian Biography Online.*

3   *Jesuit Relations*, ed. Thwaites, XXVIII:165,185-87.

4   *Jesuit Relations*, ed. Thwaites, XXVIII:195-97.

5   Mahoney, *Marie of the Incarnation: Selected Writings*, 271.

6   Tanguay, *À Travers les Registres*, 31.

7   *Jesuit Relations*, ed. Thwaites, XXXIV:39.

8   *Jesuit Relations*, ed. Thwaites, XXVIII:141.

9   *Programme de recherche en démographie historique (PRDH) Genealogical Database.* Between 1650 and his death in 1664, Abraham Martin stood as witness at three marriages recorded in the church archives.

10 Simpson, Patricia. *Marguerite Bourgeoys and Montréal, 1640-1665*, 219 (End-note).

11 "Evolution of juvenile justice in Canada," *Department of Justice Canada.*

12 "Evolution of juvenile justice in Canada," *Department of Justice Canada.*

13 "Evolution of juvenile justice in Canada," *Department of Justice Canada.*

14 "Evolution of juvenile justice in Canada," *Department of Justice Canada.*

15 "Evolution of juvenile justice in Canada," *Department of Justice Canada.*

16 Tanguay, *À Travers les Registres*, 58.

17 Tanguay, *À Travers les Registres*, 58.

18 Isabelle Bertault would have two more husbands. In 1673, at the age of four-teen, she married Noël Laurence in Boucherville and had six children with him. In 1688, she married Jean-Baptiste Lafortune in Repentigny and had

five more children. Isabelle died in Repentigny in 1736, at the age of seventy-seven. (*Programme de recherche en démographie historique (PRDH) Genealogical Database*)

19   Pinkard, *A Revolution in Taste: The Rise of French Cuisine, 1650 – 1800*, 211.

20   Pinkard, *A Revolution in Taste: The Rise of French Cuisine, 1650 – 1800*, 211-12.

21   Vachon, "Talon, Jean," *Dictionary of Canadian Biography Online*.

22   Pinkard, *A Revolution in Taste: The Rise of French Cuisine, 1650 – 1800*, 212.

23   *Jesuit Relations*, ed. Thwaites,, XXVIII: 189, 237.

24   Vachon, "Talon, Jean." *Dictionary of Canadian Biography Online*.

25   *Jesuit Relations*, ed. Thwaites, V:47, 49.

26   Mahoney, *Marie of the Incarnation: Selected Writings*, 262.

27   Trudel, *Introduction to New France*, 195; Vachon, "Laval, François De," *Dictionary of Canadian Biography Online*.

28   Simpson, *Marguerite Bourgeoys and Montréal, 1640-1665*, 95-96, 172-74; Trudel, *Introduction to New France*, 58-59.

29   *Jesuit Relations*, ed. Thwaites, XLVII:89.

30   Registers of Notre-Dame des Quebec and the Journal des Jesuits, as quoted in Tanguay, *À Travers les Registres*, 42; *Programme de recherche en démographie historique (PRDH) Genealogical Database*, Burial Record # 68917 (Nicolas) and # 94089 (Guillaume).

Chapter Sixteen

1   As quoted in Repplier, *Mére Marie of the Ursulines*, 199-200.

2   *Jesuit Relations*, ed. Thwaites, XLVIII:39, 41.

3   *Jesuit Relations*, ed. Thwaites, XLVIII:47,49. The US Geological Survey confirms the severity of this earthquake, noting that it was probably a magnitude 7 quake and was felt over an area of some 750,000 miles, including all of eastern Canada and throughout New England. At Trois-Rivières, significant rock-

slides modified several waterfalls. The St. Lawrence River remained muddy for a month. In New England, the aftershocks did not cease until July. If the quake had occurred at a later date, when the land was more densely populated, there would have been much more damage. (Historic Earthquakes: St. Lawrence Valley region, Quebec, Canada, February 5, 1663; USGS Earthquake Hazards Program Web 7 November 2012)

4   *Jesuit Relations*, ed. Thwaites, XLVIII:49.

5   As quoted in Repplier, *Mère Marie of the Ursulines*, 202-03.

6   *Jesuit Relations*, ed. Thwaites, XLVIII:205, 207.

7   Louis XIV had become the King of France in 1643, at the age of four. He did not personally begin governing until 1661. Known as the Sun King, his reign would last seventy-two years.

8   Tanguay, *À Travers les Registres*, 47.

9   The term was first used by Marguerite Bourgeoys, founder of the Congregation of Notre-Dame in Montreal, in her autobiographical writings (Runyan, "Daughters of the King and Founders of a Nation: Les Filles du Roi in New France," 4).

10   Charbonneau et al., *The First French Canadians: Pioneers in the St. Lawrence Valley*, 38. According to this source, the *filles du roi* accounted for half of the 1400 French women who settled in Canada before 1680.

11   Charbonneau et al., *The First French Canadians: Pioneers in the St. Lawrence Valley*, 31, 212-13 (footnote).

12   Vachon, "Talon, Jean." *Dictionary of Canadian Biography Online*.

13   Charbonneau et al., *The First French Canadians: Pioneers in the St. Lawrence Valley*, 28; Runyan, "Daughters of the King and Founders of a Nation: Les Filles du Roi in New France," 25-26.

14   Runyan, "Daughters of the King and Founders of a Nation: Les Filles du Roi in New France," 8-10, 18, 37; Charbonneau et al., *The First French Canadians: Pioneers in the St. Lawrence Valley*, 28, 70.

15   Charbonneau et al., *The First French Canadians: Pioneers in the St. Lawrence Valley*, 28.

16 Runyan, "Daughters of the King and Founders of a Nation: Les Filles du Roi in New France," 35-40.

17 Chapais, Thomas. "The Great Intendant: A Chronicle of Jean Talon in Canada 1665-1672," *Chronicles of Canada*. VI: Ch 2; Runyan, "Daughters of the King and Founders of a Nation: Les Filles du Roi in New France," 5; Charbonneau et al., *The First French Canadians: Pioneers in the St. Lawrence Valley*, 28; Simpson, *Marguerite Bourgeoys and Montréal, 1640-1665*, 165-68.

18 Hamelin, "Bourdon, Jean." *Dictionary of Canadian Biography Online;* Chapais, Thomas. "The Great Intendant: A Chronicle of Jean Talon in Canada 1665-1672." *Chronicles of Canada*. VI: Ch 2.

19 Simpson, *Marguerite Bourgeoys and Montréal, 1640-1665*, 105. Rumors have persisted since the seventeenth century that the girls were prostitutes from the streets of Paris and other French cities. In a book written in 1952, the historian Gustave Lanctot presented evidence that these girls were carefully selected and that the *filles du roi* were "respectable and virtuous." (Simpson, *Marguerite Bourgeoys and Montréal, 1640-1665*, 166)

20 As quoted in Simpson, *Marguerite Bourgeoys and Montréal, 1640-1665*, 167.

21 As quoted in Charbonneau et al., *The First French Canadians: Pioneers in the St. Lawrence Valley*, 93-94.

22 From the *Memoires of Talon to Colbert*, Quebec, 10 Nov 1670, as quoted in Charbonneau et al., *The First French Canadians: Pioneers in the St. Lawrence Valley*, 28.

23 Runyan, "Daughters of the King and Founders of a Nation: Les Filles du Roi in New France," 23, 58, 64-65. Many of the girls married soldiers from the Carignan-Salières regiment which arrived in 1665, thus providing incentive for the soldiers to remain in the colony ("King's Daughters." La Société des Filles du roi et soldats du Carignan, Inc).

24 *Programme de recherche en démographie historique (PRDH) Genealogical Database*, Marriage Contract, Record # 94311.

25 *Programme de recherche en démographie historique (PRDH) Genealogical Database*, Marriage Contract, Record # 94320; *Pistard Database*. Bibliothèque et Archives nationales du Québec (BAnQ). Civil marriage record dated November 17, 1667.

26   *Programme de recherche en démographie historique (PRDH) Genealogical Database,*
     Marriage record # 66909; Le Clercq, "Normand, Marie-Madeleine" and
     "Normand, Catherine." *Fichier Origine Database.* Quebec Federation of Gene-
     alogical Societies.

27   Chapais, Thomas. "The Great Intendant: A Chronicle of Jean Talon in
     Canada 1665-1672." *Chronicles of Canada.* VI: Ch 2; Vachon, "Talon, Jean."
     Dictionary of Canadian Biography Online; Runyan, "Daughters of the King and
     Founders of a Nation: Les Filles du Roi in New France," 35.

28   Bennett, "Couillard De Lespinay, Louis," *Dictionary of Canadian Biography Online.*

29   Hamelin, "Bourdon, Jean," *Dictionary of Canadian Biography Online;* Burke-
     Gaffney, "Canada's First Engineer Jean Bourdon (1601-1668)," *Canadian
     Catholic Historical Association (CCHA), Report.* On his last trip, Bourdon would
     spend two years in France, returning in July of 1665, the summer that the
     Carignan-Salières regiment arrived at Quebec.

30   Pinkard, *A Revolution in Taste: The Rise of French Cuisine, 1650 – 1800,* 51-53.

31   Pinkard, *A Revolution in Taste: The Rise of French Cuisine, 1650 – 1800,* 52-53.
     The residence belonging to Cardinal Richelieu is known as the *Palais Royal*
     today.

32   Pinkard, *A Revolution in Taste: The Rise of French Cuisine, 1650 – 1800,* 52-54.

33   Pinkard, *A Revolution in Taste: The Rise of French Cuisine, 1650 – 1800,* 53-54.

34   Pinkard, *A Revolution in Taste: The Rise of French Cuisine, 1650 – 1800,* 58. In the
     sixteenth century, the ambassador from Venice remarked that in Paris, within
     an hour of ordering, guests could sit down to a sumptuous dinner, be it for
     ten or for one hundred people (Pinkard, 58).

35   Pinkard, *A Revolution in Taste: The Rise of French Cuisine, 1650 – 1800,* 59.

36   Lewis, *The Splendid Century: Life in the France of Louis XIV,* 204-209.

37   Lewis, *The Splendid Century: Life in the France of Louis XIV,* 172-73.

38   Lewis, *The Splendid Century: Life in the France of Louis XIV,* 172-73.

39   Lewis, *The Splendid Century: Life in the France of Louis XIV,* 49, 210.

40   Trudel, *Introduction to New France,* 225-227.

Chapter Seventeen

1 Charbonneau et al., *The First French Canadians: Pioneers in the St. Lawrence Valley*, 28-29; Trudel, *Introduction to New France*, 160; Chapais, "The Great Intendant: A Chronicle of Jean Talon in Canada 1665-1672," *Chronicles of Canada*.

2 Trudel, *Introduction to New France*, 58-62; Vachon, "Talon, Jean," *Dictionary of Canadian Biography Online*; Sulte, Fryer, and David, *A History of Quebec*, 40-42.

3 Charbonneau et al., *The First French Canadians: Pioneers in the St. Lawrence Valley*, 30-31,198-99.

4 Sulte, Fryer, and David, *A History of Quebec*, 38.

5 Charbonneau et al., *The First French Canadians: Pioneers in the St. Lawrence Valley*, 27.

6 In the early years of the French colony, the word *"habitant"* was used to indicate a permanent resident; in later years it was applied to one who operated a small farm or paid a cens for his land concession from his seigneur. (Harris, *The Seigneurial System in Early Canada: A Geographical Study*, viii)

7 *Programme de recherche en démographie historique (PRDH) Genealogical Database*, Census Record #95976.

8 *Programme de recherche en démographie historique (PRDH) Genealogical Database*, Census Record # 96813.

9 Langlois, *Dictionnaire Biographique Des Ancêtres Québécois (1608-1700)*, 483.

10 Vachon, "Talon, Jean," *Dictionary of Canadian Biography Online*; Trudel, *Introduction to New France*, 140.

11 Vachon, "Talon, Jean," *Dictionary of Canadian Biography Online*; Trudel, *Introduction to New France*, 140.

12 Vachon, "Talon, Jean," *Dictionary of Canadian Biography Online*; Trudel, *Introduction to New France*, 140.

13 Tanguay, À Travers les Registres, 48; *Programme de recherche en démographie historique (PRDH) Genealogical Database*.

14 Mahoney, *Marie of the Incarnation: Selected Writings*, 264.

15 Dickinson and Young, *A Short History of Quebec*, 22.

16   Charbonneau et al., *The First French Canadians: Pioneers in the St. Lawrence Valley*, 31, 212-13 (footnote).

17   Harris, *The Seigneurial System in Early Canada*, 22-23; Sulte, Fryer, and David, *A History of Quebec*, 32.

18   On page 7 of his book *The Seigneurial Regime*, Trudel states that, between 1623 and 1653, there were sixty-two seigneuries en fief granted in New France; an additional fifty-three seigneuries were granted between 1653 and 1663. In his *Introduction to New France*, on page 58, Trudel gives a different number, stating that by 1663, forty-five seigneuries had been granted on the two banks of the St. Lawrence River. On page 32 of *A History of Quebec*, Sulte, Fryer, and David state that the Company of One Hundred Associates granted about sixty seigniorial estates in New France between the years 1633 and 1663. Harris, on page 22 of his book *The Seigneurial System in Early Canada: A Geographical Study* states that the Company granted "some seventy seigneuries."

19   Harris, *The Seigneurial System in Early Canada*, 22-23; Sulte, Fryer, and David, *A History of Quebec*, 32.

20   *Jesuit Relations*, ed. Thwaites, IV:268-9 (Notes section).

21   Trudel, *Introduction to New France*, 171-75; Harris, *The Seigneurial System in Early Canada*, 22-23; Sulte, Fryer, and David, *A History of Quebec*, 32.

22   Trudel, *Introduction to New France*,179; Dickinson and Young, *A Short History of Quebec*, 41-43; Sulte, Fryer, and David, *A History of Quebec*, 32; Harris, *The Seigneurial System in Early Canada: A Geographical Study*, 42-43, 62. Other income came in the form of tithes, donations, royal subsidies, and fees paid by the state for the care of the sick and poor.

23   Provost, "Giffard de Moncel, Robert," *Dictionary of Canadian Biography Online*.

24   Jetté states that Noël was given the "concession du fief Morin 15-11-1653, reconcedé en arrière-fief de St-Luc dans la Rivière-du-Sud 15-11-1663, réuni au domaine après 15-10-1683." (Jetté, *Dictionnaire Généalogique des familles du Québec*, 834); According to Harris, upon coming to New France, Intendant Talon "reconceded several smaller seigneuries which had existed only on paper during the proprietary period." (Harris, *The Seigneurial System in Early Canada: A Geographical Study*, 27) Michel Langlois, in *Dictionnaire Biographique Des Ancêtres Québécois*, III:483, also states that Noël was granted a fief in Montmagny on the 15 of November 1653. With respect to Jetté's comment,

"réuni au domaine après 15-10-1683," this was after Morin's death and probably refers to any land not developed at that time.

25 *Parchemin Notary Records (1626-1789), Bibliothèque et Archives nationales du Québec* (BAnQ) Notary record dated May 17 1655; Langlois, *Dictionnaire Biographique Des Ancêtres Québécois.* III: 483.

26 Trudel, *The Seigneurial Regime,* 10-11; Trudel, *Introduction to New France,*175.

27 Harris, *The Seigneurial System in Early Canada: A Geographical Study,* 26-27.

28 Vachon, "Talon, Jean," *Dictionary of Canadian Biography Online.*

29 Dickinson and Young. *A Short History of Quebec,* 22.

30 Trudel, *Introduction to New France,* 171-75; Dickinson and Young. *A Short History of Quebec,* 31-32, 87.

31 Trudel, *Introduction to New France,* 136.

32 Trudel, *Le Terrier Du Saint-Laurent en 1663,* 176.

33 Poirier, "Martin Boutet," The Canadian Encyclopedia/ The Encyclopedia of Music in Canada; *Programme de recherche en démographie historique (PRDH) Genealogical Database.*

34 Dickinson and Young. *A Short History of Quebec,* 81-82.

35 Trudel, *Introduction to New France,* 163-65.

36 Dickinson and Young. *A Short History of Quebec,* 25.

37 Simpson, *Marguerite Bourgeoys and Montréal, 1640-1665,* 173-74.

38 Dollier de Casson, as quoted in Simpson, *Marguerite Bourgeoys and Montréal, 1640-1665,* 97.

39 Dickinson and Young. *A Short History of Quebec,* 25.

40 Letter from Marie de l'Incarnation, as quoted in Tanguay, *À Travers les Registres,* 56.

41 Mahoney, *Marie of the Incarnation: Selected Writings,* 248.

42   Chapais, "The Great Intendant: A Chronicle of Jean Talon in Canada 1665-1672," *Chronicles of Canada.*

43   Charbonneau et al., *The First French Canadians: Pioneers in the St. Lawrence Valley,* 172.

44   Charbonneau et al., *The First French Canadians: Pioneers in the St. Lawrence Valley,* 28-29; Trudel, *Introduction to New France,* 160, 163; Chapais, "The Great Intendant: A Chronicle of Jean Talon in Canada 1665-1672," *Chronicles of Canada.*

Chapter Eighteen

1   According to the historian Marcel Trudel, land development on the south shore of the St. Lawrence River lagged behind because of a lack of French settlers and threats from the Iroquois. (Trudel, *Introduction to New France,* 58)

2   Langlois, *Dictionnaire Biographique Des Ancêtres Québécois (1608-1700) Tome III,* 484. A seigneur was entitled to an act of foi et hommage (faith and homage) from anyone who held land under him. (Harris, *The Seigneurial System in Early Canada: A Geographical Study,*viii)

3   Harris, *The Seigneurial System in Early Canada: A Geographical Study,* 30.

4   Langlois, *Dictionnaire Biographique Des Ancêtres Québécois (1608-1700),*484. Jetté states that the fief Morin was returned to the [Royal] domaine after October 15, 1683, three years after Noël's death (Jetté, *Dictionnaire Généalogique des familles du Québec,* 834). Presumably, this refers to any land on the fief that was undeveloped.

5   *Parchemin Notary Records (1626-1789),* Bibliothèque et Archives nationales du Québec (BAnQ). Document of R. Becquet, Notary of Quebec, February 25, 1668.

6   *Parchemin Notary Records (1626-1789).* Bibliothèque et Archives nationales du Québec (BAnQ).

7   Harris, *The Seigneurial System in Early Canada: A Geographical Study,* 46-47; Dickinson and Young. *A Short History of Quebec,* 86-87. (Note that in the latter source, it is stated that all children inherited equally.)

8   Dickinson and Young. *A Short History of Quebec,* 86-87.

[9] Langlois, Michel. *Dictionnaire Biographique Des Ancêtres Québécois (1608-1700)*, 484.

[10] In 1683, several of Marie-Madeleine's siblings donated their portions of the arriere-fief of Saint-Luc to Gilles Rageot and Marie-Madeleine. (*Pistard Database*, Bibliothèque et Archives nationales du Québec)

[11] *Programme de recherche en démographie historique (PRDH) Genealogical Database.* Baptism, marriage and death records for Hélène's children.

[12] Langlois, Michel. *Dictionnaire Biographique Des Ancêtres Québécois (1608-1700)*, 484.

[13] *Programme de recherche en démographie historique (PRDH) Genealogical Database.* Baptism records.

[14] Mahoney, *Marie of the Incarnation: Selected Writings*, 273; Charbonneau et al., *The First French Canadians: Pioneers in the St. Lawrence Valley*, 37.

[15] Mahoney, *Marie of the Incarnation: Selected Writings*, 273. Letter written by Marie de l'Incarnation to the Ursuline Superior at Mons, dated October 1, 1669.

[16] Charbonneau et al., *The First French Canadians: Pioneers in the St. Lawrence Valley*, 18, 31-34, 40-41, 199; Trudel, *Introduction to New France*, 132-33, 203; Brault, *The French-Canadian Heritage in New England*, 110.

[17] Vachon, "Talon, Jean," *Dictionary of Canadian Biography Online*.

[18] In 1681, the population of Quebec City itself was listed as 1,345 (Douglas, "Education in Quebec in the 17th Century").

[19] Charbonneau et al., *The First French Canadians: Pioneers in the St. Lawrence Valley*, 18, 31-34, 37,40-41, 199; Trudel, *Introduction to New France*, 132-33; Brault, *The French-Canadian Heritage in New England*, 110.

[20] Dickinson and Young. *A Short History of Quebec*, 22 -23; Trudel, *Introduction to New France*, 30-32.

[21] Le Clercq, *First Establishment of the Faith in New France*, I:256, 406-07. The Récollet missionaries who had been in New France from 1615 to 1629 returned to the colony in 1670 at the request of Intendant Talon. They were able to regain their property and the Convent of Notre-Dame-des-Anges in Quebec. (Sulte, Fryer, and David, *A History of Quebec*, 37; Vachon, "Laval, François De," *Dictionary of Canadian Biography Online*)

22   *Lands of Promise and Despair. eds.* Beebe and Senkewicz, 153.

23   Jesuit power and influence declined in the eighteenth century, after the conquest by Great Britain. Jesuit land was confiscated by the British in 1763. The old college fell into a state of disrepair and was razed in the late eighteenth century. It was never rebuilt.

24   Chapais, "The Great Intendant: A Chronicle of Jean Talon in Canada 1665-1672," *Chronicles of Canada.* VI: Ch 2.

25   Zoltvany, "Aubert De La Chesnaye, Charles," *Dictionary of Canadian Biography Online.*

26   Chapais, "The Great Intendant: A Chronicle of Jean Talon in Canada 1665-1672." *Chronicles of Canada.* VI: Ch 2; Trudel, *Introduction to New France,* 207.

27   Dickinson and Young, *A Short History of Quebec,* 38.

28   Vachon, "Laval, François De," *Dictionary of Canadian Biography Online.* The monsignor was born in April of 1623 at Montigny-sur-Avre, in the diocese of Chartres, France. Laval was descended from the younger branch of the Montmorencys, one of the noblest families in France. The young Laval attended the Jesuit College at La Flèche and the College de Clermont in Paris, two of the most prestigious schools in France. There, he was greatly influenced by his Jesuit teachers. His interest in the priesthood and in the missions of New France sprang from his school days with the Jesuits. Laval was ordained a priest in 1647. From this family came several cardinals, as well as a number of civil, naval and military officers. Through his mother, Bishop Laval belonged to the legal nobility which had provided the parliament of Rouen with several officers of the crown and the church with many prelates. (Vachon, "Laval, François De," *Dictionary of Canadian Biography Online*)

29   Vachon, "Laval, François De," *Dictionary of Canadian Biography Online;* Sulte, Fryer, and David, *A History of Quebec,* 38-39;

30   Mahoney, *Marie of the Incarnation: Selected Writings, 28-29, 257-58*; Vachon, "Laval, François De," *Dictionary of Canadian Biography Online.*

31   Simpson, *Marguerite Bourgeoys and Montréal, 1640-1665,*121-125, 175-78; Mahoney, *Marie of the Incarnation: Selected Writings,* 28-29; Sulte, Fryer, and David, *A History of Quebec,* 38-39; Vachon, "Laval, François De," *Dictionary of Canadian Biography Online.*

32 Information noted on a plaque on the grounds of the Seminary of Quebec in August, 2011.

33 Dickinson and Young, *A Short History of Quebec*, 42.

34 Vachon, "Laval, François De," *Dictionary of Canadian Biography Online*. Laval had made strong inroads in establishing a national Church before his death on May 6, 1708 at the age of eighty-five. Laval was buried on May 9 in his beloved Cathedral of Notre-Dame in Quebec. (Vachon, "Laval, François De")

35 Douglas, "Education in Quebec in the 17th Century."

36 Mahoney, *Marie of the Incarnation: Selected Writings*, 264-65.

37 Mahoney, *Marie of the Incarnation: Selected Writings*, 6, 272-74.

38 Chabot, "Guyart, Marie dite Marie de l'"Incarnation," *Dictionary of Canadian Biography Online*.

39 Mahoney, *Marie of the Incarnation: Selected Writings*, 6, 272-74; Chabot, "Guyart, Marie dite Marie de l'"Incarnation," *Dictionary of Canadian Biography Online*.

40 On display at the Ursuline Museum in August of 2011 were two exquisite altar frontals embroidered in the latter half of the seventeenth century. They are woven in wool and silk thread and edged in bobbin lace. In the center of each piece is a medallion featuring a beautifully detailed religious scene. These works are a testament to the fine needlework produced by the sisters and students living in this cloistered community in the late 1600s. ("Marie LeMaire Des Anges and her Workshop: The Fine Art of Embroidery", *Ursuline Museum*, Quebec City, on display in August of 2011)

41 Exhibition, "Marie LeMaire Des Anges and her Workshop: The Fine Art of Embroidery" and L' Exposition L'Académie des demoiselles," *Ursuline Museum*, Quebec City; "Repplier, *Mére Marie of the Ursulines*, 240.

42 Charbonneau et al., *The First French Canadians: Pioneers in the St. Lawrence Valley*, 172-73,177.

43 Hamelin, "Bourdon, Jean," *Dictionary of Canadian Biography Online*.

44 Bennett, "Hébert, Guillemette," *Dictionary of Canadian Biography Online*. The legal battles initiated by the Hébert descendants concerning the sale of the

family property would continue into the twentieth century (Bennett, "Hébert, Guillemette").

[45] *Programme de recherche en démographie historique (PRDH) Genealogical Database*, Family Record #85; Charbonneau et al., *The First French Canadians: Pioneers in the St. Lawrence Valley, 141.*

[46] *Programme de recherche en démographie historique (PRDH) Genealogical Database.*

[47] Provost, "Giffard de Moncel, Robert," *Dictionary of Canadian Biography Online.*

[48] *Jesuit Relations*, ed. Thwaites, XXV:107.

[49] Dickinson and Young, *A Short History of Quebec*, 28, 72-74.

[50] Vachon, "Talon, Jean," *Dictionary of Canadian Biography Online.*

[51] Vachon, "Talon, Jean," *Dictionary of Canadian Biography Online.*

[52] The Château Frontenac, which opened in Quebec in 1893, was named after the Comte de Frontenac. The luxury hotel became an iconic image of Quebec.

[53] Eccles, "Buade de Frontenac et de Palluau, Louis De," *Dictionary of Canadian Biography Online.*

[54] Dickinson and Young, *A Short History of Quebec, 58-59.*

[55] Vachon, "Talon, Jean," *Dictionary of Canadian Biography Online.*

[56] *Programme de recherche en démographie historique (PRDH) Genealogical Database*, Baptism record for Louis Jolliet.

[57] Vachon, "Jolliet, Louis," *Dictionary of Canadian Biography Online.*

[58] Vachon, "Jolliet, Louis," *Dictionary of Canadian Biography Online.*

[59] Charbonneau et al., *The First French Canadians: Pioneers in the St. Lawrence Valley,* 169-171.

[60] According to the *Programme de recherche en démographie historique* (PRDH), the date of Hélène's death is known by an annotation in the "registre de la Confrerie de la Sainte-Famille "(Register of the Confraternity of the Holy Family, established by Bishop Laval in Quebec in 1666), which was discovered by

Archange Godbout. It was cited by Léon Roy in a 1946 article on the descendants of Pierre Desportes in the *Mémoires de La Société Généalogique Canadienne-Française,*165.

61 *Programme de recherche en démographie historique (PRDH) Genealogical Database,* Burial Record # 69207.

62 Langlois, *Dictionnaire Biographique Des Ancêtres Québécois (1608-1700),* 484.

63 *Quebec Catholic Parish Registers 1621-1900: Notre-Dame-de-Quebec, 1679-1690,* Family Search.org, Image 22; Roy, "Pierre Desportes et sa descendance," *Mémoires de La Société Généalogique Canadienne-Française,* 168.

64 In 1688, the church Notre-Dame-des-Victoires was built over what was originally Champlain's Habitation at Quebec.

65 Charbonneau et al., *The First French Canadians: Pioneers in the St. Lawrence Valley,* 161. "That scarcely one thousand women, who married within a half century [the seventeenth century], could end up fifty years later with fifty thousand descendants is quite astonishing" (Charbonneau et al., *The First French Canadians: Pioneers in the St. Lawrence Valley,* 205).

66 The historian Marcel Trudel claims that in 1663 Hélène Desportes was the "most fruitful" woman in the colony, that is, the woman who had produced the most children before 1663 (Charbonneau, "Reconstitution de la population du Canada au 30 juin 1663 suivant Marcel Trudel").

Chapter Nineteen

1 Information on the children of Hélène Desportes and Guillaume Hébert comes from the following sources: Jetté, *Dictionnaire Généalogique des familles du Québec; Programme de recherche en démographie historique (PRDH);* the *Parchemin – Banque de données notariales (1626-1789)* and *Pistard Database,* both located at the Bibliothèque et Archives nationales du Québec (BAnQ). Baptism, marriage and burial records are also found in the *Quebec Catholic Parish Registers 1621-1900,* digitized and available at Family Search.org.

2 Tanguay lists Guillaume Fournier as co-seigneur of the parish of St. Charles in his *Dictionnaire Genealogique des Familles Canadiennes,* 239.

3 Based on her date of birth, Françoise would have been 76 years old; however, she was listed as 86 on her death certificate.

4   Information on the children of Hélène Desportes and Noël Morin comes from the following sources: Jetté, *Dictionnaire Généalogique des familles du Québec; Programme de recherche en démographie historique (PRDH)*; the *Parchemin – Banque de données notariales (1626-1789)* and *Pistard Database*, both located at the Bibliothèque et Archives nationales du Québec (BAnQ); *Dictionary of Canadian Biography Online;* and Beaupré's "Agnés Morin et ses Parents." Baptism, marriage and burial records are also found in the *Quebec Catholic Parish Registers 1621-1900,* digitized and available at Family Search.org.

5   Tanquay, *Clergé Canadaien*, 47; Provost, "Morin, Germain," *Dictionary of Canadian Biography Online.*

6   *Pistard Database*, Bibliothèque et Archives nationales du Québec (BAnQ), document dated February 25, 1663.

7   Langlois, *Dictionnaire Biographique Des Ancêtres Québécois (1608-1700)*, 483.

8   *Parchemin – Banque de données notariales (1626-1789)*, Bibliothèque et Archives nationales du Québec (BAnQ). Document of R. Becquet, Notary of Quebec, February 25, 1668; Langlois, Michel. *Dictionnaire Biographique Des Ancêtres Québécois (1608-1700)*, 484.

9   Historian Marchel Trudel points out that in New France the bourgeoisie were not a well-defined class; in general, a man's prosperity and standing in the business community could earn him the title of bourgeois. (Trudel, *Introduction to New France*,141-42)

10 Bernier, "Morin, Marie," *Dictionary of Canadian Biography Online.*

11 Vachon, "Rageot, Gilles," *Dictionary of Canadian Biography Online.*

BIBLIOGRAPHY

Beaupré, Gaston. "Agnès Morin et ses Parents." *L'Ancetre*. Sainte Foy, Quebec: Société de généalogie de Québec. 10.3 (Nov. 1983): 87-92.

Beebe, Rose Marie and Robert M. Senkewicz, Eds. *Lands of Promise and Despair: Chronicles of Early California, 1535-1846*. Berkeley, CA: Heyday Pub, 2001.

Belanger, Raymond. *François Bellenger: Seigneur de L'Islet-de-Bonsecours*. Québec: Presses de l'Université Laval, 2010.

Bennett, Ethel M. G. "Couillard De Lespinay, Louis." *Dictionary of Canadian Biography Online*. Canada: University of Toronto/Université Laval, 2000. Web. 25 May 2012.

---. "Desportes, Hélène." *Dictionary of Canadian Biography Online*. Canada: University of Toronto/Université Laval, 2000. Web. 25 Aug. 2008.

---. "Hébert, Guillemette." *Dictionary of Canadian Biography Online*. Canada: University of Toronto/Université Laval, 2000. Web. 14 Nov. 2012.

---. "Hébert, Joseph." *Dictionary of Canadian Biography Online*. Canada: University of Toronto/Université Laval, 2000. Web. 25 Aug. 2008.

---. "Hébert, Louis." *Dictionary of Canadian Biography Online*. Canada: University of Toronto/Université Laval, 2000. Web. 17 June 2010.

Bernier, Hélène. "Bourgeoys, Marguerite." *Dictionary of Canadian Biography Online*. Canada: University of Toronto/Université Laval, 2000. Web. 9 Oct. 2011.

---. "Morin, Marie." *Dictionary of Canadian Biography Online*. Canada: University of Toronto/Université Laval, 2000. Web. 25 Aug. 2008.

Best, Henry B. M. "Martin, Abraham." *Dictionary of Canadian Biography Online*. Canada: University of Toronto/Université Laval, 2000. Web. 25 Aug. 2008.

Biggar, H.P. *The Early Trading Companies of New France*. Toronto: University of Toronto Library, 1901. *Google Books*. Web. 29 Sept. 2011.

Bosher, J.F. "French Ports and North America before 1627: The View from La Rochelle." Ontario: York University. Web. 27 April 2011.

Bourgeault, Ivy Lynn, Cecilia Benoit, and Robbie Davis-Floyd. *Reconceiving Midwifery*. Montreal: McGill Queen's University Press, 2004.

Brault, Gerard J. *The French-Canadian Heritage in New England*. Hanover: University Press of New England, 1986.

Burke-Gaffney, M.W. "Canada's First Engineer Jean Bourdon (1601-1668)." *Canadian Catholic Historical Association (CCHA), Report* 24 (1957): 84-104. Web. 17 Feb. 2012.

Campeau, Charles Vianney. "Navires venus en Neuvelle-France gens de mer et passagers des origines á la Conquête." Web. 16 May 2011.

Campeau, Lucien, S.J. "Roman Catholic Missions in New France." *Handbook of North American Indians*. 20 vols. Washington D.C.: Smithsonian Institution, 1988. 8: 464-467.

---. "The Jesuits of Early Montreal." Willaim Lonc and George Topp, trans. *Early Jesuit Missions in Canada*. vol. II. Web. 29 Aug 2009.

Chabot, Marie-Emanuel, O.S.U. "Guyart, Marie dit Marie de l'Incarnation." *Dictionary of Canadian Biography Online*. Canada: University of Toronto/Université Laval, 2000. Web. 17 June 2010.

---. "Chauvigny De La Peltrie, Marie-Madeleine De." *Dictionary of Canadian Biography Online*. Canada: University of Toronto/Université Laval, 2000. Web. 29 Feb. 2012.

Champlain, Samuel de. *Voyages of Samuel de Champlain*. Ed. Rev. Edmund F. Slafter. Trans. Charles Pomeroy Otis. 3 vol. Boston: The Prince Society, 1880. *Google Books*. Web. 26 Aug. 2008.

---. *The Works of Samuel de Champlain in Six Volumes*. Ed. H. P. Biggar. Trans. H.H. Langton. vol. 4 & 6. Toronto: The Champlain Society, 1932. *Internet Archive*. Web. 23 July 2011.

Chapais, Thomas. "The Great Intendant: A Chronicle of Jean Talon in Canada 1665-1672." *Chronicles of Canada*. Toronto: Glasgow, Brook and Co., 1914. Vol. 6. *Project Gutenberg e-book*. Web. 19 Jan. 2012.

Charbonneau, Hubert. "Reconstitution de la population du Canada au 30 juin 1663 suivant Marcel Trudel." *Revue d'histoire de l'Amérique française.* 27. 3 (Dec 1973):417-24. *érudit.* Web. 20 July 2011.

Charbonneau, Hubert, Bertrand Desjardins, André Guillemette, Yves Landry, Jacques Légaré, and François Nault. *The First French Canadians: Pioneers in the St. Lawrence Valley.* Trans. Paola Colozzo. Ontario: Associated University Press, 1993.

Charlevoix, Pierre François Xavier de. *History and General Description of New France.* Trans. John Gilmary Shea. Vol. 2. Chicago: Loyola University Press, 1866. *Google Books.* Web. 15 Sept. 2009.

Cushner, Nicholas P. *The Jesuits in Colonial America: 1565-1767.* Buffalo: State Univ. of New York, 2000. Web. 3 Oct. 2011.

Daveluy, Marie-Claire. "Chomeday de Maisonnueve, Paul de." *Dictionary of Canadian Biography Online.* Canada: University of Toronto/Université Laval, 2000. Web. 9 Oct. 2011.

---. "Mance, Jeanne." *Dictionary of Canadian Biography Online.* Canada: University of Toronto/Université Laval, 2000. Web. 9 Oct. 2011.

Debian, G. "Engagés pour le Canada au XVIIe siècle vus de La Rochelle." *Revue d'histoire de l'Amérique française.* 6. 2 (1952): 177-233. *érudit.* Web. 21 Jul. 2011.

---. "Liste des engagés pour le Canada au XVIIe siècle (1634-1715)." *Revue d'histoire de l'Amérique française.* 6.3 (1952): 374- 407. *érudit.* Web 21 Jul. 2011.

Deroy-Pineau, Françoise. "Marie Guyart de l'Incarnation." *Canada: Portraits of Faith.* Canada's Christian Heritage. Web. 12 Feb. 2010.

Dickinson, John and Brian Young. *A Short History of Quebec.* Montreal: McGill-Queen's University Press, 2003.

Dionne, N.E. *The Makers of Canada: Champlain.* London: T.C. & E.C. Jack, 1905. *Google Books.* Web. 26 Aug. 2008.

Doughty, Arthur G. *The Cradle of New France: A Story of the City Founded by Champlain.* London: Longmans, Green and Company, 1909. *Internet Archive: Canadian Libraries.* Web. 16 Sept. 2009.

Douglas, James Jr. "Education in Quebec in the 17th Century." *Transactions.* New Series, No. 25 (1903). Quebec: Literacy and Historical Society of Quebec. Online at *Literacy and Historical Society of Quebec: Early Publications 1824-1924.* Web. 4 Aug. 2011.

---. *Old France in the New World: Quebec in the Seventeenth Century.* Cleveland: The Burrows Brothers Company, 1905. *Google Books.* Web. 20 Jan. 2012.

Durant-Gasselin, T. "Huguenot Pirates in the Seventeenth Century." *Musée virtual du protestantisme français.* Web. 11 Jan. 2011.

Eccles, W.J. "Buade de Frontenac et de Palluau, Louis De." *Dictionary of Canadian Biography Online.* Canada: University of Toronto/Université Laval, 2000. Web. 4 May 2012.

"Evolution of juvenile justice in Canada." *Department of Justice Canada.* Web. 27 July 2011.

Fillion, Konrad. "Essai sur l'évolution du mot habitant (XVIIe-XVIIIe siècles)." *Revue d'histoire de l'Amérique française.* 24.3 (1970): 375-401. érudit. Web. 21 July 2011.

Fischer, David Hackett. *Champlain's Dream.* New York: Simon and Schuster, 2008.

Fiske, John. *New France and New England.* Boston: Houghton Mifflin Co. 1902. *Google Books.* Web. 25 Aug. 2008.

Foisset, Bernadette and Gail Moreau-Desharnais. "Martin/L'Ecossais, Abraham." *Fichier Origine Database.* Quebec Federation of Genealogical Societies. Web. 17 June 2010.

Fournier, Marcel. "Samuel de Champlain de Brouage ou de La Rochelle? – Les deux!" No. 34 (August 2012). *Commission franco-québécoise sur les lieux de mémoire communs.* Web. 19 Sept. 2012.

Fraser, Antonia. *Love and Louis XIV: The Women in the Life of the Sun King.* New York: Anchor Books, 2007.

Gagnon, Ernest. *Le Fort et Le Chateau Saint-Louis (Quebec).* Montreal: Librairie Beauchemin, 1908. *Internet Archives.* Web. 23 June 2011.

Garneau, F.X. *History of Canada.* Trans. Andrew Bell. Vol. 1. Montreal: Richard Worthington, 1866. *Google Books.* Web. 4 Oct. 2010.

Glimpses of the Monastery: Scenes from the History of the Ursulines of Quebec during the Two Hundred Years 1639-1839. Second ed. Quebec: L.J. Demers & Frère, 1897. *Google Books.* Web. 20 June 2011.

Goubert, Pierre. *The French Peasantry in the Seventeenth Century.* Trans. Ian Patterson. Cambridge: Cambridge University Press, 1986.

Hamelin, Jean. "Bourdon, Jean." *Dictionary of Canadian Biography Online.* Canada: University of Toronto/Université Laval, 2000. Web. 13 May 2011.

---. "Huault de Montmagny, Charles." *Dictionary of Canadian Biography Online.* Canada: University of Toronto/Université Laval, 2000. Web. 1 Oct. 2012.

Harris, Rev. W. R. *Practice of Medicine and Surgery by the Canadian Tribes in Champlain's Time.* Reprint from the Archeological Report. Toronto: William Briggs, 1915. Web. 27 July 2011.

Harris, Richard Colebrook. *The Seigneurial System in Early Canada: A Geographical Study.* Montreal: McGill-Queen's University Press, 1966.

Haudrère, Philippe. "Royal College de Flèche, Wellspring of Missionary Zeal". *Encyclopedia of French Cultural Heritage in North America.* Web. 23 May 2010.

Hayes, Derek. *Canada: An Illustrated History.* Vancouver: Douglas and McIntyre, 2004.

---. *Historical Atlas of Canada: Canada's History Illustrated with Original Maps.* Vancouver: Douglas and McIntyre Ltd., 2006.

"Historic District of Old Québec." *UNESCO World Heritage Center.* Web. 11 August 2011.

"History: Dieppe." *Monastère Communauté Augustines Malestroit.* Web. 16 Feb 2012.

Horn, James. *Adapting to a New World English Society in the Seventeenth-Century Chesapeake.* Chapel Hill, NC: UNC Press Books, 1996.

Hussey, Andrew. *Paris: The Secret History.* New York: Bloomsbury, 2006.

Jesuit Relations and Allied Documents(The): Travels and Explorations of the Jesuit Missionaries in New France. Ed. Reuben Gold Thwaites. *71 vol.* Cleveland: The Burrows Brothers Co, 1897. *Internet Archive: Canadian Libraries.* Web. 22 Oct. 2009; *Google Books.* Web. 30 Aug. 2009; *Creighton University.* Web 9 Dec. 2009.

Jetté, René. *Dictionnaire Généalogique des familles du Québec*. Montreal: University of Montreal. 1983.

Johnston, A. J. B. *Life and Religion at Louisbourg 1713-1758*. Montreal: McGill-Queen's University Press. 1996.

Kallman, Helmut. "Martin, Charles-Amador." *Dictionary of Canadian Biography Online*. Canada: University of Toronto/Université Laval, 2000. Web. 19 Feb. 2012.

"King's Daughters." Chantilly, VA: *La Société des Filles du roi et soldats du Carignan, Inc*. Web. 8 Aug. 2005.

Kingsford, William. *The History of Canada*. Vol. 1. Toronto, Can: Rowsell & Hutchison, 1887. *Google Books*. Web. 30 Aug. 2009.

Labine, M. Gustave. *Histoire des Premiers Travaux des Péres Récollets en la Nouvelle France, 1615-1629*. Montreal: Imp. de L'Institution des Sourds-Muets, 1893.

Laforce, Hélène. *Histoire de la sage-femme dans la région de Québec*. Quebec: Institut Québécois de Recherche Sur la Culture, 1985.

--- "L'Univers de la sage-femme aux XVIIe aux XVIIIe siècle." *Cap-aux-Diamants: la revue d'histoire du Québec*. 1. 3 (Autumn 1985): 3-6. *érudit*. Web. 9 May 2012.

Langlois, Michel. *Dictionnaire Biographique Des Ancêtres Québécois (1608-1700) Tome III Lettres J à M*. Sillery: La Maison Des Ancêtres Québécois, 2000.

Laverdiére, Charles. *Samuel De Champlain*. Quebec: Imprimerie A. Coté, 1877. *Google Books*. Web. 10 Sept. 2009.

Le Blant, Robert. "Le testament de Samuel Champlain, 17 novembre 1635." *Revue d'histoire de l'Amérique francaise*. 17.2 (1963): 269-286. *érudit*. Web. 22 Feb. 2010.

---. "Le triste veuvage d'Hélène Boullé." *Revue d'histoire de l'Amérique francaise*. 18.3 (1964):425-437. *érudit*. Web. 7 Oct. 2010.

Leblond de Brumath, Adrien. *The Makers of Canada: Bishop Laval*. London: T.C. & E.C. Jack, 1906. *Google Books*. Web. 8 Sept. 2009.

Le Clercq, Christian. *First Establishment of the Faith in New France*. Trans. John Gilmary Shea. New York: John G. Shea. 1881. 2 vols. *Internet Archive: Canadian Libraries*. Web. 15 Sept. 2009.

'L' Exposition Marie Lemaire des Anges et son atelier: Le grand art de la broderie." *Musée des Ursulines de Quebec.* Quebec, Canada. 2 Aug. 2011.

'L' Exposition L'Académie des demoiselles." *Musée des Ursulines de Quebec.* Quebec, Canada. 2 Aug. 2011.

Le Moine, J.M. *Quebec Past and Present: A History of Quebec 1608-1676.* Quebec: Augustin Coté and Co., 1876. *Google Books.* Web. 29 Sept. 2009.

Lescarbot, Marc. *The History of New France.* Trans. W. L. Grant. Vol. 1 Toronto: The Champlain Society, 1907. *Google Books.* Web. 22 Aug. 2008.

Lessard, Renald. "De France à Nouvelle-France: la practique médicale canadienne aux XVIIe et XVIIIe siècles." *Annales de Bretagne et des pays de l'Ouest.* 1988. 95. 4: 421-33. Web. 9 May 2012.

Lewis, W.H. *The Splendid Century: Life in the France of Louis XIV.* Long Grove, IL: Waveland Press, 1953.

Machar, Agnes Maule and Thomas G. Marquis. *Stories of New France: Being Tales of Adventure and Heroism from the Early History of Canada.* Boston: D. Lothrop Company, 1890. *Google Books.* Web. 22 Aug. 2008.

Macouin, Jean-Paul. "Hébert, Louis." *Fichier Origine Database.* Pub: Quebec Federation of Genealogical Societies. Web. 17 June 2010.

Mahoney, Irene, O.S.U., ed. *Marie of the Incarnation: Selected Writings.* NY: Paulist Press, 1989.

Mann, Charles C. *1491: New Revelations of the Americas Before Columbus.* New York: Vintage Books, 2006.

McLeod, Susanna. "Hôtel-Dieu of Quebec, Canada's First Hospital." *Canadian Settlement.* Web. 15 June 2010.

Miethe, Terrance D and Hong Lu. *Punishment: A Comparative Historical Perspective.* New York: Cambridge University Press, 2004.

Moir, John S. "Kirke, Sir David." *Dictionary of Canadian Biography Online.* Canada: University of Toronto/Université Laval, 2000. Web. 4 October 2011.

Montagne, Madame Pierre. *Tourouvre et les Juchereau: Un chapitre de l'émigration percheronne au Canada.* Québec: Société Canadienne de Généalogie: 1965.

Moreau-Desharnais, Gail F. "Exiles from Québec Found in the Parish of St-Jacques de Dieppe During the Kirke Occupation (1629-1632)." *Michigan's Habitant Heritage.* 24.2 (April, 2003): 77-78.

---. "Langlois, Francois." *Fichier Origine Database.* Pub: Quebec Federation of Genealogical Societies. Web. 17 June 2010.

Morin, Marie. *Annales de L'Hôtel-Dieu de Montreal.* Collationées et annotées par AE Faiteix, E.Z. Massicotte, and C. Bertrand. Montreal: L' Imprimerie Des Editeurs, 1921. Web. 11 Sept. 2009.

Morton, Thomas. *The New English Canaan.* Introductory matter and notes by Charles Francis Adams, Jr. Ed. Boston: Prince Society, 1883. *Google Books.* Web. 5 Nov. 2010.

Munro, William Bennett. "The Seigneurs of Old Canada: A Chronicle of New World Feudalism." Toronto, 1915. Pub. in *Chronicles of Canada*, Vol. 5. *Project Gutenberg e-book.* Web. 19 Jan. 2012.

New Peoples: Being and Becoming Métis in North America (The). Eds. Jacqueline Peterson & Jennifer Brown. Winnipeg: The University of Manitoba Press, 1985.

Parchemin – Banque de données notariales (1626-1789). Bibliothèque et Archives nationales du Québec (BAnQ). Quebec, Canada.

Parent, France. "Au-delá des rôles, la place des femmes." *Cap-aux-Diamants: la revue d'histoire du Québec.* 204: 25-29. érudit. Web. 20 July 2011.

Parkman, Francis. *France and England in North America.* Part Second. Boston: Little, Brown, and Company, 1867. *Google Books.* Web. 20 June 2011.

---. *Pioneers of France in the New World.* Boston: Little, Brown, and Company, 1918. *Google Books.* Web. 10 Sept. 2009.

Paul, Louise. "The Servants of God in Canada." *The Pilgrim of Our Lady of Martyrs.* Vol. XXI. New York: Pub 27 & 29 West 16th St., 1905.

Pepper, Mary Sifton. *Maids and Matrons of New France.* Boston: Little, Brown, and Company, 1901. *Google Books.* Web. 11 Sept. 2009.

Pinkard, Susan. *A Revolution in Taste: The Rise of French Cuisine, 1650 – 1800.* New York: Cambridge University Press, 2009.

"Pioneers and Immigrants: New France (1608–1763)." *Canada in the Making.* Canadian Institute for Historical Microreproductions: Early Canadiana Online. Web. 27 Sept 2011.

Pistard Database. Bibliothèque et Archives nationales du Québec (BAnQ), Quebec, Canada. Web. 20 July 2011.

Poirier, Lucien. "Martin Boutet." *The Canadian Encyclopedia/The Encyclopedia of Music in Canada.* Web. 21 Oct. 2011.

Pouliot, Léon. "Lalemant, Charles." *Dictionary of Canadian Biography Online.* Canada: University of Toronto/Université Laval, 2000. Web. 16 May 2011.

---. "Lalemant, Jérôme." *Dictionary of Canadian Biography Online.* Canada: University of Toronto/Université Laval, 2000. Web. 7 Mar. 2012.

---. "Le Jeune, Paul." *Dictionary of Canadian Biography Online.* Canada: University of Toronto/Université Laval, 2000. Web. 20 Nov. 2010.

Programme de recherche en démographie historique (PRDH) Genealogical Database, University of Montreal, 2005. Web. 1 Nov. 2012.

Provost, Honorius. "Cloutier, Zacharie." *Dictionary of Canadian Biography Online.* Canada: University of Toronto/Université Laval, 2000. Web. 13 May 2011.

---. "Giffard de Moncel, Robert." *Dictionary of Canadian Biography Online.* Canada: University of Toronto/Université Laval, 2000. Web. 26 Oct. 2010.

---. "Le Sueur, Jean." *Dictionary of Canadian Biography Online.* Canada: University of Toronto/Université Laval, 2000. Web. 17 Feb. 2012.

---. "Morin, Germain." *Dictionary of Canadian Biography Online.* Canada: University of Toronto/Université Laval, 2000. Web. 25 Aug. 2008.

---. "Prévost, Martin." *Dictionary of Canadian Biography Online.* Canada: University of Toronto/Université Laval, 2000. Web. 17 Feb. 2012.

Repplier, Agnes. *Mère Marie of the Ursulines.* Garden City, NY: Country Life Press, 1931.

Rider, Nick. *Short Breaks in Northern France.* London: Cadogan Guides, 2005.

Rioux, Jean de la Croix. "Sagard, Gabriel." *Dictionary of Canadian Biography Online.* Canada: University of Toronto/Université Laval, 2000. Web. 16 Jan. 2012.

Robinson, Ivan. "New France's First Child? It's a Girl!" *Connecticut Maple Leaf.* 12.1 (Summer, 2005): 5-6.

Rousseau, Jacques. "Sarrazin, Michel." *Dictionary of Canadian Biography Online.* Canada: University of Toronto/Université Laval, 2000. Web. 10 May 2012.

Roy, Léon. "Pierre Desportes et sa descendance." *Mémoires de La Société Généalogique Canadienne-Française.* 2. 3 (Jan. 1947): 165-68.

Rubin, Alissa J. "For Punishment of Elder's Misdeeds, Afghan girl pays the price." *The New York Times.* Web. 16 Feb. 2012.

Runyan, Aimie Kathleen. "Daughters of the King and Founders of a Nation: Les *Filles du roi* in New France." Master's Thesis, University of North Texas, May, 2010. Web. 13 Mar. 2012.

Sagard, Gabriel. *Histoire Du Canada Et Voyages Que Les Freres Mineurs Recollects y Ont Faicts Pour La Conversion Des Infidelles.* Paris: Chez Claude Sonnius, 1636. *Project Gutenberg* Web. 2 July 2010.

Sedgwick, Henry Dwight, Jr. *Samuel de Champlain.* Boston: Houghton, Mifflin and Company, 1902. *Google Books.* Web. 25 Aug. 2008.

Simpson, Patricia. *Marguerite Bourgeoys and Montreal, 1640-1665.* Montreal: McGill-Queens University Press, 1997.

Sister Mary of Jesus. "Ursulines." W. Stewart Wallace, ed. *The Encyclopedia of Canada.* Vol VI. Toronto: University Association of Canada, 1948:221-224. Web. 17 June 2010.

Slafter, Rev. Edmund F. "Memoir of Samuel de Champlain." De Champlain, Samuel. *Voyages of Samuel de Champlain.* Ed. Rev. Edmund F. Slafter. Trans. Charles Pomeroy Otis. Vol. I. Boston: The Prince Society. 1880. *Google Books.* Web. 26 Aug. 2008.

Small, H. Beaumont. *Chronicles of Canada.* Ottawa: G.E. Desbarats, 1868. *Google Books.* Web. 17 June 2010.

Stock-Morton, Phyllis. "Control and Limitation of Midwives in Modern France: The Example of Marseille." *Journal of Women's History,* Vol. 8, 1996.

Sulte, Benjamin, C. E. Fryer, and L. O. David. *A History of Quebec: Its Resources and People.* Vol. 1. Montreal: The Canada History Company, 1908. *Google Books.* Web. 30 Oct. 2008.

Tanguay, Cyprien. *À Travers les Registres*. Montreal: Librairie Saint-Joseph, 1886. *Google Books*. Web. 15 Sept. 2009.

---. *Dictionnaire Genealogique des Familles Canadiennes*. Quebec: Eusebe Senecal, Imprimeur, 1871. *Google Books*. Web. 21 Feb 2010.

---. *Répertoire Général du Clergé Canadien Par Ordre Chronologique Depuis La Fondation de La Colonie*. Quebec: C. Darveau, Imprimeur-Editeur, 1868. *Google Books*. Web. 15 Sept. 2009.

"The Carignan-Salieres Regiment of Canada, 1665-1671." *Civilization.CA. Museum of New France*. Canadian Museum of Civilization Corporation. Web. 6 Sept. 2001.

"The Servants of God in Canada: Hélene Boullé." *The Pilgrim of Our Lady of Martyrs, A Monthly Magazine*. Ed and Pub 27 & 29 West 16th Street, New York, Vol. XXI (1905). *Google Books* Web. 27 Jan. 2010.

Thompson, CJS. *Mystery and Art of the Apothecary*. Montana: Kessinger Pub. Co., 2003.

"Three Saintly Ladies." *World's Columbian Catholic Congress*. Chapter XII. Chicago: J.S. Hyland and Company, 1893. Web. 17 June 2010.

Tooker, Elizabeth. *An Ethnography of the Huron Indians, 1615-1649*. Syracuse: Syracuse University Press, 1991.

Tremblay, Victor. "Quen, Jean De." *Dictionary of Canadian Biography Online*. Canada: University of Toronto/Université Laval, 2000. Web. 17 June 2010.

Trudel, Marcel. "Caën, Émery De." *Dictionary of Canadian Biography Online*. Canada: University of Toronto/Université Laval, 2000. Web. 22 Oct. 2011.

---. "Caën, Guillaume De." *Dictionary of Canadian Biography Online*. Canada: University of Toronto/Université Laval, 2000. Web. 22 Oct. 2011.

---. "Champlain, Samuel." *Dictionary of Canadian Biography Online*. Canada: University of Toronto/Université Laval, 2000. Web. 17 June 2010.

---. "Charité, Espérance, Foi." *Dictionary of Canadian Biography Online*. Canada: University of Toronto/Université Laval, 2000. Web. 18 Jan. 2012.

---. *Introduction to New France*. Rhode Island: Quintin Publications, 1997.

---. "La rencontre des cultures." *Revue d'histoire de l'Amérique française*. 18.4 (1965): 477-516. *érudit*. Web. 23 July 2011.

---. *Le Terrier Du Saint-Laurent en 1663*. Ottawa, Ca: Editions De L'Université D'Ottawa, 1973.

---. *The Seigneurial Regime*. Ottawa: The Canadian Historical Association, 1976. Web. 11 July 2011.

Vachon, André. "Jolliet, Louis." *Dictionary of Canadian Biography Online*. Canada: University of Toronto/Université Laval, 2000. Web. 14 May 2011.

---. "Laval, François De." *Dictionary of Canadian Biography Online*. Canada: University of Toronto/Université Laval, 2000. Web. 8 Dec. 2010.

---. "Marsolet De Saint-Aignan, Nicolas." *Dictionary of Canadian Biography Online*. Canada: University of Toronto/Université Laval, 2000. Web. 12 Jan. 2012.

---. "Rageot, Gilles." *Dictionary of Canadian Biography Online*. Canada: University of Toronto/Université Laval, 2000. Web. 8 Dec. 2010.

---. "Talon, Jean." *Dictionary of Canadian Biography Online*. Canada: University of Toronto/Université Laval, 2000. Web. 13 Oct. 2011.

Warrick, Gary A. "European Infectious Disease and Depopulation of the Wendat-Tionontate (Huron-Petun)." *Archeology of the Iroquois: Selected Readings and Research Sources*. Jordan Kerber, Ed. NY: Syracuse University Press. 2000.

Winks, Robin W. *The Blacks in Canada: A History*. Montreal: McGill-Queen's University Press, 1997.

Zoltvany, Yves F. "Aubert De La Chesnaye, Charles." *Dictionary of Canadian Biography Online*. Canada: University of Toronto/Université Laval, 2000. Web. 14 Nov. 2012.

INDEX

32839077R00214

Made in the USA
Lexington, KY
06 March 2019